EMILY LAWLESS 1845–1913

EMILY LAWLESS 1845–1913
Writing the Interspace

HEIDI HANSSON

First published in 2007 by
Cork University Press
Youngline Industrial Estate
Pouladuff Road, Togher
Cork, Ireland

British Library Cataloguing in Publication Data
A CIP catalogue record for this book is available from the British Library.

ISBN 978-1-85918-413-4

Typesetting by Red Barn Publishing, Skeagh, Skibbereen, Co. Cork
Printed by ColourBooks Ltd., Baldoyle, Dublin

www.corkuniversitypress.com

Published with the support of the Swedish Research Council

Contents

Acknowledgements

I first heard about Emily Lawless when I came to Northern Ireland in 1999 to spend a year as a postdoctoral research fellow at the Centre for Irish Literature and Bibliography, University of Ulster. My intention was to study Irish women's writing, and Lawless was one of the writers whose name turned up again and again in bibliographies and overviews. There was almost never any real information, however, and I began to be intrigued by the continual references to an author who seemed to have been so important, yet had managed to become almost completely forgotten. I became curious both about Emily Lawless's contributions to Irish literature and the reasons for her disappearance from the canon, and found myself unable to resist embarking on a project that was not at all what I had originally planned.

There are many people whose help and encouragement have been invaluable over the years it has taken me to complete the study. First, I would like to thank Dr Anne McCartney for the innumerable discussions we had on Emily Lawless, Irish women's writing and any number of other subjects and for her generosity and friendship. I am especially grateful for the many trips we took together to the interspace of Donegal. I also wish to express my sincere gratitude to the Swedish Research Council for the grant that allowed me to spend a year in Northern Ireland and for supporting the publication of this book, to the University of Ulster for giving me research space and to the staff at the Centre for Irish Literature and Bibliography for sharing ideas with me. I am very grateful to the Swedish Foundation for International Cooperation in Research and Higher Education for awarding me a grant that allowed me to continue working with scholars in Ireland. I wish to thank my colleagues at Umeå University for providing me with a friendly work environment and the staff at the University Library and the Research Archives, Umeå University, for helping me locate obscure material. My gratitude to colleagues in various universities in Ireland for accepting that I sometimes descended on them out of the blue and needed help with library access and other matters. A special thank you to Dr Tina O'Toole, University of Limerick, Dr Margaret Kelleher, NUI Maynooth, Dr Riana O'Dwyer, NUI Galway, Dr Anne Fogarty, UCD and Dr Julie Anne Stevens, Trinity College Dublin and St. Patrick's College, Drumcondra, Dublin for their help and interest in the project. I also want to thank Professor Marianne Thormählen, Dr Birgitta Berglund and the postgraduate seminar in English literature, Lund University, Sweden, for their valuable comments on chapter 'Negotiating authority'.

I gratefully acknowledge the permissions to quote from the following manuscripts: Horace Plunkett, Letters to Emily Lawless 30 Jul. 1902 and 3 Oct. 1902; Margaret Oliphant, Letter to Emily Lawless, Jul. 1890, Lawless Papers, Marsh's Library, Dublin, quoted with the permission of the Governors and Guardians of Archbishop Marsh's Library. Emily Lawless, Letter to Clement K. Shorter, 11 Apr. 1895, quoted with the permission of the James Joyce Library, University College Dublin. Elizabeth Cloncurry, Letter to W. E. H. Lecky, 20 Jul. 1887, Emily Lawless, Letter to W. E. H. Lecky, 30 December 1890, Emily Lawless, Letter to W. E. H. Lecky 13 May [1895?], Emily Lawless, Letter to W. E. H. Lecky, Aug. 24 [1887?], Emily Lawless, Letter to W. E. H. Lecky 5 Nov. [1895?] quoted with the permission of the Board of Trinity College Dublin. The following letters are the property of the Board of the National Library of Ireland and have been quoted with the permission of the board: Emily Lawless, Letter to Lord Castletown 2 Aug. n. y., Emily Lawless, Letter to Lord Castletown, 10 Aug. n. y., Emily Lawless, Letter to Lord Monteagle, 31 Aug. 1907. Emily Lawless, Letter to A. V. Dicey 24 July, n. y. has been quoted with the permission of the University of Glasgow Library. Emily Lawless, Letter to Rhoda Broughton 9 Oct. n. y., has been quoted with the permission of the Depositor of DDB M/L/2, Cheshire and Chester Archives and Local Studies. The following manuscripts have been quoted by permission of the British Library: Emily Lawless, Letters to Macmillan's 1883–1904, British Library manuscript number Add.54966 f128–f129, f 134, f140–f141, f143–146, f153–f156, f165–166, f172–f173, f176–f178, f180–f183, Emily Lawless, Letter to W. E. Gladstone, 22 Oct. 1894, British Library manuscript number Add. 44519/149 and Emily Lawless, Letter to Sir Alfred Lyall, 27 Oct. [1902], British Library [London, India Office Library and Records] manuscript number Eur.F.132/109/25. The cover portrait of Emily Lawless is reproduced with the permission of the Governors and Guardians of Archbishop Marsh's Library and I am grateful for the permission to use the picture.

Chapter 3, 'Interspatial identities', contains material previously published in the article 'Writing the Interspace: Emily Lawless's Geographical Imagination' which is included in *Engaging Modernity: Readings of Irish Politics, Culture and Literature at the Turn of the Century*, ed. Michael Böss and Eamon Maher (Dublin: Veritas, 2003) pp. 121–140. I am grateful for the permission to reprint this material.

Finally I want to thank my children, Marit, Nils and Jerker for their willingness to come to Northern Ireland for a year and for surprising me every day with their insights and abilities. And Per, thank you for always being the best part of everything.

Behind the book

The Hon. Emily Lawless (1845–1913) was one of the most prominent figures on the Irish literary scene around the turn of the nineteenth century. Yet today she is mostly known as the author of a few romantic poems celebrating Ireland's past, despite the substantial body of fiction and other prose works that constitutes her main literary contribution. She was the daughter of the third Baron Cloncurry, and consequently a member of the Protestant aristocracy, and this family background almost certainly damaged her literary reputation after the proclamation of the Irish Free State. Poems that could be read in patriotic terms were acceptable, but works attempting to be fair to both England and Ireland, unionists and nationalists, were probably more difficult to praise. Most of Lawless's writings are characterised by the double voice of a writer reluctant to provide an easy solution or a final answer. Such a feature may be regarded as unconstructive in a country's nation-building phase, but it has a lot to offer for a culture attempting to move beyond polarisation.

Among the Emily Lawless papers in Marsh's Library, Dublin, there is a book of sketches containing a drawing of a woman reading. The woman's face is hidden behind the book. It is a fitting illustration of Lawless's claim that 'I have a relish, I might almost say a passion for obscurity'.[1] Obscurity, as Lawless defines it in *A Garden Diary* (1901), 'means that you belong to yourself; that you have your years, your days, hours, and minutes undisposed of, unbargained for, unwatched, and unwished for by anybody. It means that you are free to go in and out without witnesses; free as the grass, free rather as the birds of the air.'[2] Obscurity in this sense is liberating. The obscurity that constitutes Lawless's reputation today, however, is more the result of confinement than freedom, since, as a writer, she has become the victim of a political classification that she resisted in all her works.

Lawless's first publication is a contribution to the *Entomologist's Monthly Magazine* in 1867.[3] The 'poor little note' resulted in a letter to Lawless requesting further details about her observations, an event she remembers as 'a minute, but quite imperishable point of glory in an otherwise dim and unnoticeable Past'.[4] She remained an amateur entomologist, botanist, geographer, geologist and marine zoologist throughout her life. Her interest in natural phenomena suffuses all her subsequent writing, with the consequence that most of her work crosses the borders between literary genres. Her novels and stories are interspersed with accounts of the naturalist's pursuits and detailed botanical descriptions, and her early articles on Irish insects and plants anticipate the themes and attitudes of her fiction, particularly the understanding that Ireland is an *interspace,* a place where normal categories do not apply and rational explanations do not suffice. But although Ireland is constantly celebrated in her works, it is rarely idealised, and her view of the country is too ambiguous to fully answer the needs of the new nation.

As an Anglo-Irish woman writer who combined nationalist feelings with unionist sympathies Lawless was an unsuitable subject for canonisation in the new Irish state, and her position as a writer was therefore far more secure outside Ireland than in her own country. To a large degree she became a victim of the 'patriotic sentiment' that propelled the Irish canonisation process, according to the contemporary critic Stephen Gwynn: 'We desire a Walter Scott that he may glorify our annals, popularise our legends, describe our scenery, and give an attractive view of the national character.'[5] Lawless was in fact compared to Walter Scott,[6] but the double outlook that characterises her writing produces narratives where any glorification of Irishness is offset by sympathetic descriptions of English characters, and criticism is evenly distributed. Her themes are often taken from the Irish past, but, as Gwynn makes clear, the political situation complicates matters, since to 'write on anything connected with Irish history is inevitably to offend the Press of one party, and very probably of both'.[7] But while Gwynn is alert to the pitfalls of political criticism, he shows no awareness of the consequences of gender bias; although he acknowledges that the 'roll of Irish novelists is more than half made up of women's names', he confesses to 'a preference for men's work'.[8] Both the critical approach based on nationalist-political considerations and the conscious or unconscious privileging of men's writing have contributed to relegating Emily Lawless to the margins of the Irish literary canon.

This was not always the case. Lawless's fame grew steadily from the publication of her first novel in 1882, and by the turn of the century her novels and poems were read in most parts of the English-speaking world. She published in prestigious magazines such as the *Nineteenth Century, The Gentleman's Magazine,* and *Belgravia,* and was part of the literary establishment of her time. Her novel *Grania: The Story of an Island* (1892) appears on the list of one hundred books towards the formation of a village library, published in the *Irish Homestead* in 1900.[9] In 1905 she received an Honorary Doctorate in Literature from Trinity College, Dublin. It was the crowning moment of a long career and represented her recognition by the intellectual elite of her country. The *Irish Times* obituary called her 'perhaps, the most distinguished literary Irishwoman of her time'.[10] In an *Irish Times* article from 2000 about what writers will be likely to be read in the year 2100, Fintan O'Toole considers what a similar list, drawn up in the year 1900 might have looked like:

> It is interesting to speculate, for example, on what choices a panel of experts, asked a century ago to draw up a similar list of then-living Irish writers, might have imagined we would now be reading. Bernard Shaw might just have squeezed in, though he was not then a particularly successful playwright.
>
> W. B. Yeats might just have made it on the basis of his new volume, *The Wind Among the Reeds,* though a sceptic might have wondered whether all his Celtic Twilight stuff wasn't just another passing fad. George Moore would almost certainly have made it. But Oscar Wilde would probably have been left out as a shameful and best-forgotten figure. Bram Stoker? Too trashy. Augusta Gregory?
>
> On the other hand, Emily Lawless, Edward Dowden, George Egerton, Aubrey De Vere, Sir John Mahaffy, Shan Bullock and G. F. Armstrong might well be just the sort of writers who would seem destined to find an appreciative audience in the year 2000. After all, the basic assumption would have been that Irish literature would still be essentially a branch of British imperial culture. The Ireland we now inhabit would have been literally inconceivable.[11]

In the year 1900, the main criticism directed at Lawless might have been that her works were too Irish to be proper expressions of 'British imperial culture', and her position as a member of the Protestant upper class would probably have been regarded as totally unremarkable. The conclusion that her unionist sympathies made her a target of the processes of erasure after 1922 seems inevitable. Yet her work is not political – on the contrary, it is remarkably balanced and was received as free from partisan motives: 'Although by no means a nationalist, Miss Lawless cannot be called a unionist', writes the Brighton-based *Southern Weekly Review*, 'the bent of her mind is strictly judicial and impartial, and she is more concerned with the truth of things than with the warfare of parties'.[12] Her contemporaries generally commended this feature of her writing, but the few, powerful, voices that criticised her denounced her for not being sufficiently committed to an Irish cause.[13] Yeats includes Lawless's historical novel *Maelcho* in his selection of the hundred best Irish books[14] and lists her other novel of Elizabethan times, *With Essex in Ireland* – 'though with much doubt' – as one of the thirty most valuable books about Ireland.[15] Nevertheless, he regards her as being 'in imperfect sympathy with the Celtic nature' and attacks her 'commonplace conception of Irish character'.[16] If only Lawless could 'cast off a habit of mind which would compress a complex, incalculable, indecipherable nation into the mould of a theory invented by political journalists and forensic historians', she would be a good writer, he suggests.[17] Significantly, Lloyd R. Morris accords her only two lines in his chapter on prose writing in *The Celtic Dawn* (1917): 'The Hon. Emily Lawless has also written of the west coast and of the legend connected therewith.'[18] It seems clear that Lawless's writing did not fit the assumptions about what Irish literature should be at the time.

Lawless was certainly much more appreciated as a writer in both England and America than in Ireland, and the brief notice in the *Daily Sketch* published after her death bears the headline 'The Irish Did Not Understand Her'.[19] This view seems to be supported in the obituary in *The Irish Book Lover* where it is noted that neither *Hurrish* nor *Grania* met with much favour in Ireland.[20] Probably she was also more widely read outside her home country, where the names of Pierre Loti, J. M. Barrie and Thomas Hardy were much more familiar to the reading public – at least this is what the *United Ireland* newspaper suggests: 'It is one of the misfortunes of this country that while we complain that we have no present-day literature, we really have, but do not know it. For we do not read our own books.'[21] If Irish literature is not allowed to transcend political categories, it can never flourish, the writer continues:

> There is really – to speak, perhaps, a little bluntly – one thing which
> Irishmen who would like to see their country with a literature of her own
> must bear in mind: namely, that they will never have such if it is to consist
> solely of books which flatter our National vanities, glaze over our National

defects, and exaggerate our National virtues. Let us have an end of this. We do not know whether Miss Emily Lawless is a Nationalist or the reverse – nor do we care; but we do believe that in 'Hurrish' and the beautiful story now under review [*Grania: The Story of an Island*] she has given to Irish literature works which will add immensely to its reputation, and place her own name beside the first two or three of Ireland's foremost novelists.[22]

There was still some interest in Lawless's work in 1916, when the Irish Literary Society held an 'Emily Lawless Night' on 15 January. Lieutenant Lynan's paper on her Irish fiction, sent to the Society from the trenches, goes some way towards explaining why her writing met with such contradictory responses in her own country:

Emily Lawless' novels are as individual and as hard to classify as the people they describe; and they can hardly be appreciated fully until her object in writing them has been understood. To her the Munster forests of the sixteenth century and their dark tragedies and the struggle of existence on the rocky western seaboard in modern years were symbolic of all Ireland and Irish life.[23]

Since it defies categorisation, Lawless's work could not be claimed by the nationalist movement and, despite all the eulogies from abroad, Yeats's negative assessment of her writing prevailed.

In 1944 Seamus Fenton attempted to re-establish Emily Lawless's literary reputation in a lecture delivered to the Women's Social and Progressive League in Dublin. From the report of the ensuing discussion it is clear that Lawless was at that time no longer known.[24] Fenton praises her poems for their national sentiment and sense of place and several of the listeners – among them Rosamond Jacob and Hannah Sheehy-Skeffington – proposed that they should be used to teach Irish history. Mrs Carthy, a former professor in Carysfort Training College, went so far as to claim that if 'such ballads were properly taught there would be no need of compulsion to learn Irish'.[25] One poem by Lawless was indeed included in the secondary-school English literature course, together with a poem each by Aubrey de Vere, D'Arcy Magee and James Clarence Mangan.[26] Lawless was consequently reclaimed within a nationalist framework that previously excluded her, the ambiguous politics and double vision of her work suppressed or overlooked in another way.

Fenton's lecture did not spark any widespread interest in Lawless's writing and it took until 1965 before a selection of her poetry was

reissued, edited by Padraic Fallon for the An Chomhairle Ealaíon/Series of
Irish Authors. Little else than the bare facts of genealogy was known about
Lawless at this time, and Fallon outlines the Cloncurry family's
involvement in the struggle for Catholic emancipation and Irish
independence to 'explain why a daughter of the Gods of the time should
appear to be so born a rebel'.[27] In contrast to previous anthologisers,
however, he finds Lawless's national poems rather trite, and considers her
more thought-provoking poetry of ideas her best work.

In the late 1970s, Lawless's Irish fiction was republished in the
Garland series of Irish and Anglo-Irish nineteenth-century writing.
Understandably, the editor Robert Lee Wolff is mainly concerned with the
Irishness of Lawless's work, and like Fallon he traces her family history to
show her connections with the nationalist cause, downplaying her
unionist leanings.

Her resistance to political labelling has made Lawless a problematic
object of study in a critical climate primarily concerned with questions of
cultural and national identity. The preoccupation with identity politics in
Irish Studies has consequently ensured her continued absence from the
Irish literary canon. Cultural Studies could provide an escape from the
concern with national identity, but, so far, this type of criticism has been
remarkably unsuccessful in retrieving women's contributions, since it has
mainly been concerned with writers involved in the public domain –
scholars, priests, journalists, politicians and other (male) intellectuals.
Lawless remained outside the more public networks that shaped Irish
culture at the end of the nineteenth and beginning of the twentieth
centuries and may therefore easily be overlooked.

A biographical study by Marie O'Neill appeared in 1995, and was
awarded the Old Dublin Society's Medal,[28] and it seems clear that interest
in Lawless is growing. The few critical studies that have appeared in recent
years have highlighted her importance as a woman writer,[29] but, although
the commentators are united in their opinion that Lawless has been
unfairly overlooked and deserves a place in the Irish literary canon, this has
only rarely led to a retrieval of her work. The complexity of Lawless's
writing makes her a less than ideal nationalist icon, but she is equally
unsuitable for celebratory feminist retrieval, since her gender politics are
just as complex as her national politics. The lack of explicit feminist
declarations in her works means that she was not really a suitable object
for the early versions of feminist criticism that were intent on finding

subversive subtexts and rebellious ideas in the texts.[30] The subtitle of volumes IV and V of the *Field Day Anthology of Irish Writing: Women's Writing and Traditions* (2002) indicates a change to a more open variety of feminist criticism, however. Critics like Angela Bourke, Gerardine Meaney, Margaret Kelleher, Claire Connolly and others represent a feminist approach that acknowledges diversity and accepts both that literary women did not necessarily see themselves as feminists and that the face of feminism has changed considerably over the years. Instead of searching for evidence of textual transgressions, a new generation of feminist critics has begun to recognise the value of retrieving different kinds of women's traditions, and it is within this framework that Lawless and her contributions can be reclaimed.

What is required is consequently an interpretative model that acknowledges complexity and avoids the constrictions of traditional political interpretations. Emily Lawless does not speak for a unified group of 'women' or 'Irish'. Instead, her writing is double-voiced, representing 'a multiplicity of fluid positions linked by in-common body form' or in-common national origin in its broadest terms.[31] From a conventional feminist point of view, such fluidity is undesirable because it seems to defy political action, but, as Margrit Shildrick makes clear, ambiguity does not necessarily lead to 'the dead end of permanent fragmentation'; rather, it is a means to suggest 'multiple possibilities for agency'.[32] In a more general sense, the double voice may even be an expression of the Irish mind itself, which, according to Richard Kearney, 'does not reveal itself as a single, fixed, homogeneous identity' but as double or dialogic.[33]

In an article about North Clare, Emily Lawless uses the neologism *interspace* to summarise the indefinable qualities of the west of Ireland.[34] The notion of the interspace can be associated with the feminist concept 'paradoxical space', defined by Gillian Rose as 'multi-dimensional, shifting and contingent', simultaneously both central and marginal.[35] It can also be connected to Michel Foucault's idea of *heterotopia* as a 'disorder in which fragments of a large number of possible orders glitter separately in the dimension, without law or geometry'.[36] Heterotopias are 'spaces whose functions are different or even the opposites of others', where things not usually found together are juxtaposed and where spatialised processes of resistance and transgression can take place.[37] It is both a liberating and a disturbing image and, as Foucault envisages them, heterotopias are also fragmented, dissolving and destructive regions. As opposed to utopias, they are incoherent and uncomfortable, and can certainly not function as uniting images for a group or a nation. However, as a disorganised environment, a heterotopia is closer to the unpredictability of the natural world, and its fluid form involves the positive elements of tolerance, freedom, ambiguity and difference. A utopian world may be perfect, but its perfection usually relies on a uniformity whose negative pole is constraint.

Like parallel space and heterotopia, the term 'interspace' can be used as an interpretative tool and an enabling concept. It expresses indefiniteness and contradiction, negotiation and complexity, and it can be extended to refer to Lawless's place as an Anglo-Irish author, to her situation as a woman writer in nineteenth-century society and to the dialogic mode of writing resulting from these positions. The interspace can be used as a metaphor for the political ambiguity evident, for instance, in Lawless's early fiction, where she addresses women's issues but avoids taking a clear stand. It can illustrate her unwillingness to subscribe to any kind of taxonomical system, be it botanical, zoological or national. It can be used to describe the peculiar style resulting from the strategy of addressing issues of public concern such as national history through a privatising discourse. Moving between male and female, English and Irish, rational and fantastic positions, Lawless interrogates the nature of gender definitions, national identity, and the privileged role of logic and reason in Western thought by choosing the interspace and its metaphorical correspondences before a final answer. In the language of postmodernism, she opts for *both and neither* rather than either-or.[38] Descriptions of individuals reveal the effects of both patriarchal and colonial oppression, but her openly dialogic narration collapses the opposition between categories without establishing new systems. As far as politics go, it is potentially more radical than a focus on the male–female – or English–Irish – power struggle, because it attacks the foundational concept of hierarchy itself.

At first glance the reading woman in the sketch kept in Marsh's Library, Dublin, seems to be hiding behind her book, but the pose can also be viewed as a definite foregrounding of the book. Understood as an illustration of the circumstances of nineteenth-century women writers, the drawing sends an ambiguous message. On the one hand it suggests the invisibility of woman, on the other it gives precedence to the work before the producer, indicating that the identity of the writer should not be the main focus. This could be taken to suggest that to read Lawless in terms of her biography will conceal the full complexity of her work. Like the book that covers the features of the woman in the sketch and leaves her forever indefinable, Lawless's writing permits her a multitude of imagined options.

Read closely, without a drive towards either/or aesthetic judgements or easy political pigeon-holing, Lawless's writing reveals a dialogue where contradictory positions are contained. This dialogue manages to encompass a society in flux, while confrontation and clear-cut positioning – the corollaries of a hierarchical logic – would have to suppress part of the truth. It is not an apolitical strategy, nor is it evidence of political innocence. The negotiations Lawless introduces into her texts must be read as the conscious choice of a writer who is aware of the complicated nature of the political and social relationships she treats, and so rejects reductive stereotyping. Lawless writes the interspace, where identities, social structures and even geographical contours are unstable, accepting that contradictions and uncertainties are not only unavoidable, but necessary.

Chapter 1

Family and friends

The Hon. Emily Lawless (1845–1913) was born into the Irish aristocracy as the daughter of Lord Cloncurry, and grew up at Lyons estate near Dublin. She spent long periods of time with her mother's family outside Galway and learned to love the rugged landscape of the west of Ireland. She never married, and after her father died in 1869 she appears to have been the constant companion of her mother, travelling with her to England and the Continent and sharing houses with her in London, Ireland and abroad. After her mother's death, Lawless spent more and more time in London and, some time around the middle of the 1890s, she moved permanently to England and settled in Surrey. She suffered from what may have been arthritis, and was bed-ridden for long periods of time in the final years of her life until she died in 1913. Nevertheless, she continued to visit Ireland every year until 1911.

Lawless's first work, some observations on Irish moths, was published in 1867, but she seems not to have attempted a literary career until rather late in life. Some articles about outdoor experiences in Ireland and abroad appeared in journals like the *Nineteenth Century* and *Belgravia* in the early 1880s, and her first novel, *A Chelsea Householder* was published in 1882, followed by the publication of *A Millionaire's Cousin* a few years later in 1885. These first novels were set outside Ireland, but, with the exception of *Major Lawrence, F. L. S.* (1887) and *A Garden Diary* (1901) the rest of her longer works deal with Irish themes. Her best-known novels are *Hurrish: A Study* from 1886 and *Grania: The Story of an Island* from 1892, followed by her historical novels *With Essex in Ireland* (1890) and *Maelcho: A Sixteenth Century Narrative* (1894). Her history *Ireland* (1887) and her biography of Maria Edgeworth (1904) also enjoyed considerable success, and she published two collections of short stories, *Plain Frances Mowbray and Other Tales* (1889) and *Traits and Confidences* (1897). In

10

1905 she received an Honorary Doctorate from Trinity College, Dublin, in recognition of her literary contributions. Her illness became more pronounced in the 1890s, which meant that she began to find it difficult to write longer prose narratives. She produced the rather slight novels *A Colonel of the Empire: From the Private Papers of Mangan O'Driscoll, Late of the Imperial Service of Austria, and a Knight of the Military Order of Maria Theresa* (1895) and *The Book of Gilly: Four Months Out of a Life* (1906), but in the main she turned to poetry. Her first collection of poems, *With the Wild Geese* (1902), contains her most frequently anthologised poems 'After Aughrim', 'Clare Coast', 'Fontenoy. 1745' and 'Dirge of the Munster Forest. 1581', much admired as capturing the Irish atmosphere and often read as patriotic celebrations of Irish history. Her second volume, *The Point of View* (1909), mostly contains philosophical musings and was privately printed. Her last works, the novel *The Race of Castlebar: Being a Narrative Addressed by Mr. John Bunbury to His Brother Mr. Theodore Bunbury* (1913), written in collaboration with Shan Bullock, and *The Inalienable Heritage and Other Poems* (1914), were published after her death.

In the years after the proclamation of the Irish Free State Lawless was dismissed as a conservative unionist whose works had little or nothing to offer for the new nation. One result of this dismissal is that very little information about her has survived. Although she had a great number of friends and was acquainted with many of the important political and literary figures of her time, Lawless also appears to have been a very private person, and information about her personal life is sparse. As a result, the account of her biography is unavoidably sketchy and incomplete, since the available sources contain quite a lot of detail on certain aspects and periods of her life and none at all on others. Obituaries and newspaper articles obviously give important information and a particularly valuable source is Edith Sichel's tribute in the *Nineteenth Century and After* (1914), where Sichel provides a sketch of Lawless's life and acquaintances and also quotes some private letters at length. William Linn's unpublished thesis from 1971, 'The Life and Works of the Hon. Emily Lawless, First Novelist of the Irish Literary Revival', is admirably thorough in its listing of obscure and often quite unexpected sources of information. Conducting his research in the 1960s, Linn was also able to interview people who had known Lawless, and though some of his conclusions seem too much influenced by the 1970s tendency to search for the writer's psychology in the works, Linn's account of material and the biographical details included are invaluable. Information about the Cloncurry family background can be found in memoirs of contemporaries, such as the reference to Lawless's great-grandfather in the *Hamwood Papers of the Ladies of Llangollen and Caroline Hamilton* located by William Linn. A more detailed although perhaps not entirely objective account of the first two generations of the Cloncurrys is available in the autobiography of Emily Lawless's grandfather Valentine, the second Baron Cloncurry. Information about the second Lord Cloncurry can also be gleaned from histories of the 1798 Rising of the United Irishmen, where he played a minor part or in works about his more famous acquaintances Lord Edward Fitzgerald and Daniel O'Connell. Incidental facts about Lawless herself can be found in works by or about her contemporaries, such as the autobiography of Elizabeth, Countess of Fingall, or Lady Gregory's diaries, though the information in such sources is of course tinted by the author's personal views. Further material, albeit scant, can be found in biographical works such as Margaret Digby's biography of Horace Plunkett or Alfred Lyall's biography of Lord Dufferin and Ava. Finally, Marsh's Library holds the papers donated to the library by her brother Frederick after Lawless's death, primarily newspaper cuttings and reviews, and a number of letters to or from Lawless are published in works by or about some of her friends, like Margaret Oliphant or George Tyrrell, or survive in various archives in Ireland, England and the United States. However, even though there are no comprehensive sources, it is possible to piece together if not a complete biographical account of the woman Emily Lawless, at least enough information about her background and connections to provide a context for her writing.

The early categorisation of Lawless as a conservative unionist ignores the complexities of her writing, and fails to take account of the intricacies of her family history. Nicholas Lawless (*c.* 1735–1799), the first Baron Cloncurry, grew up as a Catholic. His prospects of advancement were slight under the penal laws and he left Ireland for France in the hope of finding there the 'liberty to enjoy those privileges of property and talent from which they were debarred in their native land', as his son Valentine Browne Lawless, the second Baron (1773–1853), expresses it in his autobiography.[1] After some years abroad Nicholas Lawless became disappointed with life in France and returned to Ireland, where he conformed to the established church in 1770 to be able to 'hold a territorial stake in the country'.[2] In 1789 he was elevated to the peerage and in 1796 he bought Lyons estate from Sir Michael Aylmer, whose family had owned the land for 500 years.[3] In relation to the Aylmers, Sir Nicholas Lawless was perceived as a nobody, as the comment in the *Hamwood Papers of the Ladies of Llangollen and Caroline Hamilton* makes clear:

> Aylmer of Lyons is in a worse situation. Lyons was seized on by Sir Nicholas Lawless, who in the memory of thousands was a carpet man in Thomas St., Dublin. He is suddenly become fearfully opulent and like a Harpy availing himself of it, seizes on all the estates within his reach. Lyons was a very large estate and for many generations in the Aylmer family. By the inattention and extravagance of the present gentleman it has become the prey of the upstart Lawless.[4]

Sir Fenton Aylmer reports a story of how the Lawless family attempted to eradicate every trace of the Aylmers, going so far as to levelling their graves, but admits that he cannot vouch for the truth of the tale, and that there might be other satisfactory explanations.[5] Nicholas Lawless became a member of the Irish House of Commons and subsequently the House of Peers, but it seems clear that he never wholly forgot his humble past.[6] Like many other Irishmen with a similar background, he became one of the 'champions of the oppressed, from whose ranks they found themselves so lucky as to have risen'.[7] The main blot on his reputation as an Ireland-friendly politician is that he voted for the 1800 Union with England.

The family atmosphere appears to have been one of liberalism, tolerance and concern for the situation of the Irish Catholics. Before he succeeded to the title in 1799, Nicholas Lawless's son Valentine spent some time in Switzerland, where he met French refugees from the Revolution.[8] In their company, he writes:

> it was natural that my thoughts should dwell upon the rights of men, the abuses of party domination, and especially of that form of the latter, which had so long held Ireland back in the progress of civilization. Thus my residence in Switzerland sent me home to Ireland more Irish than ever; I lamented her fate, ardently desired to be able to aid in ameliorating it, and became filled with a passionate love of country, which neither persecutions, nor disappointments, nor even the efflux of time, have, I am happy to say, rooted out from my heart.[9]

After his return to Ireland in 1795 he involved himself in Irish politics. His mother, Lady Cloncurry, seems to have been sympathetic to the cause of the United Irishmen, at least so far as to loan £1,500, a large sum in 1796, to Lord Edward Fitzgerald, one of the key figures in the organisation and her son's dear friend.[10] His sisters also joined the society and managed to help United Irish prisoners by making it possible for their friends to visit them in gaol after dark.[11] Their brother, meanwhile, was elected to the Leinster Executive of the society.[12] In 1797 Valentine Browne Lawless wrote a pamphlet where he criticised English rule in Ireland and opposed the proposed Union with England,[13] and he was the principal sponsor of the United Irishmen's propaganda sheet *The Press,* edited by Arthur O'Connor.[14] Some time in 1797 he was in London, acting as a centre for the Irish patriots and relaying messages from the United Irish agent in Paris.[15] Although such rather minor tasks may have been his main contribution to the 1798 Rising, he was twice arrested and imprisoned in the Tower of London for treason.

Some letters from the first Baron to the Duke of Portland included in Valentine Lawless's autobiography indicate that Nicholas Lawless's decision to vote for the Union was mainly an attempt to obtain a pardon for his son. On 13 May 1799, the first Lord Cloncurry wrote to the Duke:

> I am very sorry to find that [my son] has again incurred the observation of his Majesty's government. I trust, however, that it arises merely from precaution, in consequence of his former indiscretion, and the persons with whom he had, at that time, the misfortune to connect himself. God forbid; that I should ever allow myself to consider him as criminal. That he may have entertained vain and idle notions of liberty and reform, I am perfectly aware, from the principles of certain persons with whom he kept company, which I always disapproved as well by my example as by my advice. [. . .] If my Lord, your Grace's warrant for again confining him was granted, which I trust in God it was, merely as a measure of precaution, in consequence of any former indiscretion, and that he has not been guilty of any act of a serious tendency, I hope your Grace and his Majesty's ministers will think him sufficiently punished, and permit him to return to his family.[16]

Apparently Lord Cloncurry's first letter on behalf of his son met with no success, and three months later he addressed the Duke of Portland again, this time pointing out his loyalty and adding that he had voted for the Union. On 20 August 1799, only nine days before he died and Valentine Lawless succeeded to the title, the Baron wrote:

> During your Grace's residence here I heartily supported your
> administration; and your Grace well knows that I claimed no merit for it.
> [. . .] Your Grace may know that I voted in the House of Lords for
> receiving the proposition for a Union; I also gave it my interest in the
> county of Limerick, where I have some property, and which, perhaps, few
> would have done, treated as I have been.[17]

Despite his father's assurance that his association with people who 'entertained vain and idle notions of liberty and reform' was a thing of the past, the second Baron continued to be interested in social change. He corresponded with the champion for Catholic emancipation, Daniel O'Connell, for example,[18] and received him at Lyons.[19] In time, O'Connell seems to have become disappointed with the Baron, since in 1831 he published an open letter to Lord Cloncurry in *The Times* where he urges him to fight for immediate repeal of the Union but fears that the 'heartlessness of aristocracy' has come over him.[20] Nevertheless, Valentine Lawless was known as a 'liberal and considerate landlord'.[21] He continued to work for the rights of the Irish Catholics in Parliament and was, for instance, very critical of groups like the Kildare Place Society, because its members engaged in proselytising rather than educational activities.[22] He also protested against the system that obligated Catholics and Protestant Dissenters to pay tithes to support the Church of Ireland.[23] Reporting his death, *The Times* quotes the *Evening Post* obituary: 'From an early age he had taken an active part in public affairs, entering with zeal and energy upon the political arena, always on the popular side, at a period when patriotism was unfashionable and often most perilous.'[24] The second Lord Cloncurry's name was also closely connected with scandal, however. In 1807 he sued Sir John Piers for seducing his wife, born Elizabeth Georgiana Morgan, allegedly for a bet. The case caused considerable public interest as one of the juiciest scandals of the day.[25] Cloncurry won, but he divorced his wife on 26 June 1811.[26]

Against a family background ranging from a Catholic background only two generations back to involvement in the United Irishmen and Catholic Emancipation, the view that Emily Lawless was only a conservative unionist needs to be reconsidered. Although Valentine Browne Lawless certainly wished to present himself and his family in a favourable light in his autobiography, his granddaughter was probably at least as much influenced by his idealised pictures as by any objective description of the family's past. In *A Garden Diary* she writes that she used to regard England as the great enemy:

> In my eyes she stood visibly out as the Great Bully, the Supreme Tyrant, red with the blood of Ireland and Irish heroes. [. . .] I had quite a respectable capacity for hatred in those days, and England – that historic England of which I knew absolutely nothing – enjoyed the greater part of it.[27]

But 'it was only by keeping up the fiction of an incarnate Saxondom that indignation could be retained at the proper boiling point',[28] and not even Lawless's historical novels offer clear divisions between friends and foes in terms of nationality. She came to reject the idea of national identity as stable and unchanging and, as a consequence, the image of England as the perpetual villain. At the same time, she fully acknowledged English oppression as a historical fact, and thus managed to combine the nationalist outlook her grandfather represented with the unionism she later embraced.

Emily Lawless's mother, Elizabeth Cloncurry, belonged to the unionist side of the political spectrum as one of the Kirwans of Castlehacket, Galway. The Kirwan family was one of the original Tribes of Galway, the fourteen families who dominated the political, social and commercial life of the city between the fifteenth and eighteenth century. Like the Lawlesses, the Kirwans were originally a Catholic family, and the only Tribe of Galway that had a Gaelic background, but John Kirwan of Castlehacket converted to the established church in 1740, presumably for much the same reasons as the first Baron Cloncurry.[29] According to Margaret Oliphant, the Castlehacket branch of the family were high Tories by the early decades of the nineteenth century, and rather concerned to see Elizabeth join 'the very household of a former rebel'.[30] The Kirwans seem to have been good landlords,[31] something that may have contributed to Lawless's portrayal of the relationship between landlord and tenant in, for instance, her first Irish novel, *Hurrish* (1886).

Lawless's parents were married in 1839, and in 1853 Edward Lawless (1816–1869) succeeded to the title as the third Baron Cloncurry. In 1869 the Baron threw himself out of a window after what appears to have been a period of mental instability. According to *The Times,* the Lord's doctor had advised 'him to be kept under constant surveillance', and it is stated that he 'had made other attempts on his life'.[32] Valentine Lawless (1840–1928) succeeded his father as the fourth Baron, and was himself succeeded by his brother Frederick (1847–1929). The title became extinct on 18 July 1929.

A further family tragedy occurred in November 1891, when Emily Lawless's sister Rose was found drowned in a pond. The jury returned a verdict of 'Accidentally drowned',[33] but there were soon rumours of suicide. Lady Gregory seems to have taken it for granted that both Lord Cloncurry and Rose Lawless killed themselves, noting in her journal that 'the streak in Emily's family that led to the suicide of her father and sister turned to genius in her'.[34] Emily Lawless remained close to her mother, and travelled with her across Europe and shared various houses with her in London for many years. When Lady Cloncurry died in 1895, Lawless described it as a 'crushing' blow, even though her mother had been ill for quite some time and her death had been expected.[35]

It is clear that Lawless operated within a privileged framework, socially as well as politically. According to Elizabeth, Countess of Fingall, one of her greatest friends was Hermione, Duchess of Leinster.[36] The Duchess was known for her beauty, and the two women were apparently very unlike each other. The Countess's description of Lawless is certainly not flattering: 'She was pale and flaccid, with half-closed, near-sighted eyes and limp white hands. Her speech was slow and she was very delicate and rather hypochondriachal and untidy in her dressing.'[37] Lady Gregory was similarly critical of Lawless's physical attributes and social graces:

> She was young when I first saw her at St. Clerons, but she had no trace of the beauty of her mother Lady Cloncurry, of whom it was said, I don't know with what truth, in my childhood, that once when she went into the House of Lords the whole assembly had stood up in tribute to that beauty, perhaps a gift from the Sidhe, who inhabit the hill of Cruachmaa, at the foot of which was her home. Emily had then a hard, decided manner.[38]

When asked for a photograph of herself to be used in the American promotion of *Maria Edgeworth* (1904), Lawless declined, indicating that she was not particularly pleased with her own looks: 'I received a letter from your American branch a little while ago, asking for a photograph to accompany, I understand, circulars. Will you mind explaining for me that I really do not possess such a thing, except some very antediluvian ones, & do not think that they would be special encouragement if I did. (The last remark, by the way is private!).'[39] Lennox Robinson gives a sympathetic description of her appearance, however:

> She was very tall with red-gold hair, full of laughter and humour. An artist, a great walker, a horse-woman and a swimmer, diving deeply into the wild Atlantic and bringing to the surface strange sea-creatures and sea-plants no Clare fisherman had ever seen.[40]

The active life Robinson describes is very different from the infirmity and seclusion that seem to have characterised Lawless's later years. Whether she was a hypochondriac as the Countess of Fingall intimates is of course impossible to determine. She often refers to her ill-health in her letters, writing to Rhoda Broughton that she has 'been utterly hors de combat for nearly two months past',[41] to Edmund Gosse that she is 'sofa-bound',[42] to William Edward Hartpole Lecky that her doctor has advised her to spend 'the very cold months in the south of France'.[43] In a letter to Mr Macmillan she gives the cause of her suffering as arthritis: 'I am a complete cripple at present, and fear I have little chance of being anything else, as the doctors have all decided that it is arthritis, & seem to have no means of really arresting it.' [44]

Despite her illness, she managed to maintain her many contacts, however, and she took a particularly keen interest in Irish affairs. She was quite close to her cousin Sir Horace Plunkett, founder of the Irish Agricultural Organisation Society. As her friend Edith Sichel saw it, the cousins were politically akin to each other in being 'Irish first and political afterwards'.[45] Edward E. Lysaght defines Plunkett as one of the few representatives of political neutrality in Ireland:

> If he was a Unionist at all it was of that rare type which, while recognizing the indisputable nationality of Ireland, has so little fear of its absorption or disappearance that the alleged material advantages of Union with England appear more desirable than the chances of self-government and the perhaps rather empty satisfaction of the public recognition of a national entity too self-evident to require any such adventitious assistance.[46]

A similar love of Ireland combined with doubt in the country's ability to govern itself characterises Lawless's writing. It seems Plunkett involved Lawless in the work to establish Irish village libraries,[47] and she supported the United Irishwomen, the women's branch of the Agricultural Organisation, and contributed material to the organisation's journal the *Homestead*. While Plunkett was working on his *Ireland in the New Century* (1904) he corresponded frequently with Lawless, referring to her letters as 'most helpful',[48] and accepting her offer to go through the proofs.[49] Nevertheless, Lawless did not always agree with Plunkett's politics. In a letter to Lord Monteagle she writes:

> I so entirely agree with you about H. P.'s new political developments, which seemed to me when I was with him wholly utopian & possible in a world where the lion & the lamb agree, & where party has vanished away with all other ugly human developments, but quite impossible at present in this one![50]

The letter indicates that Lawless regarded Plunkett's attempts to combine nationalist sentiment and unionist politics as naïve, although it could be argued that her own works exemplify precisely the same attitude. In her biography of Horace Plunkett, Margaret Digby writes that Emily Lawless 'understood the emotional content of Irish Nationalism even while remaining herself a Unionist'.[51]

Another Lawless cousin was Bernard Fitzpatrick, the second Baron Castletown, a member of the Gaelic League credited with having brought the kilt back to Ireland. Lord Castletown tried to involve Lawless in a Pan-Celtic congress he was apparently planning, but only got her promise for a small subscription and the loan of those of her books that had Irish themes. In a letter to the organisers she writes that she will send the subscription directly to her cousin, as 'I do not wish my name to appear in the list of subscribers'.[52] Her reluctance to be publicly recognised as a supporter is symptomatic of her unwillingness to be drawn into a camp.

Lawless was acquainted with many distinguished scholars and politicians of the time. The Irish historian W. E. H. Lecky was a particularly valued friend, as their correspondence indicates and as Elizabeth Lecky makes clear in her memoir of her husband.[53] The Earl of Dufferin, later Marquis of Dufferin and Ava, Viceroy of India, and Sir Alfred Lyall, civil servant in India, poet and biographer of Lord Dufferin, were also among Lawless's friends.[54] Another friend with experience of imperial government was Sir Mountstuart Elphinstone Grant Duff, Under Secretary of State for India and for the Colonies between 1868 and 1880 and Governor of Madras. During a visit to Mount Trenchard, the home of the Monteagle family, Lawless met Bertrand and William Russell, Douglas Hyde, Sir Roger Casement and the Protestant nationalist historian Alice Stopford Green, among others.[55] She corresponded with

George Tyrrell, the Irish-born Jesuit priest and philosopher connected with the 'Modernist' Catholic movement which attempted to bring the church closer to contemporary developments in science and society.[56] A more distant acquaintance, perhaps, was Edmund Gosse. Lawless wrote to him in 1894 to praise his biography of his father,[57] and again in 1908 to tell him how much she appreciated *Father and Son: A Study of Two Temperaments* (1907).[58] She begins the second letter by writing '[w]e have not met for so long & even then in such a passing fashion, that you will likely enough be puzzled even to recall my name', which indicates that they did not know each other well.[59] The letter contains a vivid description of a visit Lawless made to Philip Henry Gosse as a child, making her 'perhaps one of the very few surviving people who penetrated to your father's seclusion!'[60]

Among the friends Edith Sichel enumerates in her reminiscence of Lawless are Sir Henry Blake, born in Limerick and later Governor of Bahamas, Newfoundland, Jamaica, Hong Kong, and Ceylon, and his wife Lady Blake. The Blakes accompanied Lawless on her travels to the Aran Islands when she was collecting material for *Grania: The Story of an Island* (1892).[61] Other friends mentioned by Sichel are Lady Blake's sister Grace, Duchess of St Albans, Lady Evelyn de Vesci, married to the fourth Viscount de Vesci in the Irish peerage, and Mary Studd, a woman Lawless met at Castlehacket.[62] Her mother's friends, Lady Ritchie, daughter of the writer William Thackeray, and the Scottish writer Margaret Oliphant, were also important to her.[63]

Other writers in her circle were the sensation novelist Rhoda Broughton, Maria Catherine Bishop and Ella Fuller Maitland. According to Sichel, Fuller Maitland's *Pages from the Day-Book of Bethia Hardacre* (1895) was Lawless's favourite bedside book.[64] She met Mary A. Ward, whose novels appeared under the name Mrs Humphry Ward, during a winter stay in Valescure, and the two became friends[65] – too much so, as Lady Gregory saw it: 'I think her close association with London, with Mrs. Humphrey [sic] Ward, Mrs. Bishop, did not serve her as a writer. She did not let herself go as in her three fine poems, but tried to keep a balance and so lost passion.'[66] Lady Gregory seems not to have admired the writing styles of Mary A. Ward and M. C. Bishop, and probably she also felt that Lawless's association with her English friends influenced her writing in a negative way, so that it became too impassioned to be considered truly Irish.

The nineteenth-century Irish cultural sphere was not exclusively Irish, of course. The Anglo-Irish community obviously had strong links with England, the northern counties had close relations with Scotland, the Catholic Church was connected to Rome and Irish nationalists were influenced by French revolutionary philosophy. London journals were read alongside the *Dublin University Magazine,* and Irish writers commonly published in London or Edinburgh and could expect their work to be reprinted for the American market. Thus, intellectual and popular discourses were exchanged between Ireland and England, the European continent and the growing Irish populations in America and Australia. Emily Lawless usually spent part of the year in London, regularly travelled to France, Italy or Spain during the winter and had friends in many places in the world.[67] In this way she gained an international perspective that can sometimes be seen also in the novels where she deals with Irish themes.

Lawless clearly regarded herself as an intellectual, as borne out by a note in Margaret Oliphant's autobiography:

> There are kinds of foolishness I like for my own part, as there is also a kind of benignant gentle dulness [*sic*] which always soothes me, and which I constantly recommend to Miss Lawless as so good a relief from the intellectualism she loves; but then she does love the intellectual, and I don't – much.[68]

Though she certainly saw herself as Irish, her writings indicate that she felt a need to transcend a purely national identity. She was part of a British and sometimes international literary establishment as well as an Irish one, and there were consequently a number of different audiences she could expect. As an Irish writer she would be read in an Ireland where nationalist sentiment steadily grew stronger, but also in an England where opposition to Irish Home Rule was widespread. She was reluctant to become involved in the Irish revival, and her unwillingness to support the Irish theatre seems to have been partly an effect of her conviction that Irish themes and subjects were unlikely to find favour with the public. She writes to Lady Gregory in 1894, explaining her position:

> I enclose a cheque for £1, but confess it is more as a proof of my regard for <u>you</u> than of belief in the Drama, for I cannot with the best wish in the world to do so, feel hopeful on that subject. My experience has been that

any attempt at treating Irish history is a fatal handicap, not to say absolute
<u>bar</u>, to anything in the shape of popularity, and I cannot see how any
drama can flourish which is not to some degree supported by the public,
as it is even more dependent on it than literature is.[69]

There were probably also political reasons for her scepticism. In a letter
to Horace Plunkett, Lawless writes:

I had a long and very amiable letter from – lately, who asserts that I 'helped
them' – i. e. the Gaelic Theatre and circle! I was not aware of it, but it
shows that I'm not at least antagonistic. I am not *anti-Gaelic* at all so long
as it is only Gaelic *enthuse* and does not include politics.[70]

Apparently Lawless did not have a very good relationship with W. B.
Yeats and, in a letter to Lord Castletown, she refers to him as one of the
'disloyals', though she does not elaborate on what she means by the term.[71]
She often seems to have been on opposite sides to Yeats, however. Lady
Gregory writes in her journal:

I wish she and Yeats had not quarrelled all the time here. The British,
perhaps the commercial, side of the first holder of the title, the blanket
manufacturer, made her indignant that he was not writing articles every
week that would enable him to help and support his family.[72]

During the weekend party in question, according to Lady Gregory, Yeats
vehemently defended the artist who put his art first, whereas Lawless's
view was that an 'artist or poet should lay aside his gift if by working at
an ordinary trade he could better help his family'.[73] Though she was not
as prolific as some of her contemporaries, she made sure that her writing
yielded as much as possible by having her poems and articles republished
as collections or in other journals, and her books published in American
editions. Sichel mentions that she had 'a concrete mind with a turn for
affairs; with a man's business outlook'.[74] She was very careful to find out
what terms would apply when a work was published, as her
correspondence with Macmillan's about *A Millionaire's Cousin* (1885)
makes clear:

Since coming home one or two things have occurred to me that I forgot
to touch upon this morning. One is about copyright. Messrs Sampson Low
who published my first (& only) novel, also on half profits, told me that
although they had a legal claim to half copyright of future editions it was

not a claim they enforced, and that if I wished to bring out another edition I could do so independently of them, or under a new arrangement. I have a letter to that effect. Will you kindly let me know if this will hold good in this case also? and how many copies there will probably be in the first edition? In all probability there will be <u>no</u> call for a further edition, but it seems as well to provide for future contingencies beforehand. Should the 'Millionaire's Cousin' have any success it might perhaps be worth while some day to have another edition of the first book, as I believe no copies exist. Another little point I should like to feel clear about is how soon after publication a statement is usually furnished? and another still smaller one is how many copies I should be able to lay hands on for my own behoof?[75]

Despite the somewhat girlish tone of the letter and despite the fact that the issues raised should normally have been dealt with during the meeting referred to, Lawless seems to have been well aware of the commercial side of publishing. Another example of her business-like attitude is the effort she put into making sure that she received as good terms as possible for the American copyright of her books.[76] She actively tried to sell her work, as is indicated in, for instance, a letter to Clement K. Shorter: 'I am putting together a volume of short stories to come out this year, & have been writing one or two to make it long enough. It occurs to me that you might care for one for the "English Illustrated magazine".'[77] When a book was nearing its publication she took great care to ensure that everything was in good order. There are thirteen letters in the Macmillan Archive about the manuscript of *Maria Edgeworth* (1904), concerning matters like the best kind of type to use for quoted material, printers' corrections, the proper form of names appearing in the text and requests for additional proof-reading: 'I should be very glad if the whole could go through some careful hands after I have corrected it myself. Is there anyone in your office who would be likely to undertake this? Errors of fact I can correct, & for the style of course I alone am responsible, but small oversights are very apt to be passed over, & disfigure a book.'[78] She also wished to influence matters like cover, binding and price, and wrote several letters to Macmillan's about the appearance of *A Millionaire's Cousin* (1885): 'Your idea of having the book got up something like Shorthouses' "Little Schoolmaster" seems to me excellent but I think that the printing ought not to be too close. I suppose it could be turned out for 2/6 or 3/?'[79] When the proposed binding did not meet with her approval, she suggested changes:

I am sorry to say I do not like the brown & buff binding now that I see it <u>at all</u>. Neither does my mother who declares that it looks as it was meant to bind 'Magnall's questions' or 'Lindley Murray'! You said there would be no objection to using the one you have bound 'Miss Bretherton' in & I think therefore that we could not do better. If it was necessary to vary it we could have the backs the <u>deep</u> red & the sides the <u>light</u>. I am sorry if this gives any extra trouble but I am certain that the cover sent would not be suitable for a novel.[80]

In contrast to such examples of business acumen, Lawless did not treat her writing as a profession, at least not in the sense that she devoted her time wholly to her work. A description of her work habits is included in the *Irish Book Lover:*

Her method of composition was peculiar to herself. She would not plan out her work from start to finish, as other novelists do, even as an architect plans a house. She would write a portion of a story, then tire of it and set it aside, whilst she commenced another, which frequently met the same fate. Then, as the humour seized her, she would take up one or other and complete it. Thus, she frequently had two or three books 'on the stocks' at once, consequently the number of unfinished and unpublished MSS. she has left behind must be very great.[81]

It is possible, even probable, that Lawless did leave a good number of unfinished pieces behind, but since she left instructions that most of her papers should be burnt after her death, and her brother Frederick carried out her wish, very little remains.[82] There are a few poems in the Lawless collection in Marsh's Library, but no longer manuscript seems to have survived.

After her mother's death, Lawless stopped travelling between Ireland, London and various places in Europe. The main reason for this seems to have been that her rheumatic complaint made the wet climate of Ireland difficult for her. It is not entirely clear from the sources exactly when she took up permanent residence in England, but the *Literary World* notes that in 1895 she occupied a farmhouse known as the Borough Farm on Thursley Common in Surrey, previously a favourite retreat of Mrs Humphry Ward.[83] She subsequently moved to Gomshall, Surrey, where she built a cottage with Lady Sarah Spencer, daughter of the fourth Earl Spencer and sister to the Irish Viceroy, John Poyntz. The house, 'Hazelhatch', was finished in December 1898, and Lawless lived there until her death, though up until 1911 she still visited Ireland every year.[84]

Emily Lawless died on 19 October 1913. Sir Horace Plunkett writes in his diary: 'Emily Lawless died peacefully yesterday. Poor thing. Her life had been one of constant nerve torture for many years. It is a happy release. But what a break with the past.'[85] In her autobiography, Katharine Tynan describes meeting Lawless's brother at a concert shortly after his sister had died:

> I met Emily Lawless's brother, a very gentle, refined-looking, elderly man. It was just after Miss Lawless's death. He told me she had died in her sleep. The maid, entering the room in the morning and drawing up the blind, was struck by the rigidity of the sleeper, and approaching found her dead, wearing the utmost placidity of countenance. He spoke of her as 'my dear' and 'my dear one'. It was pleasant to know that she was so much loved.[86]

At the time of Lawless's death, the Anglo-Irish Ascendancy world that she had belonged to had already begun to disappear. As Irish literary criticism grew more nationalist in tone, sometimes excluding even such previously recognised literary heroes as Yeats on the grounds of impure nationality,[87] Lawless's politically ambiguous writing began to be dismissed as conservative or even anti-Irish. A few years after her death she was almost completely forgotten.

Chapter 2

Anti-suffragist and New Woman: early fiction

The woman question was one of the most burning issues in the late nineteenth century, and the new awareness of women's lack of opportunities and rights in society vitally influenced both social life and literature. Emily Lawless's dates correspond exactly to the definition Ann Heilmann gives of the first generation of New Women: 'writers born around the mid-century whose main work falls in the 30-year period between 1880 and 1910'.[1] However, even though her early novels deal with some of the themes prominent in New Woman fiction, Lawless combines the feminist scrutiny often found in this type of literature with a reluctance to offer a sustained challenge to the prevalent gender ideology. To place her early novels in the context of New Woman fiction reveals the inherent duality of her gender politics; that is, how she both criticises and upholds the values of the patriarchal society she belongs to. To the extent that writing is an expression of identity, Lawless seems to reject a gendered foundation of selfhood to express an identity that is more a matter of intellectual choice – a wish to be objective, to belong to the cultured elite, to be both Irish and European, both a woman and an intellectual.

At the same time, the very act of writing and publishing can be seen as evidence of an emancipated life, and the relation between a woman writer's life and the gender politics expressed in her writing can be quite complex. As a woman writer Lawless was certainly a powerful symbol for the feminist movement, but to be taken seriously by the literary establishment she would have had to dissociate herself from issues that defined her as oppositional. The double voice of Lawless's writing reflects the intellectual woman's dilemma as both inside and outside the cultural institutions of her time, as well as the conflict between the protection offered by the traditional feminine role and the autonomy promised by a professional life. Her reluctance to take sides is not primarily evidence of objectivity, nor is it a sign of uncertainty or political instability. Rather, it functions as a textual accommodation of the contradictions and tensions in a patriarchal society under pressure, and as an expression of how a woman writer negotiated her social and literary spaces. Lawless's early fiction is thoroughly ambivalent where gender issues are concerned.

As the 1905 Trinity Doctorate demonstrates, Lawless did indeed create a space for herself in public life. Given the fact that it was only in 1904 that female students were admitted to Trinity College,[2] the appointment was a triumph for women and showed that female intellectuals were well able to participate in the cultural sphere on the prevailing terms. Even so, the honour draws attention to a central question for the woman writer (and for the feminist critic): what is the price of public recognition? For critics anxious to find evidence of subversion in women's work such a sign of official approval may be seen as compromising the political messages of the texts. Could it be that Lawless was appointed because she accepted, perhaps even embraced, the patriarchal values that underwrote the public sphere? Is it radical or conservative to write oneself into the mainstream? Must a professional woman not automatically be a feminist? Conservative and anti-feminist views are easily seen as ludicrous, because today they usually represent the losing side – at least officially. It is important to remember that this was not always the case. For many women writers, a patriarchal organisation of society was simply regarded as the natural order. For others, the ostensible conformism of their works alleviated the threat they embodied as independent women. Hence, what may look like conventionality in the present critical light may have been a very strategic choice. Apparent support of the *status quo* could function as a safeguard against reprisals in the form of social ostracism or publishers' rejection slips.

The time when the New Woman writers flourished is also what Gaye Tuchman describes as 'the period of redefinition' and 'the period of institutionalization';[3] that is, the years between 1880 and 1917, when the novel changed from having been a literary form predominantly used by women to becoming men's business. This development carried with it a rise in the status of the novel but also an increasing contempt for what began to be seen as 'womanish writing', domestic and romantic as well as feminist and proto-feminist. As the novel became more and more a masculine preserve, women were 'edged out', as Tuchman puts it, and success – in cultural if not necessarily in popular terms – became a matter of adopting what was perceived as a more masculine style. According to her friend Edith Sichel, Lawless had

> a concrete mind with a turn for affairs; with a man's business outlook, large and lucid, not over-concerned with detail; still more with a gift for natural science, her 'ruling passion' from seven years old onwards, and for the methods of minute research.[4]

This enumeration of late Victorian masculine virtues suggests that Lawless did not quite fit her society's definitions of womanhood. In a story based on an episode from her childhood, Lawless describes herself as a child as full of contempt for those activities considered suitable for girls and painfully aware of the opportunities denied her because of her sex:

> Even for this aspiring naturalist, for this embryo discoverer, life had its drawbacks. If less pressing upon her than upon others, there still were certain respects in which the long-recognized limitations of her sex continued to assert themselves. The most formidable, perhaps, of these was the early recognition of the fact that under no circumstances, by no possible stretch of indulgence, would this coming Cuvier or Buffon in short frocks ever be entrusted with a gun! This plainly tyrannical, and heartless regulation had the natural effect of curtailing at one fell swoop the entire realm over which her future activities were to range, and in which she was to record her triumphs.[5]

Instead of pursuing her dream to become a new Darwin, Lawless had to be satisfied with entomology, and underneath the humorous tone of the account there is a real sense of lost opportunity. But Sichel glosses over the problems faced by the woman intellectual, and indeed, even Lawless's womanhood. Overvaluing her masculine attributes, she claims that Lawless was capable of separating her identity as a woman from her art:

> Perhaps there are few people in whom the two strains of artist and of woman kept so distinctly alongside – seldom fusing, touching occasionally, yet without causing the conflict, the clash of emotions which has troubled so many creators.[6]

'Writing as a woman' is consequently seen as problematic, and at least in Sichel's view it added to Lawless's greatness that her femininity did not contaminate her work. This judgement is of course a product of a belief in the possibility – and desirability – of an objective style and, by adjusting her interpretation to prevalent cultural ideals, Sichel neutralises the complexity of Lawless's works. For Sichel, the dilemma of being a woman writer is easily overcome if the woman simply suppresses her feminine identity.

The question is whether this solution is at all desirable and, further, whether it is possible for a woman writer to completely eliminate her function as a feminist role model. With Maria Edgeworth as her example and Margaret Oliphant as her mentor, Lawless was part of a female tradition that was different from mainstream male writing at the time. James M. Cahalan even argues that the 'work of twentieth-century writers such as Kate O'Brien and Jennifer Johnston would be unimaginable if Lawless had not come before'.[7] The importance of female predecessors for creative women should certainly not be underestimated. On the other hand, Lawless had an extensive network that included many male intellectuals, and there is no indication that she privileged women's work or women's questions. Not every turn-of-the-century woman writer thought of herself as a feminist, and in Ireland women's issues were overshadowed by the struggle for Irish nationhood. There was a conflict between nationalism and feminism from the very beginning, since the suffragettes fought for the right to vote for a parliament that the nationalists would not accept. Many women who would otherwise perhaps have campaigned for suffrage therefore chose to support nationalist groups instead.[8] Other women, like the Countess of Fingall, Susan L. Mitchell and the Hon. Mary Lawless, worked for the improvement of rural life through associations like the United Irishwomen, an offshoot of the Irish Agricultural Organisation Society instigated by Lawless's cousin Sir Horace Plunkett. In a pamphlet about this women's branch of the society, Plunkett makes clear that he viewed working for the association as an alternative to the struggle for the vote:

> Here, then, is the real mission of the United Irishwomen. They will find in social work an outlet for some of that abundant energy which has been displayed by women on the other side of the channel in the campaign for the suffrage.[9]

However, although the organisation encouraged women to focus on social rather than political work, the gender ideals of the United Irishwomen were not necessarily conservative. In many ways, they were quite radical,

and in the third part of the pamphlet George W. Russell argues for
women's rights to fulfilling occupations:

> to-day the starved soul of womanhood is crying out over the world for an
> intellectual life and for more chance of earning a living. If Ireland will not
> listen to this cry, its daughters will go on slipping silently away to other
> countries, as they have been doing – all the best of them, all the bravest,
> all those most mentally alive, all those who would have made the best wives
> and the best mothers.[10]

There is a clear contradiction between Russell's insistence on women's right
to fulfilling work on the one hand and his continued view of women as
primarily wives and mothers on the other. It is obvious that the basic idea
of the movement was that there was a clear division between women's and
men's work, although, in this, the organisation only reflected public
opinion. Lawless supported the United Irishwomen and may have shared
Plunkett's opinion that women's 'housekeeperly instincts' were of greater
value to the modern nation than their votes.[11] She was already an
established writer when the United Irishwomen appeared, however, and her
decision to avoid the women's movement was probably more influenced by
her mother and perhaps by the family friend Margaret Oliphant, who was
firmly against both feminist action and feminist fiction, though some of her
portraits of women certainly emerge as feminist today.[12]

Part of the problem is how to define the meaning of the term
'feminist' in the nineteenth century. For many women, it was the public
commitment that was perceived as the problem. According to Oliphant,
Lawless's mother, Lady Elizabeth Cloncurry, was impatient 'with the
flutter of feminine agitations which have been so general' but frequently
and compassionately talked about 'those deprivations women have to bear,
and which no suffrages nor freedoms, political or otherwise, can help
them out of'.[13] This was Oliphant's opinion as well. Elizabeth Jay
summarises her position by saying that Oliphant was 'painfully aware of
the limitations imposed upon women's lives by the unthinking tyranny of
cultural tradition, but wanted to distinguish these from the sacrifices
which, consciously embraced, might bear fruit in the refinement of the
moral spirit'.[14] As Arlene Young sees it, like 'other women writing in the
second half of the nineteenth century, Oliphant consistently tries to move
beyond the stereotypes in her representations of women, without ever
overturning the conventions'.[15] In Lawless's circle, women's problems were

somehow seen as natural, albeit regrettable, parts of being a woman that could not be remedied by group action. Apart from a sceptical attitude to the efficacy of legal measures, held by, for instance, Oliphant, there was also the widespread feeling that women who campaigned for suffrage endangered their femininity.[16]

The main problem was the methods employed by women activists, and even though Emily Lawless continued to be deeply interested in women's conditions she never took an active part in the struggle for the vote. In a letter to Edith Sichel, she clarifies her position:

> I have no sympathy with Suffragette methods, I need hardly say, and have personally no wish for a vote, but the helplessness of great bodies of women-workers even against *admitted* wrongs, simply because there is no one whose *interest* it is to speak for them, is too plain a fact for any fair-minded person, man or woman, to deny.[17]

The phrase 'I need hardly say' shows that Lawless was by no means alone when she dissociated herself from the militant suffragettes, and in 1889 she signed 'An Appeal Against Women's Suffrage', thus making public her refusal to support the most important cause of the late nineteenth-century women's movement.[18] The appeal expresses a firm belief in the complementary gender ideology, stressing women's natural difference from men and maintaining that women should be satisfied with remaining in the domestic sphere: 'the care of the sick and the insane; the treatment of the poor; the education of children'.[19] The document was signed by more than a hundred influential women, many of them titled, many using their husbands' names, like Lady Randolph Churchill, Mrs Leslie Stephen, Mrs Humphry Ward and Mrs Matthew Arnold. The appeal was anti-suffrage, however, not anti-feminist, and at least Mary A. Ward, or Mrs Humphry Ward as she called herself when she published her fiction, actively supported attempts to involve women in public life.[20] It is symptomatic of the complex attitudes to the woman question that Ward's anti-suffrage novel *Delia Blanchflower* (1915) in many ways can be read as a feminist text. Ward certainly denounces the violence of the militant branches of the suffragette organisations, but the novel also shows how women's suffering is caused by patriarchal oppression and the pressures of an inhuman industrialised society.[21] Mary Ward was a friend of Emily Lawless, and it is reasonable to assume that their views on women's issues may have coincided, at least to some extent.

Some years after 'An Appeal Against Women's Suffrage', Lawless's opinion appears to have changed somewhat, judging by a letter she wrote to Professor A. V. Dicey to thank him for his 'little book'.[22] The content of the letter indicates that the book in question is Dicey's pamphlet *Letters to a Friend on Votes for Women* (1909). Lawless begins by writing that she finds herself in agreement with Dicey, especially as concerns his argument that only those able and willing to defend and die for a country should have a right to a part in its government. Yet, the letter also acknowledges that the patriarchal system is an important reason why women cannot vote, and Lawless doubts whether any man 'would willingly pass from a condition in which that vote (the women's) wd have after all a very restricted influence, to one in wh it would, if exercised collectively, swamp his <u>own</u>'.[23] Lawless's argument meanders considerably, and her own conclusion that she is 'rather a facer-of-both-ways' seems a good description of her position.[24] The letter ends with a curious mixture of deference and defiance:

> It will really be very kind if you will waste a few minutes of your time in answering me on some of those points? Observe the instinctive deference with which my appeal is made! That is no doubt partly <u>hereditary</u>; as well as mainly & honestly <u>personal</u>! To put the matter in a nutshell. I expect that the present sole possessors of Power will be wisest in their own interest to retain that power in their own hands. The few instances of a voluntary surrender we have any of us known (such as Majuba for instance) do not probably encourage <u>repetitions</u>. Predominant physical strength is unquestionably a big factor in <u>Nature</u>, therefore in <u>History</u>. It is not a noble, generous or chivalrous factor, & nothing will make it so, but at least both 'classes' had better face it frankly & with widely-open eyes![25]

On the one hand, Lawless assumes the position of the 'little woman' in relation to Dicey, in line with nineteenth-century gender conventions, but, on the other, she appears to be very critical of male power and its foundation on masculine strength. Like most of her writing, Lawless's letter to Dicey is double-voiced.

In one sense, public repudiation of a movement that attracted so much hostility was a tactical move for women writers, ensuring that they did not lose their platform, at the same time as it made more moderate feminist claims less objectionable, but it can also be seen as a wish to avoid categorisation. Instead of entering the political scene, Lawless resorted to the particular. Her works contain poignant stories of women's suffering that recognise oppression as many women's lot, but never really amount to a feminist statement. Despite her awareness of the repressive gender order, she did not commit herself to any cause, nor did she see herself as a member of a unified category of women. Her attitude is perhaps best summarised in the words 'I'm not a feminist, but . . .' This position can be seen particularly clearly in her early novels.

*

Emily Lawless's first three novels are set outside Ireland and explore issues of class, gender and individual freedom in Victorian culture. The emphasis is particularly on the problem of female autonomy and, for this reason, the works can be grouped together with the New Woman fiction that evolved into a genre of its own at the end of the nineteenth century. According to Ann Heilmann, this literature can be defined as:

> a white, western, middle-class, humanist, predominantly heterosexual genre which, to varying degrees and depending on individual writers' shifting positions, articulated the belief in women's difference from or essential equality with men, thematizing the expediency and/or the problems of separatism, and arguing for women's social and political emancipation.[26]

The focus on women's emancipation was not universal, however, and New Woman fiction was used by both feminists and anti-feminists to support or discredit the women's movement. The immense popularity of the books meant that writers aspiring to succeed in the literary market-place were drawn to the genre regardless of their political affiliations, and the New Woman herself can obviously function as both an inspiring example and a negative stereotype. Common themes are the predicament of the woman artist, the conflict between love and a professional life and the effects of an unhappy marriage, but the outcomes differ according to what ideology the writer wishes to disseminate. Lawless's three New Woman novels, *A Chelsea Householder* (1882), *A Millionaire's Cousin* (1885) and *Major Lawrence, F. L. S.* (1887),[27] explore questions connected with women's liberation, but do not attack the patriarchal order as a system primarily upheld by men. On the contrary, Lawless shows that restrictions on women's liberty are often sustained by women, and she is clearly pessimistic about the possibilities of womanly solidarity.

The heroine of Lawless's first novel, *A Chelsea Householder*, combines the traits of the classical romantic heroine with those of the New Woman. Muriel Ellis is a young and beautiful orphan, but also an artist with her own house in Chelsea. The possession of a latch-key is an obvious sign of independence, but supportive sisterhood, a common feature of New Woman fiction, is conspicuous by its absence.[28] Unlike the writers who described female utopias, Lawless offers a very critical description of Muriel's attempt to share her house with her sister-in-law, and, while there is also a positive example of women living together, female separatism is plainly not the solution.

Except for the tender relationship between Grania and her sister Honor in the novel *Grania: The Story of an Island* (1892), it is only *A Chelsea Householder* of all Lawless's novels that contains descriptions of female friendships. The most important of these, the relation between Muriel and her companion Miss Prettyman, demonstrates new and old attitudes to female independence. Elizabeth Prettyman is a fluttering, insecure woman whose only protection from a frightening world is proper behaviour:

> She was perfectly devoted to her companion, and regarded her as a sort of impersonification [*sic*] of all the possible and impossible talents and perfections; indeed, was in the habit of deferring to her, and accepting all her various crotchets and theories in a way that certainly was not customary at their respective ages. At the same time she never could divest herself of a certain uneasy feeling of responsibility on her account. Muriel was so terribly unconventional. There really was no knowing what vagary, or what artistic or philanthropic freak she might not take it into her head to commit. And, artist though she was herself, Miss Prettyman was a perfect priestess of the proprieties, holding everything like unconventionality in the deepest distrust. (18)

The friendship with Miss Prettyman counterbalances Muriel's unconventional behaviour and alleviates such fears as might arise from descriptions of her insistence on making her own decisions in life. For Elizabeth Prettyman, independence is dangerous, as well as a breach of propriety, while for Muriel it is a necessary part of being an artist:

> 'You are a great deal too handsome to go wandering about in this sort of way by yourself. I don't mind saying it to you, because of course you know it, and, besides, you're not vain; but it really is not the thing to do. Nobody does it – no lady, at least.'

'But my dear Elizabeth, I am an artist, and artists cannot be bound by these ridiculous conventional rules. I should die if I had to be always thinking of the proprieties.'

'I don't see that, Muriel. I am an artist too, and I hope I have never violated propriety, or even *wished* to do so; besides, at my age it is different.' (41)

The difference between the two women is emphasised by the fact that Miss Prettyman is a copyist while Muriel is a talented, original artist. There is certainly a link between copying and convention on the one hand and originality and female autonomy on the other, and symbolically, at least, it would seem as if Lawless endorses the latter combination. But not too far. Since the fusty Miss Prettyman would not have been the friend of someone who was too radical, Muriel's need for independence is contained and made to seem less threatening, and thus Lawless's text is both associated with and dissociated from feminist ideas.

If the friendship with Miss Prettyman primarily functions to downplay the threat of a feminist side to Muriel's character, the effect of another friend, Kitty King, is to strengthen this aspect:

The Kings were remarkably dull stereotyped sort of people, always excepting that wayward young lady herself, who had independence and audacity enough in her own small person to have set up a whole household. Indeed, it was currently asserted, and that, too, by others besides Elizabeth Prettyman, that Kitty had taken up the career of art student, not because she cared one single button about art, but simply as a sort of cloak under the cover of which she might the better carry out her own emancipation. (105–6)

Where Miss Prettyman is staid and conservative, Kitty is frivolous and radical, and as a friend to both these characters, Muriel emerges as the golden mean.

A Chelsea Householder also contains a picture of a dysfunctional female relationship. Muriel's sister-in-law Mrs Skynner shares the house in Chelsea with her young relative, and while Muriel is away she invites her acquaintance Madame Cairioli to stay with her. It is gradually revealed that she has been gravely mistaken in her assessment of this lady, who is, in fact, 'a professional beggar; one of the best known in London' (125). When this becomes clear, Mrs Skynner throws her out, blaming the whole mess on Muriel, and Madame Cairioli later dies in squalor. The picture of Madame Cairioli shows how few options were open to single women in the late nineteenth century and in this way her imposition on the women of the Chelsea household is made to seem understandable, if not quite forgivable. Mrs Skynner, on the other hand, emerges as both unable to judge other people and unwilling to show charity, while Muriel seeks out the dying woman to see what help she may offer. As opposed to the friendships with Kitty King and Elizabeth Prettyman, which corresponded to facets of Muriel's character, Mrs Skynner's function in the story is to be Muriel's contrast.

A few descriptions of Muriel's insufficient domestic qualities could possibly be seen as mild expressions of feminist awareness, though they certainly do not amount to a feminist statement:

> Muriel's housewifely instincts were by nature, it must be owned, but slightly developed; indeed, she would any day of the week have infinitely preferred going without her dinner to having to go through the preliminary ordeal of ordering it. (119)

Lawless's class bias is clear when she makes Muriel order – not cook – her dinner and it is clear also that Muriel is able to challenge social conventions in ways not possible to some of the other women characters because she has her own money. Yet, at the end of the novel it is Muriel who sacrifices her gift and marries, not the artist Mr Wygram, who offers her a life of companionship and the opportunity to continue her work, but the overbearing and dictatorial clergyman Stephen Halliday, who requires her to give up her artistic aspirations. While the kind of union Mr Wygram suggests appeals to Muriel 'in the abstract' (173), she is not in love with him and, '[l]ike every nature which is at once strong and feminine, Muriel had a keen, almost a passionate need of loving and being loved' (145). Love, as Lawless presents it in *A Chelsea Householder,* seems to include an element of submission that the kind and considerate Mr Wygram cannot inspire. Halliday, on the other hand, is combative and 'too big somehow, mentally as well as physically' (205), and the masculine ideal he represents is incompatible with female independence. In the end Muriel's status as New Woman is thus undermined by a promise of domestication, and she is made to realise that art can never offer her the fulfilment she desires. Her choice of love before art allows a contemporary reviewer for the *Nation* to describe her as 'a girl of just that gentle independence of spirit which is so much more attractive than positive softness, or outright strongmindedness'.[29] It was common at the time to refer to intellectual women as strong-minded and, in the eyes of the *Nation* commentator at least, the traditional romantic ending proves that Muriel's independence was only a temporary aberration, and that when she has found her true place at the end of the novel there is no longer any need for her to 'play very prettily at being an artist'.[30]

While *A Chelsea Householder* touches upon critical social issues such as class and gender inequality, it cannot be described as a political novel. It was published anonymously in the old three-decker format and is longer than its rather meagre plot deserves, but, in general, it was received as a 'bright and pleasant' story, free from both sensationalism and sordid realism.[31] According to what Lawless wrote in a letter to Macmillan's in February 1883, the first edition of the novel 'nearly all sold out', so there was obviously some popular appeal.[32] Edith Sichel, however, misnames the work *A Chelsea Cousin*, which indicates that she, at least, did not know it very well, and states that the novel 'met with no success'.[33] William Linn sees it as 'an example of the worst Victorian sentimentality',[34] and it is clear that Lawless tried to conform to a rather conventional idea of what a novel should be like. The satirical descriptions of Muriel's sister-in-law Mrs Skynner, her friend Elizabeth Prettyman, the fraudulent Madame Cairioli and the flirt Kitty King made both the *Standard* and the *Spectator* reviewers compare Lawless with Jane Austen, and the descriptions of New Forest and Norfolk scenery were praised, but it is clear that the novel was not considered in any way out of the ordinary.[35]

Since the potentially provocative picture of Muriel as an independent New Woman is offset by her decision to follow Halliday's lead in the end, the novel was regarded as an inoffensive instance of domestic Victorian fiction rather than as aligned with the New Woman novels of the day:

> Muriel Ellis, with her simple good-breeding, generous nature, good-sense, and love of art, without the infection of its follies, while she is in some danger of assigning to it an undue place and importance in her life, is as happy a corrective of the artistic young woman of recent fiction as can be desired.[36]

A Chelsea Householder could be taken as an indication that Lawless indeed supported patriarchal constructions of femininity, but this is to disregard her double voice. The novel's most interesting feature are the portraits of different kinds of women or feminine positions, and the discussions about proper feminine behaviour and the pictures of female suffering still remain, albeit in uneasy tension with the conventions of the romantic novel. *A Chelsea Householder* is a novel where feminist ideas clash with the romance script, but the traditional happy ending does not necessarily mean that feminism is discarded. Rather, the two positions are in dialogue with each other, expressing Lawless's ambivalent gender politics. That the contemporary reviewers failed to notice this conflict in the text is hardly strange, given the misogynist climate of late nineteenth-century reviewing.[37]

*

Lawless's second novel, *A Millionaire's Cousin: A Story*, was initially serialised in *Macmillan's Magazine* in 1885 and published in book form later the same year. The power of the lending libraries and their preference for the three-volume format still greatly influenced the publishing world, as Lawless was clearly well aware:

> It seems to me as if your magazine was of such preeminent importance that no story (long enough for separate existence) that is considered good enough to appear in it could very well be unworthy of republication, though I can quite understand that with the strong bias of Mudie & other libraries in favour of the 3 vol forms it might very well fail to be very highly remunerative.[38]

The novel was obviously better received in its serialised form than when it appeared as a book. There is a rather offended tone in the request for reviews Lawless sent to Macmillan's:

> She [Miss Lawless] does not know whether any notices of her story have appeared either in the 'Spectator' or 'Saturday review' if so she would like to see them whether favourable or the reverse. None of those she has seen have been as cordial as the notices she read of the story while it was coming out in 'Macmillan'. Should Messrs Macmillan think any of the notices worth making extracts from to insert with advertisements of the book Miss Lawless would be much obliged by their kindly letting her first see their selection. She does not herself fancy that any of them would be much use in that direction.[39]

One of the few mentions of the novel appeared in the 'Books of the Month' list in the *Atlantic Monthly,* where the novel is described as 'a lively story' with 'a briskness about the telling which takes the place of the otherwise necessary humour'.[40] *A Millionaire's Cousin* strikes a more modern note than *A Chelsea Householder,* and this might have been one reason for the public's disfavour. An equally possible reason is that its ambiguity regarding the woman question might have made readers conclude that it was not modern enough. The book did not sell very well.[41]

An important theme in the novel is the negotiation between conflicting views of women's place in society. As the narrator Adolphus Bell sees it, gender configurations are culturally determined, not natural, and it seems probable that Lawless would be of the same opinion, despite her signature on the appeal against women's suffrage. Yet, Bell's arguments for women's independence are seriously compromised by the fact that, as a narrator, he is exposed as totally subjective and unreliable in the end. Bell never becomes the privileged voice of the author, but, precisely because of this, Lawless manages to present a strong defence for women's right to autonomy at the same time as she distances herself from this position. The issue remains unresolved and the dialogic nature of the text is emphasised by the gender difference between Lawless as the author and the male narrator Bell.

Using the voice of the other gender denies a direct correspondence between author and narrator and prevents both automatic rejection on the basis of sex and such reductive interpretations as the early feminist attempts to identify the 'real woman' in women's fiction. By blurring the borders of identity, cross-gendered writing becomes an expression of women's (and men's) discontent with conventional roles. In sexual-political terms the concept remains problematic, however, because it paradoxically both reinforces and challenges traditional gender boundaries. On the one hand, the technique presupposes an identity based on biological sex – the woman writer – and an identity based on gender as a socially constructed category – the male narrator – and both these positions reflect prevailing definitions of femininity and masculinity. On the other hand, the very fact that cross-gendered writing is possible suggests a fundamental hybridity that refutes absolute differences between the sexes and reduces the differences between what is regarded as masculine and feminine language, thought and behaviour.

Even though the author is present only as signature, the text constantly invokes two voices, sometimes in opposition, and the fissures created by the gender-switch are widened by the fact that a first-person narrator represents an individual, as opposed to a universal, position. While always qualified by subjectivity, the voice of the narrator is seldom wholly discredited, and as a result there is no total vision, but an ongoing dialogue between the narrating 'I' and the author who controls it. This dialogue inevitably involves a negotiation between conceptions of masculinity and femininity, power and silence, inside and outside perspectives, and only rarely arrives at a conclusive answer. In consequence, women's use of male voices may be seen both as an acceptance of the values of a patriarchal society and an attempt to collapse the system altogether. The gender politics of the technique remain unclear.

Emily Lawless used the device of cross-gendered narration in the short stories 'The Builder of the Round Towers: A Chronicle of the Eighth Century' and 'A Ligurian Episode' and in the novels *With Essex in Ireland* (1890), *A Colonel of the Empire* (1895), *The Race of Castlebar*, written in collaboration with Shan Bullock (1913), and *A Millionaire's Cousin* (1885). In *With Essex in Ireland* the subject matter – sixteenth-century history and war – partly warrants a male narrative perspective, but in the contemporary *A Millionaire's Cousin* there is no obvious external reason for using a man's voice, which means that the technique becomes even more integral to the meaning of the text. The novel is set in London and Algeria and almost certainly makes use of material from a visit Lawless made some time before 1882, when she records travelling from Algiers to the Bay of Biscay.[42] The story develops the theme of the woman artist, which is important also in *A Chelsea Householder*, but discussions about the place and position of women in society are much more prominent – though the issue remains unsettled. *A Millionaire's Cousin* is an unusually clear example of the double voice that permeates Lawless's fiction.

The title establishes the narrator's identity as relational – he is a millionaire's cousin, not somebody in his own right. In one sense this feminises him, since a relational identity is commonly associated with women, but the first line of the story emphasises his uniqueness, in apparent opposition to the designation given in the title: 'I, Adolphus Bell, am a painter, and the first of my family that has taken to the arts as a vocation.'[43] It is significant that the story begins with 'I', since Bell's reliability as a narrator changes according to the degree of self-centredness he displays. His struggle between a relational and a singular identity is played out when he measures himself against other men, and particularly the millionaire John Hargrave, whose main shortcoming, apart from his possession of a large fortune, is that he sometimes seems to forget Bell's existence:

> Several times lately I have had to speak to him twice and even oftener before I could rouse him sufficiently to obtain an answer, though unless he is trying to calculate what the aggregate of his fortune amounts to at compound interest, or how long it would have to accumulate before it could pay off the National Debt, I cannot see what he can have so particularly to think about. There is something oppressive about the man too, which increases the longer one is *tête-à-tête* with him; he seems to grow larger and larger somehow, and oneself in proportion to shrink and dwindle away. (94)

The problem, in other words, is that Hargrave makes Bell feel small, and to compensate for his feelings of inferiority Bell convinces himself that Hargrave's success is merely a matter of luck, while his own qualities are internal and as a consequence more valuable:

> Setting aside his money – which every one knows is a purely adventitious matter, no more a merit of his than his having large hands or being six feet high – setting aside this all inequality so far as I can see ceases, indeed but that it might seem to savour of self laudation I should be disposed to say that it began again on the other side. In maintaining that I am a cleverer man than John Hargrave I can hardly be accused of any extravagant personal eulogy seeing that he obviously is not a clever man at all, as every one who knows him is perfectly well aware. (94–5)

As male voice, Bell is an ideological rather than a linguistic construct and, while he does not represent masculinity in any general sense, it seems clear that Lawless understood power struggle as a main component of maleness. A central theme in the novel is thus the nature of equality, dramatised in Lawless's description of the condescending attitudes of French and English colonists in Algeria, the contemptuous attitude of Algerian men towards women, the debates concerning women's roles in society and Adolphus Bell's mental games of one-upmanship.

In London, Bell shares a studio with two other men, an arrangement that makes power balance one of his chief concerns. As he perceives it, equality is analogous with sameness, and, since one of the artists has spent some time abroad, it becomes imperative for Bell to travel too. Being poor, he can do so only at the invitation of his cousin Hargrave, which puts him in a position of dependence. He nevertheless accepts Hargrave's offer to receive him in Algeria, primarily so that he can restore equilibrium at home by 'flaunting Africa and its golden joys in the very face of the reluctant Judkins', his well-travelled studio mate (9). Since Hargrave's money highlights the financial aspect of his inequality, Bell tries to convince himself that his poverty somehow makes him morally superior to his relatives:

> Poor relations have, however – perhaps unwarrantly – their own opinions, and it was no small consolation to me, I remember, to mentally smile at these redundant splendours, and turn up my nose (of course quite invisibly!) at what, to my youthful and fastidious mind, seemed the somewhat barbaric character of my great-uncle Hargrave's entertainments. (5)

Bell contrasts the ephemeral quality of money with his own artistic gifts, but is unable to lose his feeling of relative inadequacy: 'why should wealth – an accident of which fate, or an untoward investment, might at any moment deprive him – weigh upon me like this, I have often wondered' (14). These emotions form the background to the familiar fairy-tale romance of the beautiful girl, the rich man and the poor artist – a typically feminine plot that achieves a certain twist by being narrated in a man's voice.

Bell's credibility may be compromised even from the beginning, but the expectations installed by the presence of the romance plot restores some of his authority, since it seems to cast him as the hero. This doubt as to the exact nature of his narrative control persists almost to the end of the story and, not entirely sure whether Bell's account is to be trusted or dismissed, the reader is led to view him in a more sympathetic light. At least for most present-day readers, Bell also appears more likeable, since he is the one who defends women's independence.

The main sub-theme of the novel is the negotiation between conflicting views of women's place in society. In a long sequence Bell debates the issue with the Anglo-French Algerian colonist Madame de la Hoche. The focus of their discussion is Hildegarde Bonson, the heroine of the romance plot, and the desirability of a union between her and the millionaire Hargrave. Miss Bonson's brother Marmaduke 'makes no secret of regarding his feminine belongings as created wholly and solely for his own behoof', an attitude that is explained at least to some extent as the result of living 'under a Moorish roof' (43). Nevertheless, there is no sense that English gender politics are any more civilised than the Algerian attitude, as it is presented in the novel. Rather, patriarchal control of women is presented as universally accepted. Thus Marmaduke and his mother view Miss Bonson as a commodity and tell her that she must marry a rich man so that they may keep her allowance. In Madame de la Hoche's opinion, this is the reason why Hildegarde Bonson has refused Hargrave's advances so far:

> They press, they drive, they persecute her – they give her no peace – they tell her that she is a wicked girl to hesitate, and that it is her bounden duty to accept him. If she does not already detest your cousin it is that her good sense tells her that it is not his fault, and that he is really nearly as much a victim in the matter as she is. (48)

Miss Bonson's dream is to go to London and earn her living as an artist, but both her mother and Madame de la Hoche ask Bell to tell her that she is incapable. Mrs Bonson's hypocritical motive is that art demands 'all or nothing', so 'when social circumstances forbid that we should thus devote ourselves absolutely to her service – then it seems to me that the more fitting part is for us to fold our hands' (104). Her primary motive, however, is that she would lose the potentially valuable merchandise her daughter comprises. Her opinion expresses the inflexible connection between gender and opportunity in nineteenth-century society: as a woman Miss Bonson is unable to pursue art in the way Bell does. The episode draws attention to how the values of a patriarchal society are internalised and transmitted by women and make them collude in maintaining social restrictions. Lawless consequently did not subscribe to a simplistic belief in a uniform community of women oppressed by tyrannical men. Rather, the passage suggests that she recognised the complex configurations behind the exercise of power. The narrative perspective also allowed her to challenge patriarchal ideology without risking society's disapproval by expressing radical ideas as herself, a woman who could be suspected of speaking on her own behalf. In this, the cross-gendered technique functions as a variety of the modesty topos in the early modern period[44] or the anxious inclusion of inoffensive ideas in eighteenth-century women's novels, which ensured that 'any criticism which might be levelled at the dubious character of the independent female author could be more easily deflected by reference to the educational and uplifting nature of their writing'.[45] Like the early women writers who disclaimed their responsibility for writing and publishing but yet managed to do both, Emily Lawless criticised and defended social norms at the same time.

While Mrs Bonson is highly unsympathetic and functions in the story as a negative example, Madame de la Hoche is quite likeable and there are no self-serving motives behind her doubts about the feasibility of women's independence. For Madame, the concept of an independent woman is simply a contradiction in terms: 'the position seems impossible, untenable, not to be conceived. A woman unmarried and independent, appears to me an anomaly – a sort of monster' (53). The solution for an unmarried woman is to enter a convent.[46] Bell, in contrast, believes that 'young women are to the full as capable of taking care of themselves as young men' (55) and that insisting on women's subordination is to insist on them being parasites (53). The problem, as he sees it, is that independent women subject themselves to a kind of social exile: '"I am not sure that they try and combine it with what you would call society," I added. "No doubt that introduces complications"' (52).

As a general statement on women's right to autonomy Bell's arguments are partly invalidated by Madame de la Hoche's suspicion that he is in love with Miss Bonson himself and simply wants to sabotage Hargrave's chances. Bell's uncertain narrative status emphasises the element of negotiation in the text, especially since neither the defenders of the *status quo* nor the proponents of more liberal attitudes stand for opinions that are unequivocal, consistent and free from ulterior motives. Madame undermines her own position when she describes her reaction to Ali Mooshid, a male Algerian acquaintance – and it is Bell who tells her so:

> 'I own I never can quite get over the oddity of finding myself conversing with a perfectly polite being, who all the time in his secret soul regards one as belonging to a different and an immeasurably lower creation from himself: something between a mongoose and a canary-bird, whose proper place at all events is in a cage.'
>
> 'And yet there, after all, you only have the extreme logical outcome of those theories of dependence you were just now propounding?' I responded maliciously. (58)

In obvious contradiction to her rejection of Algerian perceptions of women as less than human, Madame de la Hoche upholds ideals of femininity that reduce women's opportunities. She has strong feelings on proper female behaviour, very much like Elizabeth Prettyman in *A Chelsea Householder*. She regards it as strictly unacceptable for a woman to travel without a female companion, for instance, and she strongly criticises Bell's and Hargrave's proposed trip to L'Aghouat in the Atlas Mountains with Miss Bonson and her brother:

> there are certain decorums which society demands, and the breach of which, let me inform you as an old woman that knows the world, it rarely, if ever, pardons. And for a young lady, an unmarried girl – but there, the thing does not need dwelling upon! Its impropriety is upon the surface; it rushes to meet one! (131)

The problem revolves around the question of social acceptance and the danger of overstepping the boundaries. Thus Madame disapproves of her son's method of raising his daughters, because it involves a clash of social systems:

> His great idea is to harden them – have them turned into a pair of Di Vernons, or Kate Coventrys, or whoever the latest sporting ideal may be. It is quite vainly that I point out to him that they are not English girls as it happens, but French ones, that all the hardening in the world will not make them otherwise; that if it could the result would be that they would be ridiculous hybrids, without the merits which are to be acquired under either system. (127)

The English–French dichotomy is a variety of the male–female opposition, and Madame de la Hoche's belief that the systems must be kept apart parallels a patriarchal society's need to control women by tying them to a single identity. Female independence becomes monstrous, since it involves mixing socially defined gender systems. But this also means that hybridity can be empowering. As dual body, the hybrid is transgressive and indefinable, and what cannot be categorised cannot be controlled. The fear expressed through Madame is actually society's fear of the subversive quality of ambiguity, and her comment becomes an ironic note on the hybridity embodied in the cross-gendered narrative technique itself and ultimately in the professional woman writer.

During the excursion to L'Aghouat condemned by Madame de la Hoche, Hargrave demonstrates a more conciliatory, albeit patronising, attitude to female independence. He appears as a proponent of the chivalric ideal and argues for women's need of men's protection and guidance. Hence, he is furious with Marmaduke Bonson for taking his sister to an indecent café and sheepishly worried when it turns out that it was Miss Bonson's own decision to come:

> 'Certainly I went in of my own accord,' Miss Bonson corroborated, in a different tone. 'And what if I did, Mr. Hargrave?'
>
> John's anger collapsed almost as suddenly as it had arisen.
>
> 'I beg your pardon,' he answered meekly, 'but please believe me when I say it was *not* a fit place for you to go to – it was not indeed. Your brother does not know. Pray, in any similar case be guided by me in future,' he added, entreatingly.
>
> Miss Bonson continued to frown, but her frown lost its severity; an odd expression, half puzzled, half offended, yet not, as it seemed, entirely displeased, crossing her face. (145–6)

The episode exemplifies a compromise, a position between Madame de la Hoche's rejection and Bell's advocacy of women's independence, suggesting that an important aspect of the issue is the intention behind men's curtailment of women's liberty. Miss Bonson's reaction points to the redeeming quality of love and suggests the possibility of reconciliation.

The group never make it to L'Aghouat, as Marmaduke falls ill and, through his reactions to the enforced period of inactivity, Lawless shows Bell revealing his essential self-centredness, thus finally cancelling his narrative authority:

> It did seem to me, I must say, odd that no one appeared to perceive who the real victim of the whole fiasco was. [. . .] Now *I* had never been to L'Aghouat, or anywhere else in Algeria for that matter; *I* had always from the beginning expressed a desire to visit it; and *I* certainly had never dreamt of putting any impediments in the path. It must be clear, therefore, to every right-judging person, where any superfluous sympathy ought in the first instance to have been tendered. (174–5)

It also becomes clear that Bell desires to possess Hildegarde Bonson, not because he loves her but because it would prove his superiority to Hargrave and make his cousin's fortune worthless. On the train home Marmaduke Bonson intends to exploit society's condemnation of feminine impropriety by leaving his sister and Hargrave alone in a train compartment. What actually happens on the train is never disclosed, except that the result is not the announcement of an engagement. In Bell's eyes, this effectively tips the power balance in his favour:

> After all, I thought as I glanced around me in the gloaming, when a man possesses everything, literally everything else that heart can desire, courts and gardens, palm trees, lemon groves – not to speak of such prosaic things as a prodigiously successful business and a swollen balance at his banker's – is there not a certain fitness – a certain, I might almost go so far as to say, poetical justice – in his not being able to add to his other stores one which, if it doubtless lends the rest value, can hardly, even to the most romantic mind, be said to outweigh their more manifest and substantial advantages? (185)

His reflection reveals that he really regards women as objects, just like Miss Bonson's mother and brother, and therefore he is incapable of seeing love as anything else than a power game.

Six months later Miss Bonson appears in London, practising drawing in the British Museum where Bell is also working. Her work does not seem to offer her any pleasure but is 'a binding duty' (211), the price she has to pay for her independence. Ostensibly to help her, Bell takes up her crayon and amends the outline of her drawing, but in doing so he acts in a manner that contradicts his professed opinions on women's independence – he takes over. His attempts to finally defeat John Hargrave by ingratiating himself with Miss Bonson fail, and when at last he sees her with his cousin he has to realise that the two are a couple after all. Miss Bonson consequently ends up doing what most people have wanted her to do – she marries a millionaire. As a result she never becomes a feminist role model in the conventional sense, although her presence in London indicates that she has been able to make her own decisions and will be able to retain a measure of independence. Her choice does not become a general statement about masculine power or women's rights but the final outcome of the negotiations carried out in the novel, a solution valid only in the particular.

In the novel, Lawless casts a man as the strongest defender of women's rights, and in this she attaches to a tradition including among others Maria Edgeworth. Lawless saw Edgeworth as her 'literary mother' and was certainly familiar with her writings.[47] In both *A Millionaire's Cousin* and

Edgeworth's *Letters for Literary Ladies* (1795; 1798) the male voice ensures that the defence of women's rights does not become an instance of girl talk. The link between author and narrator is weakened and the author's perspective is obscured, and in both works the act of writing in a man's voice is in itself an interrogation of fixed gender boundaries that adds to the themes of women's education and independence. However, in *Letters for Literary Ladies* the very arrangement of the exchange, with a letter negative to women's education followed and refuted by a positive letter, seems to finally determine the politics of the text. The effects of Lawless's use of the strategy are more complex and the outcome ambiguous. Although Bell staunchly defends women's independence, his narrative authority is ultimately rejected, which means that the opinions of characters like de la Hoche and the Bonsons gain more weight. The cross-gendered technique provides Lawless with a double voice that allows her to both criticise and uphold social values at the same time.

*

Throughout her early works Lawless probes cultural configurations of gender but refrains from offering a conclusive answer. The result is sometimes utterly contradictory, as in *Major Lawrence, F. L. S.* The myths of 'true' femininity and masculinity were under pressure at the end of the nineteenth century, and the gender games of Oscar Wilde and other aesthetes contributed as much to the gender anxiety of the period as the feminist attacks. There was an intense debate around questions of degeneration and emasculation, and Lawless's novel, *Major Lawrence, F. L. S.*, can be read in this context.

The novel's protagonist, John Lawrence, is a soldier with no taste for heroism, engrossed in his hobby of marine zoology. The letters after his name proclaim him to be a Fellow of the Linnaean Society, but he has no hope of becoming a great scientist. He is a misfit in the army, in society and even in the world of science, but a faithful and dependable friend. His rival for the love of Lady Eleanor Mordaunt is Algernon Cathers, a sickly but beautiful youth whose shortcomings are consistently emblematised as a lack of manliness. Algernon appears to be an unsuitable companion for the energetic and outspoken child that Eleanor is at the beginning of the story, and their early relationship reverses the common pattern of active masculinity and passive femininity. However, when Lawrence meets

Eleanor as a young woman, she has lost her confidence and vigour and become shy and awkward instead. She lives only through Algernon, losing herself in the process. After their marriage she is soon disillusioned and has to realise that Algernon is untruthful, unfaithful and a domestic tyrant to boot. Her response is to make herself into a patient Griselda, seeing to her husband's comfort and obeying his every whim, driven by a guilt complex produced by her fear of her own anger and resentment. Her brother comments: "'Well, it's all very fine and devoted, and like – what was that fool of a woman's name? – Griselda, you know," he said, as he got up and lit himself a candle. "But I must say I call it rot!"' [48] Reviewers responded in a similar manner, with the commentator for the *Pall Mall Gazette* writing that 'the heroine [is] a noble slave, so noble indeed, that sometimes the reader is apt to become slightly impatient with her more than angelic patience'.[49] Through the character of Eleanor, Lawless exposes and criticises the ideal of the 'Angel in the House', but unlike many New Woman writers who emphasised a woman's right to leave her husband, she focuses on the effects of staying in a bad marriage and never suggests divorce as a solution. Instead, the novel establishes a link between corrupted masculinity and female self-sacrifice which is paralleled by a similar connection between proper manliness as represented by John Lawrence and women's attainment of true selfhood. While attacking the Victorian ideal of female submission, Lawless consequently subscribes to a John Bull-like construction of masculinity.

Although it was published in the old three-volume format, *Major Lawrence F. L. S.* is a more modern novel than *A Chelsea Householder*. William Linn detects influences from Henry James, particularly *The Portrait of a Lady*,[50] and the *Saturday Review* critic describes it as 'a novel of study of character rather than of exciting incident'.[51] More important, perhaps, is that the novel shows how Lawless was able to transcend the conventionally feminine in her writing. Nineteenth-century literary criticism was openly gender-oriented, and a woman who attempted to deal with what were considered unwomanly topics was particularly vulnerable to negative criticism, as the opening paragraph of the *Pall Mall Gazette* review shows:

> When a lady undertakes to make her hero a man who is a rising Indian officer and a naturalist, the wary reviewer looks out for a chance of setting his authoress right on several points connected with soldiering and science,

experience having taught him that as a rule a woman's ideas of military life and promotion are somewhat vague, and her application of proper names in science not always quite happy, particularly when they are given to creatures of the sea.[52]

The reviewer is unable to expose any mistakes in the treatment of military or scientific matters, however, and has to concede that Lawless is well able to deal with traditionally masculine fields. It could be said, then, that *Major Lawrence, F. L. S.* is a study of gender constructions both through the debates about what constitutes true manliness that recur throughout the text and through Lawless's choice to write about masculine occupations. This does not make the novel a feminist work, but it shows that Lawless did not accept constricting definitions of femininity.

*

Lawless apparently worked on another three-volume novel in 1883, but it seems to have been rejected by the publisher. In a postscript to a letter to Alexander Macmillan she comments on the manuscript: 'With regard to "Castle crown" I rather incline myself to your reader's judgement, and have put it aside altogether for the present and until I have time to revise it thoroughly.'[53] It is possible that she reused the material elsewhere, but none of her published works seems to fit the title 'Castle Crown'.

The short stories written between 1883 and 1888, collected in *Plain Frances Mowbray and Other Tales* (1889), mark a gradual transition from English and European themes to Irish material. The title story is a character study, set in Venice, and tells the story of how Lady Frances reacts when her brother puts an end to their life together by marrying the scheming Madame Facchino. Frances is portrayed as the stronger of the two, but her brother is nevertheless the centre of her life, so, when she feels betrayed by him, she is forced to consider whether her whole existence has been 'a series of self-deception and delusion'.[54] The defining factor of Lady Frances's character is described as her ugliness, and Lawless shows that looks determine a woman's life to a much greater extent than a man's:

> Now a man, let him be never so ugly, never so ungainly, has always the comfortable consciousness that his ugliness is hardly, after all, the most salient fact about him; other qualities and qualifications outweigh it, and

tend to throw it in the shade. As he grows older the impression wears off. The fact remains regrettable, but still not a fact of any very great consequence after all. With a woman it is otherwise. Her ugliness, if she is ugly, becomes, from the moment she is aware of it, the salient fact of her existence – the nucleus of discomfort around which every other discomfort turns. She sees it in every face she meets as she walks along the streets; she reads it upon a hundred irreproachably polite lips; let her heroism, let her philosophy be what it may, no amount of heroism or of philosophy will avail entirely to root it out of her consciousness. (9–10)

Because she is a woman, the fact that Lady Frances is 'the stronger, the clearer, the harder-willed, the broader-hearted, the larger-headed' (60) in relation to her brother is of no significance. In her review of the collection, Margaret Oliphant considers that 'the author makes too much of the ugliness of her heroine', and goes on to say that a 'woman with a beautiful soul is never ugly, however little beauty she may have; and, as a matter of fact, beauty is the last thing necessary, and ugliness one of the smallest detriments, to social success, especially after the period of youth'.[55] To the extent that 'Plain Frances Mowbray' is representative of Lawless's views on the issue, it seems clear that she did not share Mrs Oliphant's opinion. Underneath the quiet storytelling, there is an undercurrent of anger at the ways in which women are defined through their faces and bodies.

The second story in the collection, 'Quin Lough', is set in Ireland and relates a visit from Judge Theobald Quin, retired from service in India, to his widowed sister-in-law in County Clare. It is a pleasant story, without much plot. Unaware that his sister-in-law has remarried, the Judge feels slighted when he finds her home filled with other people. His sister-in-law, on the other hand, senses displeasure in the Judge's attitude and believes him to be upset about the marriage, not realising that he does not know about it. In the third story, 'A Ligurian Episode', the setting is again Italy. The narrator is a cynical Englishman, telling the story of how a young Scottish visitor is destroyed by his love for a beautiful Italian girl and her greedy relatives. Descriptions of the area, and particularly the weather, are used to emphasise the mood of the story, in the manner also employed, in particular, in the novels *Hurrish* (1886) and *Grania* (1892). Like *A Millionaire's Cousin,* 'A Ligurian Episode' is a cross-gendered narrative, though the most important function of the narrator is the way in which Lawless uses his ironical tone to balance the tragic content of the tale. The fact that he is masculine is of little importance to the story.

'Borroughdale of Borroughdale' describes a man who shares his interest in marine zoology with the main character of *Major Lawrence, F. L. S.* Unlike Major Lawrence, however, the initially shy and awkward Lord Borroughdale becomes both confident and professionally successful in the end. The final story, 'Namesakes', is the shortest in the collection but in many ways the most successful. The shorter format means that it is less a character study than the other four tales – William Linn describes it as 'impressionistic'[56] and Margaret Oliphant calls it 'curiously suggestive'.[57] The namesakes in question are the English Captain Maurice O'Sullivan and the young, Irish-speaking Mrs O'Sullivan he finds hiding with her baby in a hovel on his uncle's estate in County Kerry. When his uncle's employee attempts to throw the girl out, O'Sullivan prevents him, affected by her beauty and defencelessness. He begins to see himself as her protector and brings her blankets and food. A few days later the girl has gone, however, and nothing is disclosed about her fate. The implication is that the girl was too proud to accept his help, and preferred squatting to the semi-official status O'Sullivan's interest gave her. In Margaret Oliphant's view, the story 'gives a sudden gleam of light upon the perplexing character of that wonderful Celtic race which baffles every judgment'.[58] It is also possible to read it as a subtle questioning of charity as a system, and as a description of how independence is of greater value than comfort. The fact that the two main characters share a name draws attention to their difference in social standing, but also emphasises the fundamental similarity between the English and the Irish O'Sullivan. As in *Hurrish,* where both the landlord and the tenant are called O'Brien, characters who share a name blur the boundaries between groups in society and indicate that common dividing lines do not apply in Ireland.

The undramatic tone and the focus on character rather than plot meant that *Plain Frances Mowbray and Other Tales* was compared with Henry James's work. Lawless was acquainted with Rhoda Broughton, who was a friend of Henry James, and, although it cannot be determined whether she met him or not, she certainly must have known of him and his work.[59] The *Saturday Review* commentator prefers James's dialogue as smarter and more real than Lawless's,[60] however, whereas Margaret Oliphant sees James as too much of a skilful craftsman. In her view, Lawless's stories may be less perfectly manufactured, but display a greater interest in the people described.[61] The *Spectator* reviewer records an initial disappointment with the lack of 'obvious point or climax, or anticipated moral' in the tales, but continues to say that their 'true realism' should satisfy artistic taste.[62] The main criticism in the *Spectator* review is that Lawless's style betrays 'a consciousness of what "society" will say to her, especially when she writes about her own world'.[63] Qualifying adjectives sometimes diminish the force of her descriptions and give the impression that she is reluctant to take full responsibility for what she writes. Such negotiations may well be manifestations of the uncertain position of the Irish Ascendancy at the end of the nineteenth century, but it also seems logical to interpret them in gendered terms.

The doubleness of her early works seems to effectively check any attempt to draw Emily Lawless into the feminist camp. Although informed by feminist ideas, Lawless's early novels and stories never become programmatic and her heroines are individuals, neither representatives of their sex in the conventional, patriarchal manner nor feminist role models. In a feminist critical perspective, *A Chelsea Householder, A Millionaire's Cousin, Major Lawrence, F. L. S.* and the stories in *Plain Frances Mowbray and Other Tales* are best understood as negotiations between feminist attitudes and a predominantly misogynist culture, dialogues between opposite ideological positions where the final answer is left to the reader. Lawless was apparently both attracted to and repulsed by feminist ideas, both anxious to secure a place for herself by conforming to prevalent opinions and to challenge these opinions by highlighting women's issues. Her double voice is a sign of her double identification as a woman and an intellectual in a society where these concepts were often regarded as mutually exclusive. By setting her early novels outside Ireland she also negotiated the political situation of the time. Her refusal to complicate the Irish question by the introduction of feminist issues suggests that the concern with nationhood and national identity would eclipse any other theme interrogated in an Irish context.

Chapter 3

Interspatial identities: geography, landscape and the problem of taxonomy

In English and Irish topographical poetry from the eighteenth century the prospect view is the dominant visual principle, and the description of places as seen from a hilltop continue to be typical of landscape writing throughout the Romantic period. The feeling that there is nothing to obstruct the view often involves a gratifying sense of control. Hence, in earlier writing the open landscape conveys the surveyor's understanding of place. Positioned on a height, the viewer dominates, defines and claims the landscape, looking at the land in a way that displays control but ignores detail. Romantic writers are likely to imbue the landscape with feelings of independence and unbounded possibility, but these ideas, too, depend to a great extent on the notion that the poet is removed from the rest of the world, able to rise above and see beyond the constraints that limit those who toil below. The perspectival landscape view is ego-centred, since the viewer is always the point from which seeing takes place.[1] Thus, the most significant characteristic of the prospect view is that it places the viewer in a position of superiority.

'The controlling viewpoint', says Catherine Nash, is central to 'the colonial mapping of subject lands' as well as 'the representation of women within patriarchy'.[2] When women writers describe the landscape, an important question is therefore whether they continue the male tradition of the eighteenth and nineteenth centuries or whether they create new models that express a feminine, or perhaps feminist, understanding of the land. Emily Lawless challenges exactly the idea of mastery contained in commanding a view:

> The truth is it is not at all desirable to be so haughty. I will not go so far
> as to say that it is unchristian, but it is certainly unbecoming, for are we

54

not all fellow-creatures? What if you *can* command seven counties from your windows? What if on one particular morning – to me incredible – you did see three ships cross Shoreham gap? What if from your garden chair you can be regaled by a fantasia of changing light and shadows? be lapped into peace upon summer afternoons, or stirred by the drama of battle clouds, flung into blackness by a storm? Well, if you can, be glad of it, but for pity's sake abstain from bragging![3]

Lawless admits that she, too, has been 'haughty to the point of insupportableness', believing that the 'possession of wide prospects argued some peculiar, some ineffable superiority' in herself (*A Garden Diary*, 8). The scenery she refers to is the view of the Atlantic, however, where any sense of control is absent. The attraction is instead the openness. Away from the Atlantic, the contraction of the horizon 'seemed like a contraction of life', Lawless writes (*A Garden Diary*, 9). Seen in conjunction with the many ways women have been fettered by social constraints, such celebrations of unbounded landscapes and seascapes become particularly meaningful in women's writing. Perceptions of the landscape therefore reveal how we look upon the world, including our own place in it, and, since geography, together with history, is constitutive of national and nationalist discourse,[4] both the places described and the vantage points can be related to issues of cultural, ethnic and social identity, as well as gender identity – even in texts where such matters are not openly addressed. Irish fiction, as indeed most Irish literature from the earliest times up until today, is particularly preoccupied with 'place as an unseverable aspect of self'.[5]

*

A very clear connection between 'place' and 'self' is obviously the relationship between a landowner or tenant and the land. The last few decades of the nineteenth century in Ireland were dominated by the Land War, the organised agrarian protest against high rents and the landlord system that began in 1879 and continued intermittently until the Wyndham Land Act 1903.[6] Irish popular history at the time circulated a version of the country's past where complex political allegiances and webs of interrelationships were suppressed in favour of a linear narrative of oppression and resistance,[7] and since the corollary of a linear view of history is a fixed conception of space, this reshaping of the past also reshaped the landscape into Irish and English territories. Historical and geographical discourses helped to maintain a concept of nationality and cultural identity that was embedded in the land, so that by the 1880s landlords of the Ascendancy class were quite automatically associated with British conquest and the tenant farmers were just as automatically perceived as representatives of the 'real' Ireland.

As both landlords and Land Leaguers mobilised a rhetoric where places were defined as territories to be claimed, questions of possession, dispossession and repossession came to the fore. The landlords referred to their centuries-long land rights to legitimise their future in an increasingly nationalist Ireland, while the Land Leaguers saw ousting the landlord as one step further towards abolishing English influence and reclaiming the land for the Irish.[8] Thus, Land War oratory defended or disputed ownership, but did not question the idea of place at all. Places pre-existed, which meant that they could be measured and described, and ultimately seized. Women, however, were rarely landholders, and as a consequence they could not validate their Irishness by staking a claim to the land.[9] Instead, they needed to re-imagine the country to justify their continued existence in Ireland. The descriptions of places in many women's texts from the period reflect this circumstance.

As so many of her works illustrate, Emily Lawless viewed Ireland as an *interspace*, a place between and beyond recognisable paradigms. Her insistence on describing Ireland as indefinable can to a great extent be seen as a response to the categorical definitions of people and places that informed both nationalist and unionist thought at the time. By imagining the country as fundamentally unknowable, and therefore uncontrollable, she critiques nationalist and colonialist rhetoric as well as masculine scientific norms and conveys a particularly feminine, if not explicitly feminist, sense of nature. The Irish landscape takes on spiritual properties and becomes a historical text that can be read, a promise of liberation, a site of resistance and a source of knowledge and healing. Most importantly, she demonstrates how an indecipherable landscape can function to shape an identity beyond class, gender and race distinctions, and manages to claim an Irish identity for herself based on emotional engagement with, not possession of, the land.

Descriptions of scenery consequently have a particular resonance in Lawless's work. In familiar nineteenth-century manner, articles such as 'Notes in the Morbihan' lament the disappearance of rural environments 'under the energetic besom of civilization', but the ensuing sketch of the

Breton region is more than a nostalgic picture of a district threatened by technological change.[10] Landscape, Lawless suggests, can never be fully described, never possessed. Like Ireland, the Morbihan is an area with 'quite exceptionally difficult scenery to give a fair impression of, nay, even to gather up into a coherent whole in one's own mind'.[11] Thus, while writing herself into the male discipline of geography, Lawless challenges its discursive traditions from within by her refusal to define and control place:

> Even ourselves, sophisticated little creatures though we be, in how many ways we remain the accessories, rather than the masters, of our environment? For a time, especially in towns, we manage to conceal this truth from ourselves. We pretend that we have remodelled matters to our liking; that Nature has become our follower; that our law, not hers, runs through the planet; that we set the tune, and that she merely plays it.
> Oh rash, and hurrying ignorance! (*A Garden Diary*, 42–3)

Her unease with common measuring systems is most obvious in the article 'North Clare – Leaves from a Diary', the only time she uses the term 'interspace' in her writing. She characterises the region as 'an interspace between land and water' that does not 'strictly belong either to the one or to the other'.[12] The interspace is a constantly fluctuating landscape that defies order, and the topographical features she selects combine into a picture where the typical is the paradoxical. The first thing that strikes a visitor is the 'extraordinary extent to which land and water have here invaded, or rather, so to speak, interpenetrated, one another'.[13] The borders between land, sea and sky are blurred, which means that the landscape cannot really be understood in rational terms. The Burren is described as a truly mountainous area, even though there are no peaks higher than a thousand feet. In such a landscape, ordinary tools are insufficient: 'the measuring tape is all very well in its own place, but its place, somehow or other, does not seem to be here!'[14]

The concept of the *interspace* parallels what Gillian Rose terms 'paradoxical space', a sense of space connected with feminist thought:

> This space is multi-dimensional, shifting and contingent. It is also paradoxical, by which I mean that spaces that would be mutually exclusive if charted on a two-dimensional map – centre and margin, inside and outside – are occupied simultaneously.[15]

Rose's definition is concerned with social spaces such as the public and private arenas of workplace and home rather than spaces in a landscape, but given the view that places do not pre-exist as empirical objects but are constructed according to specific codes and norms, the term 'paradoxical space' is singularly apt for Lawless's description of the Burren and indeed most of her landscape descriptions.

Even such ostensibly organised areas as the garden are presented as interspaces in Lawless's work, with lack of order as the overarching idea. Though a garden would normally be contrasted with the wilderness and seen as a planned and controlled landscape, Lawless stresses its diversity. Instead of visualising the garden as a structured environment, she concentrates on its uncontrollable aspects:

> Lessons of course may be gathered in a garden, as in most other places. For the owner, the most wholesome of these is perhaps that he never really is its owner at all. His garden possesses him – many of us know only too well what it is to be possessed by a garden – but he never, in any true sense of the word, possesses it. (*A Garden Diary*, 40)

As James M. Cahalan says, questioning the idea that land can be owned, even when it is only a small garden that is concerned, connects Lawless to recent eco-feminist developments.[16] A central idea in eco-feminist thought is that attempts to subdue and control the natural world correspond to the subjugation of women under patriarchy or the colonialist oppression of the Other.[17] It is true that Lawless, at least on the word level, exhibits a certain ambivalence as regards land ownership. *A Garden Diary* is dedicated to 'the Garden's Chief Owner, and the Gardener's Friend', and at the beginning of the diary she writes that she and Lady Sarah Spencer have been 'two years in possession here' (12). Her overall philosophy, however, is that gardeners are hosts to the plants in their gardens, not their owners. Seeing the plants as guests rather than possessions increases their status and emphasises their individuality. Digging up oak saplings from the flowerbeds, she reflects:

> Never two living beings came into the world precisely alike, and these baby oaks differ each of them in some imperceptible fashion from its baby brother. Here is a handful plucked at random out of the flower-beds that will prove it. In this one that I hold in my fingers, it is easy to see that the future giant would have been a somewhat thick-set, and stunted colossus. This one again has already a tendency to self-division, and would probably

have ended by being forked. Yet again this one would, if it had been spared
– appropriate phrase – have grown up to be the very ideal of oaks; a glory
of the woods; star-proof; sun-proof; magnificent in its life, and in its death
destined to be converted into the very straightest and most wind-defying
of masts. (161)

Throughout her writing, Lawless stresses that there is *difference* within
every category, whether human, animal or vegetable. Every living thing
has the right to a name, to an identity of its own:

I notice in myself, and have observed in others, a lamentable lack of
accuracy as regards the proper names of weeds. Even some that I know the
best, and hate the hardest, I really cannot put any name to. Now this is
not as it should be. Everything, however detestable, has a name of its own,
and that name ought to be used. You may not like a man, but that is hardly
a reason for calling him 'What's-his-name', or 'Thingamy'. (27)

A respect for the individuality and complexity of things in nature lies
behind Lawless's descriptions of animal and plant life. Her insistence on
the uniqueness of even a common weed anticipates such eco-feminist
developments that see a relation between the naming of natural
phenomena in masculinist science and the naming of Woman under
patriarchy.[18] In both cases the process of categorisation leads to limiting
reductions, just like the overall designation 'weed' reduces the individual
nature of the plant in question.

Unlike the topographical poets who claimed the landscape with their
gaze, Lawless transfers the power back to the land. A garden, she says, 'is
a world in miniature and, like the world, has a claim to be represented by
many minds, surveying it from many sides' (13). When she recreates
Ireland in her Surrey garden it is consequently not as a unified landscape,
but as a series of disconnected plots:

I have a Burren corner, a West Galway corner, a Kerry corner, a Kildare
corner, even a green memento or two of the great lost forest of Ossory of
which only a few shadowy remnants survive to a remote, but happily not
an indifferent generation. (125)

Even within the confines of a flower garden, Ireland cannot be reproduced
in a coherent way but needs to be presented as multiple and incongruous.
Although Lawless does not explicitly connect her landscape descriptions

with questions of identity, her ambiguous topographies can be read as symbols of a self that cannot be conclusively defined. Her unstable geographies correspond to her double outlook as an Anglo-Irish aristocrat with a passionate love for her country but sceptical about its ability to govern itself, and as a woman writer aware of her insignificant place in the male-ordered hierarchy but reluctant to commit herself to feminist campaigns.[19] The interspatial landscapes she imagines embody this combination of apparently incompatible attitudes as well as the possibility to fluctuate between them.

Perceptions of geography, social space and identity are thus intertwined in Lawless's work, and are closely linked to the problem of taxonomy. Apart from constituting an early example of eco-feminist thinking, Lawless's nature writing prefigures the attitudes of late twentieth-century feminist geography, where subjectivity and sensitivity are valid ways of knowing and sources and methods beyond those of the academy are valued.[20] Spiritual union with the landscape opens possibilities of metaphysical illumination as well:

> Identity seems to go swimming about as if through a vacuum, and to have lost its relation with every other identity. As an individual one ceases in fact to be an individual at all, and becomes something else: a much more elemental something, made up of moods, dreams, impressions: cloudy and bewildering glimpses into things not only beyond one's own ken, but possibly beyond the ken of every other mortal also.[21]

The contrast between the objectifying, scientific, male gaze and such emotional knowledge is vast. Even though the natural world can be cruel, an intense relationship with nature leads to healing and awakens the spiritual dimensions in life:

> That Nature is cruel is not to be denied; the evidences of that cruelty are written out large and red in every woodland, under every hedgerow. That she can be also unaccountably pitiful, or at all events take pains to appear so, is fortunately equally true, and it is a truth that at times comes very near to the heart. This morning at a very early hour there was a tenderness, a kind of hovering serenity over everything, that appealed to one like a benediction. The air itself seemed changed; sanctified. The familiar little paths one walked along were like the approaches to some as yet invisible Temple. (*A Garden Diary*, 196)

But it is not simply a variety of the Romantic idealisation of mystical nature: Lawless is enough of a Darwinist to also employ very precise terminology when plants and insects are mentioned and, perhaps more importantly, she articulates her ideas within the framework of science and popular science – in journals like the *Nineteenth Century, Cornhill Magazine, The Gentleman's Magazine* and *Belgravia* – not only in her poetry and her fiction.

A romanticised notion of place usually entails feminisation – Mother Ireland is an obvious example, and the common binary opposition between Nature and Reason corresponding to Woman and Man is another. This means that to render place as feminine smacks of complicity with patriarchal ideology or at least naivety. But as feminist geographers have realised, there is a subversive quality to imagining place as indefinable, and Lawless's penchant for open, unbounded spaces can be productively understood in relation to the closeness and confinement of nineteenth-century women's lives. Her places are feminised, not through the familiar identification of Nature with Woman, where the mystery is simply the opposite of rationality, but in a liberating way. Yet, a freedom that relies on the indefinite is limited and only private, since communication at least to some extent depends on reductions:

> the thing that remains uncaught must, from the very nature of that fact, be better than the ones which we can pat, handle, and pass about to other people. And yet it seems a pity too; nay, even a trifle unreasonable. For why should the only part of oneself that is worth anything; the only part of what one sees, does, knows, feels that is in the least worth sharing with any one else, be exactly the very part that remains for ever incommunicable?[22]

Thus Lawless's landscape texts do not constitute a fully worked out critique of masculine scientific norms, although they certainly express a dissatisfaction with the crude taxonomies created by – predominantly male – botanists, geographers and naturalists. Instead, they subvert masculinist science by emphasising difference and imagining another, open space that cannot be measured and classified.

As an amateur entomologist, botanist, geographer, geologist and marine zoologist Lawless was well aware of both the uses and the limitations of taxonomical thought.[23] In an article about County Kerry she observes that when the skull-less fish the lancelet was classified as a vertebrate, this necessitated a new subdivision of the group, where the lancelet was alone in its class and all the other vertebrates crowded together in the other. The fish did not fit the scheme, but, instead of resulting in its exclusion, this led to a modification of the system.[24] The same lack of confidence in totalising models is present when she notes that the theory explaining the presence of so many subtropical plants in Ireland fails 'to fit entirely into *all* the facts of the case'.[25] To achieve a greater understanding, it is necessary to accumulate also the facts that seem to contradict the existing paradigms, and Ireland's flora and fauna have been insufficiently investigated because of 'the all-pervading and all-invading encroachment of politics', Lawless claims.[26] Botanical and zoological study might, of course, have been very low on the agenda among the Irish themselves in the political climate of the nineteenth century, but Lawless's comment has probably more to do with the tendency among English scholars to ignore or only superficially include Ireland even in studies that purportedly describe the flora and fauna of 'the British Isles'. That the way plants and insects have been labelled is to a great extent a manifestation of colonial thinking is indicated by Lawless's outburst in 'North Clare – Leaves from a Diary':

> Our whole authorised flora is indeed to my mind an exasperating piece of business, and I can never help wishing that if it was going to be so inadequate, its inadequacy had at least taken less provoking and unlooked-for lines. With regard to two of its departments I feel a positive sense of personal grievance. Our own mountains, and our own sea! To be told that we lag behind England – flat, prosaic England – in the number of our 'mountain' or 'highland' plants is already sufficiently trying, but when it comes to being gravely assured by Mr. Watson that out of what he calls his 'Atlantic type' we have but a miserable thirty-four plants, to Wales and England's sixty-two – Well, I can only say that I consider such a statement to be an outrage! Are we going to put up with such an invasion of our few prerogatives? Can any patriotic, any commonly self-respecting Irish botanist accept for a moment so palpably prejudiced and hostile a judgment? Let us, I say for my part, *not* accept it. Arise, botanic Celts, and glut your ire! Let us have an entirely new botany, based upon an entirely new system and classification, and let not the name of the hostile and anti-Irish botanist be so much as named in it![27]

In her nature writing she keeps returning to the idea that definitions and systematisations are suspect and lead to exclusions. Her critique is to a great extent directed against the Enlightenment principle that classifications should be based on what is visible, such as number of petals, skeletal features, size, height and breadth. This over-concern with external characteristics also informs conventional geographical and nationalist discourse. Describing a species of shellfish she notes:

> Like most freshwater shell-fish, long isolation has written its history upon them, and has given them a peculiar stamp of separateness, so that among members of the selfsame species individuals differ so widely that it needs some little faith to believe that they can be essentially the same.[28]

While the description displays a certain belief in essence, it also demonstrates a conviction that diversity, even within a very specific group, is possible. Underlying these observations is the view that Ireland is different, and that new categories must be created to accommodate this difference. The lancelet fish, like the shellfish and the incongruous plants of Kerry, can be can seen as an allegory of an identity that claims belonging without conformity, an image that is strongly charged in a political climate where the definition of Irishness is under debate.

Hence, Lawless addresses the question of identity obliquely, through naturalist observations and landscape descriptions. She constantly foregrounds the inherent instability of any definition of the land and, by extension, its occupants. Considering the persistent connection between women and space, the vision of the interspace is an important feminist idea, and the sense that an indefinable geography has the potential to shape identities beyond essentialist paradigms links it to what Susan Stanford Friedman terms 'the new geographics of identity':

> Instead of the individualistic telos of developmental models, the new geographics figures identity as a historically embedded site, a positionality, a location, a standpoint, a terrain, an intersection, a network, a crossroads of multiply situated knowledges. It articulates not the organic unfolding of identity but rather the mapping of territories and boundaries, the dialectical terrains of inside/outside or center/margin, the axial intersections of different positionalities, and the spaces of dynamic encounter – the 'contact zone', the 'middle ground', the borderlands, *la frontera*.[29]

The list of examples is deeply contradictory, in that it suggests both the mapping of territories and the spaces in-between as bases for identity and, to be truly revolutionary, Friedman's model presupposes mobility. The same is true about Lawless, where the really radical implications of an interspatial identity are available only to those who are in some sense already mobile; that is, not completely rooted in the land. Yet, the unstable nature of both the 'new geographics of identity' and the interspace ideal is precisely what makes these ideas so attractive, since they suggest the possibility of a both/and rather than an either/or foundation of self-hood.

On the understanding that the concept is fundamentally unstable, the notion of the interspace also allows for a temporary fixity of landscape, at least in emotional terms. Even though their topography remains unmappable, Lawless's landscapes possess very specific characteristics and the power to both influence and reflect human behaviour. The idea that landscape bears witness to history is prominent in several of her works, as in the reflective piece 'Famine Roads and Famine Memories', where the roads built to provide work for the victims of the potato blight now lead nowhere and are a grim reminder of the deaths and emigrations of the Great Famine.[30] The roads are inscriptions on the landscape that make the land itself a document of the disaster.[31] In a similar manner, Lawless describes the late nineteenth-century aspect of Connaught as an effect of the destruction of the forest several hundred years earlier, a visible memory of unwise farming methods and warfare.[32] That deforestation is commonly a memory of war is emphasised in the novel *Maelcho,* where cutting down the forest is symbolically linked to the defeat of the Irish in the Desmond rebellion of the late sixteenth century. Geographical records of this kind testify to human interference, and make the land a repository of the history and memory of past wrongs.

Sometimes, however, the seeds of tragedy are already present in the landscape. The opening passages of Lawless's first Irish novel, *Hurrish: A Study* (1886), describe the Burren as an 'iron land' where the hills 'are not hills, in fact, but skeletons – rain-worn, time-worn, wind-worn, – starvation made visible, and embodied in a landscape'.[33] That the first pages are taken up by an entirely spatial discourse emphasises that the setting is germane to theme and plot, and Lawless represents the land as both causing and reflecting the circumstances of the people who inhabit it. Hence, the Land War conflict that is the subject of the novel does not only have an abstract political basis, but it is fuelled by the physical nature of the land itself. The Burren is land on the edge, because there is nothing west of the Clare coast, and this extreme location is mirrored both in the difficult conditions of the local farmers and the strong feelings surrounding the land question. The region is exposed to an unpredictable and quite severe climate, and these external circumstances parallel the hot temper and rash actions of the people, so that, for example, the episode where the protagonist Hurrish O'Brien accidentally kills the land-grabber Mat Brady is immediately followed by a change in the weather (77).

*

Subtitled *A Study*, *Hurrish* describes the interaction between a man and his physical and psychological environment, combining fairy-tale characterisation with the scientific attitudes of the naturalist movement. The rather melodramatic plot charts how Hurrish kills his neighbour Mat Brady in an accident, is reported to the authorities by Brady's brother Maurice, is charged and acquitted, and is finally shot in revenge by Maurice. The story is set against the backdrop of the Land War, but the conflict is personal rather than political in a general sense. According to Lisbet Kickham, *Hurrish* is the only Land War novel by an Anglo-Irish woman writer in the period 1879–1922 where the principal character is a tenant.[34] The protagonist Horatio – Hurrish – O'Brien is a gentle hero-giant of almost mythical proportions, a successful farmer and fisherman in the infertile region of the Burren. His naïve and essentially non-violent brand of patriotism – an attraction to 'the crowd, the excitement, the waving flags' (6) – is contrasted with the zealous nationalism of his mother Bridget and the fear of violence represented by his orphan niece Alley Sheehan. In Charles de Kay's opinion, Alley is 'the material of which nuns, faithful wives, uncomplaining and tireless mothers are made', a character Lawless returned to and developed further in her portrait of Honor O'Malley in *Grania*. Bridget O'Brien, on the other hand, is a woman 'in whom a vicious system of government has concentrated the hatred of her race for centuries against all laws emanating from a foreign soil, is capable of standing close to the scaffold of a martyr for the cause, dabbling in his blood, and rousing the mob with the headlong fury of a village Danton'.[35] Hurrish is influenced both by his niece's credo of non-violence and his mother's fanaticism, and the plot revolves as much around this clash between different mentalities as around the political issue of land ownership.

Chapter 1 sets the scene for an experiment, and outlines the ruling conditions and the principal ingredients or characters. The central problem is the conflict between Hurrish's natural kindness and tolerance and the violence and unlawfulness connected with the cause he believes in – the tenant farmer's right to his land and, ultimately, Ireland's independence: 'His very good-nature and sociability were all against him. For what, it may be asked, *is* a good-natured and a naturally gregarious man to do, when all the sociability of his neighbourhood is concentrated around a single focus, and that focus a criminal one?' (14). Lawless presents Hurrish as the embodiment of the 'Celtic temperament – poetic, excitable, emotionable, unreasoning' and explains his involvement with nationalist organisations as the nourishment his 'poetic excitability' craves (15):

> Temperaments which, under happier circumstances, might very well have been the homes of a genuine fount of poetry, will often, for the lack of better aliment, feed upon the veriest garbage, and accept the most worthless of sawdust-cakes for bread. The magnificent promises, the fiery denunciations, the windy turbid patriotism of his favourite newspapers – by preference the contraband ones – were such sawdust-cakes to him. (15)

The novel is clearly written for the outsider, and its patronising tone cannot be denied. Ernest Boyd offers a scathing verdict in *Ireland's Literary Renaissance* (1916): 'Lawless wrote her book entirely as an unsympathetic outsider. The agrarian movement is seen in the darkness of anti-national prejudice, not in the light of understanding, and the caricatural rendering of Irish dialect stamps the book as intended for foreign consumption.'[36] The intrusive narrator creates a distance that forces the reader to reflect on the characters, not identify with them. Instead of being immersed in the story, the narrator and the reader embark on a project to study a peculiar life form, and are firmly placed outside the tale, as people who are familiar with 'the Mer-de-Glace glacier above Chamounix' (14) that Lawless uses as a point of comparison for the Burren landscape.

Hurrish is dedicated to the Scottish writer and family friend Mrs Oliphant, and in a letter to Lawless Oliphant expresses her admiration for the work: 'I have never said to you nor had the opportunity of saying elsewhere, how much I like "Essex". (Not, however, so well as "Hurrish", that must be clearly understood – "Hurrish" is a great work of genius and my own god-son, and if you produce a Hamlet or a Lear, I shall not give him the pas.).'[37] The novel was well received in England, as 'a vivid and striking picture of the Irish peasant as he really is, a description coloured by no political or partisan motive',[38] and 'one of the best and most impartial "studies", having for object the present condition of Ireland, that has yet appeared'.[39] The commentator for the *Overland Monthly and Out West Magazine,* likewise, praised Lawless's objectivity but expressed some annoyance at Lawless's view of American leadership:

> the author herself attributes the state of affairs unhesitatingly to the effect on the people's minds of the English government, and looks to autonomy as the only cure; yet she has not much faith in the 'new kind' of Irish leaders, whom she regards as self-seekers, after what she calls the 'American fashion', in a matter of course manner, not at all flattering to the political pride of the American reader.[40]

Lawless's impartiality was praised also in the *United Ireland,* where the reviewer maintained that *Hurrish* 'should be in the hands of every Irishman who reads books at all; first of all, because it is literature, Irish literature; and secondly, because while it contains a good deal that a Nationalist will know to be false, it is suggestive of quite as much that he must confess to be true'.[41] Maurice F. Egan's review in the *Catholic World* was considerably different, however, denouncing the novel as 'an exceedingly disagreeable book', because of the 'deliberate attempt of the author to give the impression that the Irish peasant, on his native heath, is a bloodthirsty pagan in principle and a Thug in practice'. Egan's conclusion is that *Hurrish* is 'a libel on Irish life'.[42] The same conclusion is reached in the review in the New York-based Fenian paper the *Nation:*

> The book is slanderous and lying from cover to cover, and it is slanderous and lying on a preconceived purpose so mean that only the daughter of an Irish landlord could pursue it. Literary talents have before now been prostituted to many low services; but the Hon. Emily Lawless has degraded literature to a service the lowest that could be entered on by a calumnious partisan. [. . .] From the pinnacle of her three-generation nobility this daughter of Cloncurry looks down, and there is no room for gradation of any sort among the peasants. [. . .] Men sometimes talk of the loss to Ireland should the class to whom this writer belongs be forced from among us. We ask any man who thinks there is any possible ground for community of thought and feeling between the Irish aristocrat and the Irish people to read this book.[43]

Apart from the negative picture of the land activists Lawless paints in the novel, an important reason for the vitriolic attack in the *Nation* is probably the distance created by the narrator's outside perspective. Other grounds for criticism may be – with good reason – the stage Irish dialect of the characters and the sometimes cardboard-like characterisation. Lady Gregory, for instance, denounced the work precisely for these reasons:

> Last evening, thinking I might have been wrong in condemning Hurrish, Emily's first novel, years ago, I began to read it. But I could not get through many pages. The dialect a dreadful mixture of 'Oi' for 'I' – (that except from our Waterford Archdeacon Burkitt I had never heard in Connacht). Then the judgement on characters rather than letting them develop. And the patronizing tone. I was sorry I had looked at it, and sorry to remember it had been accepted in London as a picture of Irish life.[44]

According to Betty Webb Brewer, what saves the novel from 'its one-dimensional characters and their predictable speeches delivered in embarrassing dialect' are the descriptions of the Burren.[45] The land is really the main character in the novel, though the struggle for the land is sometimes presented in what Ernest Boyd says was 'the only possible point of view in respectable circles' in 1886.[46]

On the whole, the Irish land question is figured in the novel as fundamentally a personal matter, not a social issue that can be remedied by political action. Hurrish becomes involved not because he is convinced that the system is unjust, but because he is swept away by rhetoric and because it is what is expected in his community. Politics is a matter of emotion and social belonging, not rational thought. But Lawless also shows very clearly the alienation of the Irish people from what was perceived as a biased legal system: 'Hate of the Law is the birthright and the dearest possession of every native son of Ireland' (177). This distrust of the law is given as the explanation for why Hurrish does not report crimes to the authorities (14) or why he does not name Maurice Brady as his attacker after he has been shot in retribution for the accident when Maurice's brother Mat was killed.[47] Even when he is dying, Hurrish protects Brady by making up a story about some people in a boat shooting at him:

> There was a general silence. Not a single being in the cabin, of course, believed a word that he had been listening to. Not one either but felt a pang of dismay and disgust at the thought that the murderer would, after all, escape. So deeply engrained, however, in Ireland, is the instinct under no circumstances to betray a criminal, that the very men who had dragged

Maurice triumphantly out of his hiding-place, and had accompanied him thus far, with the amiable intention of hearing that he was safe to be hanged, felt that Hurrish's conduct was only natural, and moreover, that, under similar circumstances, they would have done precisely the same themselves. (183)

It was primarily the way *Hurrish* illustrated the Irish peasant's sceptical attitude to the law that W. E. Gladstone appreciated:

> The authoress of 'Hurrish', a recently published novel, has, I think, been more successful in one matter of great importance than any writer of her class, or perhaps of any class. She has made present to her readers, not as an abstract proposition, but as a living reality, the estrangement of the people of Ireland from the law; how they are estranged from it in the mass, and in what varied shapes, rather than degrees, this estrangement exhibits itself under the many varieties of character and circumstances. As to the why of this alienation, also, she has her answer. 'The old long-repented sin of the stronger country was the culprit.'[48]

Though *Hurrish* clearly shows Lawless's negative opinion of the Land League, she does not attempt to exonerate England from blame. Hurrish is 'a martyr to a long and ugly past', the 'long-repented sin' (177) of conquest and misgovernment that led to the problems Ireland was facing at the end of the nineteenth century. Even so, she does not see political action as the answer:

> Perhaps [. . .] Ireland will have entered upon a new departure, though what precise form that departure will take, and whence its brightest hopes are to come, it is a little difficult, it must be owned, just now to discern. Enough perhaps that there are elements in it which have nothing, fortunately, to say to politics – of any complexion. Kindliness, faith, purity, are good spirits which may steer a boat through even as rough waters as any that it has travelled through, and bring it into safe anchorage at last. (196)

Instead of political action, Lawless seems to suggest that the solution to Ireland's problem lies in the kindness and good intentions of the individual. On a larger scale, this could translate as better government and a responsible landlord system. The paternalistic ideal behind Lawless's description of the relationship between landlord and tenant probably has its foundation in her own experiences of proper master–servant conduct.

A notice in *The Times* concerning her brother and his wife gives a glimpse of the world Lawless was used to:

> Among the signs of better times which are now becoming more numerous it may be of interest to mention that the return home of Lord and Lady Cloncurry was celebrated on Wednesday at Lyons, Hazlehatch, with great rejoicings. At 4 o'clock the workmen to the number of 30 were entertained at dinner. One of the workmen in proposing the 'Health of Lord and Lady Cloncurry', said he was speaking the thoughts of every one present in wishing them health, wealth, and prosperity. The toast was received with enthusiasm. 'The Health of the Dowager Lady Cloncurry' was given and warmly received. A dinner was given in the large building, decorated with evergreens, to about 400 people of the district. Before separating the company gave three hearty cheers for Lord and Lady Cloncurry.[49]

The image of the benevolent landlord, loved by his employees, comes through strongly in the notice. Yet, only a few years previously a number of tenants had been evicted from their holdings on Lord Cloncurry's estate. For Lawless and her family it was probably a central concern to re-establish the kind of relationship between landlord and tenant that was rapidly disappearing as an effect of the Land War. The *Times* notice describing the workmen's love for their employer appeared a little more than a year after the evicted tenants were reinstated.

Lawless is careful to avoid an 'us and them' division of people, however, and is more concerned with showing the fallibility of such categorisations. In *Hurrish,* she establishes a kind of local landscape identity where the symbiotic relationship between the people and their physical environment moves the plot forward and greatly determines the outcome. An early commentator notes that 'Miss Lawless is not content to get you Irish character; she must show you a Clare man or an Aran islander, and she is at infinite pains to point out how his nature, even his particular actions, are influenced by the place of his bringing up'.[50] However, since the land is an interspace, inherently indefinable and contradictory, such geographical identities necessarily fluctuate. Hurrish is certainly formed by his social environment – a product of 'that particular group of habits, customs, traditions, ways of looking at things, standards of right and wrong, which chance has presented to our still growing and expanding consciousness' (76) – but he is also an integral part of a landscape at once wild and calm, grim and beautiful, as are the other characters in the novel. The fact that he shares his last name with his landlord, Major O'Brien, suggests that personal identity transcends class or ethnic origin, and the same is true of the Major:

> The sense of country is a very odd possession, and in no part of the world is it odder than in Ireland. Soldier, landlord, Protestant, very Tory of Tories as he was, Pierce O'Brien was at heart as out-and-out an Irishman – nay, in a literal sense of the word, a Nationalist – as any frieze-coated Hurrish of them all. (48)

Categories always overlap, and neither Hurrish nor his landlord can be accommodated within a binary system of classification.

The most fundamental difference between the two O'Briens in *Hurrish* is that Pierce O'Brien is mobile, whereas Hurrish is tied to his place. Although the landscape he inhabits may help to create a fluctuating identity, his social environment is much more inflexible. Cultures erect boundaries, but nature, in Lawless's vision of the interspace, does not, and to a great extent it is Hurrish's inability to fully live up to the cultural identity expected of him that causes his downfall. If *Hurrish* is understood as *A Study* of national identity, it could be argued that what Lawless attempts to show in the novel is that the definitions of Irishness by cultural nationalists at the end of the nineteenth century were too narrow, and would only lead to conflict and tragedy.

*

A similar tension between place-defined and group-defined identity is evident in Lawless's second novel about the west of Ireland, *Grania: The Story of an Island* (1892). The main character, Grania O'Malley, grows up on Inishmaan, one of the Aran Islands. Her father, Con, is drinking himself to death and her sister, Honor, is dying from consumption and, although the family's standing is described as high in island terms, most readers would regard their situation as one of the utmost poverty and hardship. Grania is fiercely in love with Murdough Blake, who is her hero more or less by default, since there are few alternatives on the island. It is taken for granted that Grania and Murdough will eventually marry, but Grania is vaguely dissatisfied, since Murdough does not give her the love and affection she needs. The climax of the novel is the night when Honor lies dying and Grania sets out in the thick fog for a neighbouring island to fetch a priest to administer the last rites. Murdough refuses to go with her and instead she is accompanied by the crippled Phelim Daly. They get lost in the fog, and Grania drowns. The barren landscape of the islands and the unpredictable weather mirror the events of the story. In a conversation with Sir Mountstuart Elphinstone Grant Duff, Lawless said that 'the weather there [. . .] plays, as it does in my story, the part of Fate in a Greek tragedy'.[51]

Since all the characters are assumed to be Irish-speaking, the stage Irish that marred *Hurrish* is absent. Possibly Lawless had taken note of the criticism directed at her unsuccessful rendering of the Irish dialect, because in the dedicatory note to 'M. C.'[52] she introduces *Grania* as 'an Irish story without any Irish brogue in it – that brogue which is so tiresome always, and might surely be dispensed with [. . .] in a case where no single actor on the tiny stage is supposed to utter a word of English'. Commenting on J. M. Synge's *The Tinker's Wedding* (1909), Lawless says in a letter to Lady Gregory:

> as for the dialogue it is of course a *convention* but that one cannot blame it for since all literature is a convention, your own plays no doubt more or less so, and certainly my poor old *Grania* was, as it was merely an attempt to escape from the brogue and all its tiresome and stale conventions.[53]

The choice to abandon Irish dialect resulted in a poetic style where Gaelic tones and expressions echo in the dialogue, but there are no attempts to reproduce regional pronunciation. This solution of the language problem was appreciated also outside Ireland: 'it will please many readers to find the language exempt from dialect, only enough local flavour being retained to convey the idea of the translation of the native Erse into English'.[54]

Though the plot is simple, the picture of the little-known Aran Islands and the vivid portrayal of, above all, the main character, Grania, ensured that the novel was very well received. Favourable reviews appeared in the *Spectator*,[55] the *Atheneum*,[56] the *Bookman*,[57] the *Nation*,[58] and a number of other newspapers and journals in Ireland, England and America. The *Atlantic Monthly* reviewer's opinion is that the book is 'vastly better than the average novel'.[59] Among the very few negative comments are R. E. Prothero's view that '[f]or the length of the story it is possible that there are too many subsidiary figures, just as there are scenes which may be deemed superfluous, passages that, in spite of their remarkable beauty, may appear excessive, and a gloomy atmosphere which may seem too persistently melancholy'.[60] The gloomy atmosphere is commented on also in the *Overland Monthly and Out West Magazine:* Lawless 'grinds through the novel in a dreary, listless manner that is suggestive of the space writer on a San Francisco daily' and has dedicated the book to M. C. 'with an apology for its gloominess, as if some reparation was due for the outrage to his or her feelings'.[61] The *United Ireland* reviewer, on the other hand, regarded the novel as one of the most significant pieces of literature of the century:

> We have nothing to equal this in Irish literature. Nay, it is perhaps safe to say that it would be difficult to find its like for perfect art and most authentic human nature and human pathos in any book of the century written in any country. This, of course, will be its interest for the world's readers. But there is an added interest for us Irishmen and Irishwomen in 'Grania'. It is the most *Irish* piece of literature since the publication of 'The Welshmen of Tirawley'. It is Celtic through and through.[62]

The *North British Daily Mail* observed what might today be seen as the feminist theme of the novel:

> [T]he vital element in the story is the drawing of the two sisters. The one is full of passion for which the only object is an unworthy one, hindered by conventional ideas from giving expression even to this, feeling intensely within the narrow range which circumscribes her, unable to find compensation for the troubles of this world in the ideas taught her about the next.[63]

Grania and Honor are each other's contrasts, but their relationship is depicted as warm and loving – in fact, it is the most positive picture of women's relationships in all of Lawless's writing.

In her autobiography, Mrs Humphry Ward notes, in connection with meeting Lawless and Lady Cloncurry in Italy, that 'Miss Lawless's "Grania" is there to show how delicate and profound might be their sympathy with the lovely things in Irish Catholicism'.[64] Honor is the character representing Catholicism in the novel. She is a development of Alley Sheehan in *Hurrish,* a woman whose thoughts and actions are all defined by a deep religious faith. According to Sir Mountstuart Elphinstone Grant Duff, at least Honor was based on real women Lawless had met:

I asked if she had ever known an Honor in real life: 'Oh yes,' she said, 'I have known four or five. That sort of born nun is not by any means a very rare type among the Irish peasantry. Catholicism, when it falls on a favourable soil, is very apt to produce it; much oftener, I should think, in northern than in southern countries. No refinement, no purity which can be met with in the higher ranks is even equal to what may now and then be found in a West of Ireland cabin, amidst the most squalid surroundings. You come across people who are not merely fit for heaven; they are in heaven already.'[65]

The Inishmaan woman in the poem 'Honor's Grave' in *With the Wild Geese* (1902) also shares the characteristics of Grania's sister:

> Tender soul of womanhood,
> All her silent suffering past,
> Pious, pitiful, and good,
> Safe at last;
> Sheltered from the rough wind's blast.[66]

Honor is described as a saint and Grania a 'born rebel',[67] so much less devout than her sister that William Linn describes her as 'almost a pagan'.[68] There are episodes when Honor's piety comes across as quite cloying, and her unquestioning belief in the authority of priests is set against Grania's need for independence, her 'silent suffering' the opposite of Grania's frustration and anger. As Honor sees it, 'everyone that ever was born into this world, man or woman, must obey a priest', while Grania answers 'I would not be bid, no, not by anyone' and, moreover, maintains that 'the priests arn't all so good as you say' (vol. 1, 166). To Honor's horror, Grania would even hit a priest back if she was struck by him (vol. 1, 169). Exchanges like this illustrate the different attitudes of two women, where one has accepted her fate and her position in life, while the other fights for autonomy and self-realisation. In her conversation with Grant Duff, Lawless said that Grania did not really correspond to anyone she knew: 'A Grania [. . .] I have never known in that rank of life. The idea is taken from something a good deal higher up in the social scale.'[69] The character of Grania consequently transcends her social context.

Lawless visited the Aran Islands, together with Sir Henry Blake and his wife, to collect material for the novel,[70] several years before John Millington Synge's much more well-known visit in 1898. The poem 'Looking Eastward' in *With the Wild Geese* is given as 'Written in 1885', which seems to place Lawless's visit to the islands in the mid-eighties.[71] Synge criticised Lawless for founding her work on too short a stay and wrote in his notebook:

> I read *Grania* before I came here, and enjoyed it, but the real Aran spirit is not there. [. . .] To write a real novel of the island life one would require to pass several years among the people, but Miss Lawless does not appear to have lived here. Indeed it would be hardly possible perhaps for a lady for more than a few days.[72]

A letter from Violet Martin (Martin Ross) to Hildegarde Coghill indicates that at least the plot and characters of *Grania* were Lawless's own creation, and not based on stories she might have heard during her stay on the islands: 'The old parson of the island says that Miss Lawless drew much upon her imagination in Grania – in fact almost altogether and a woman here did not recognise the name Grania under any pronunciation that Edith could impart to it.'[73] A comment in the *Irish Book Lover* suggests that the novel's main character was Lawless's idea of essential Irishness:

> 'Grania' and 'Maelcho' were to her the eternal Irish people. In them she got down to elemental nature. Her elemental Irishman is not an animal of passion, fear and cunning, like the primitive man of the text-books, but a creature of imagination all compact, in whom bodily needs and desires are subordinated to moods as strange and vivid as that indefinable spirit of their island which Emily Lawless has expressed so lovingly and so delicately.[74]

Lawless was very ambivalent regarding national types. Discussing caricatures of Dutch and Boer people circulated during the Boer War, she writes:

> Centuries rise, and grow, and fade away; wars are made and cease again, but probably few things in this fluctuating world change so little, or with such a snail-like slowness, as the few broad lines upon which the characteristics of any given race have once got themselves legibly inscribed. (*A Garden Diary*, 115)

On the other hand, she criticises the way countries are represented through a symbolic person like, for instance, John Bull or Hibernia:

> What an odd convention it is, when one thinks of it, that habit of embodying a country in an individual! Considered seriously the whole contention is absurd. To talk of a nation as a person is to talk sheer nonsense. If one handles the idea a little it tumbles to pieces in one's fingers. The fiction of unity resolves itself into a mere vortex of atoms, all moving in different ways, and moreover with a different general drift in each successive generation. (*A Garden Diary*, 68)

The idea of a unified national identity is completely rejected. Thus, if Grania can be said in any way to embody Lawless's conception of Irish nationality, it becomes immensely important that she is portrayed as both an insider and an outsider in her community. It is not, then, simply the fact that she is a Catholic, Gaelic-speaking woman from the west of Ireland that signifies her Irishness, but the circumstance that she belongs to the land, to Irish nature rather than Irish culture.

Like Hurrish, Grania is closely identified with the landscape. To her,

> Inishmaan was much more than home, much more than a place she lived in, it was practically the world, and she wished for no bigger, hardly for any more prosperous, one. It was not merely her own little holding and cabin, but every inch of it that was in this peculiar sense hers. It belonged to her as the rock on which it has been born belongs to the young seamew. She had grown to it, and it had grown to her. She was a part of it, and it was a part of her. (vol. 1, 103)

Even her inner characteristics replicate the features of the Aran Islands: 'If all humans are themselves islands, as the poet has suggested, then this tall, red-petticoated, fiercely-handsome girl was decidedly a very isolated, and rather craggy and unapproachable, sort of island' (104, vol. 1). Nevertheless, the novel both begins and ends between the Aran Islands and the mainland, in the Atlantic, which is 'almost [Grania's] element' (vol. 1, 91). Her access to the sea and a hypothetical means of escape means that her identification with the land can be wholly positive, while the poor Daly family, who are unable to leave and are trapped by their position in the island's hierarchy as the family of a thief, are negatively identified with their surroundings:

> Seen in the twilight made by the big rock you might have taken the whole group for some sort of earth or rock emanation, rather than for things of living flesh and blood, so grey were they, so wan, so much the same colour, so much apparently the same texture as what they leaned against. (vol. 1, 62)

Desolation is part of Kitty Daly and her children, just like the open air and the unbounded seascape are part of Grania, and the starving family have allowed the land to swallow them, and have in a sense already been buried.

The difference between Grania and the Dalys is partly a matter of class, since Grania belongs to the island's aristocracy, partly a matter of agency, where starvation has made the Dalys passive and submissive while Grania is typified by activity and assertion. Yet, in the end, it is Grania who perishes. Even though she is fully part of Inishmaan she is still an outsider in the island community.[75] Like the pirate queen Grace O'Malley she shares her name with, she is a powerful and strong woman, but her kind of strength is too masculine to be really acceptable in a society where '[c]hanges, no matter of what sort or from what cause, are naturally condemned' (vol. 2, 36). Her awakening sexuality is blocked by the sense of decorum ingrained in her, and her feelings of dissatisfaction when Murdough does not show his love for her are so alien to the way she has been taught to think that she believes herself mad:

> The whole subject of love, of passion of any kind, especially from a girl and with regard to her own marriage, is such an utterly unheard-of one amongst Grania's class that the mere fact of giving utterance to complaint on the subject gave her a sense not merely of having committed a hideous breach of common decency, but of having actually crossed the line that separates sanity from madness. (vol. 2, 137)[76]

The night when she is leaving to fetch a priest for Honor, she embraces Murdough, who is shocked by her demonstration of emotion and her declarations of love: 'such conduct as this was unheard-of, was absolutely unprecedented and inconceivable! His sense of decorum was stirred to its very depths' (vol. 2, 245). Under normal circumstances Murdough is full of empty talk, whereas Grania is silent, and on the few occasions when she verbalises her feelings, he is rendered speechless (vol. 2, 163, 244–5).[77] He would prefer Grania to be a child still, and finds it hard to accept the fact that she is a woman with a mind of her own (vol. 2, 193). A trip to Galway, where she meets a haggard woman trapped in an abusive marriage, reveals to her that conditions are no better on the mainland:

> All at once an overpowering feeling of revolt overtook her, and with a bound she sprang to her feet and ran out of the cabin and down the road. Anywhere, anywhere in the world would be better than to remain an

> instant longer looking at those two, that man, that woman! Who were
> they? Were they not simply herself and him – herself and Murdough? (vol.
> 2, 121)

Since she can neither stay on Inishmaan and marry Murdough Blake
nor leave the island for a life elsewhere, Grania is caught in a double bind
where the only place she can be truly herself is in the border zone of the
Atlantic.[78] Her death by drowning is not so much a tragedy, then, as the
only possible solution and, anticipating the end, the sea speaks to her,
indicating as much:

> 'Look well at me,' it seemed to say, 'you have only to choose. Life up there
> on those stones! death down here upon these – there, you see, where the
> surf is licking the mussels! Choose – choose carefully – take your time –
> only choose!' (vol. 2, 54–5)

Just before the end she mistakes a clump of seaweed for her beloved
Murdough. Symbolically, the laminaria seaweed seems to support her for
a little while, but its elusive strength is easily dissolved into weak strands
(vol. 2, 298–9). In Bridget Matthews-Kane's view, Grania's delusional
conjuring of Murdough the moment before she dies shows that she is,
after all, unable to escape the confines of her culture and society.[79] The first
entangling and later dissolving bundle of seaweed points in another
direction, however, indicating that in the sea Grania is finally free from
all constraints. The tragedy, of course, is that this has to entail her death.

According to James M. Cahalan, *Grania* is 'the most clearly feminist
(or at least protofeminist) nineteenth-century Irish novel since those of
Sydney Owenson at the beginning of the century'.[80] If the novel is
understood as a feminist *Bildungsroman,* Grania's development can be read
in terms of spatiality rather than – as is more common – temporality.
Within a spatial model, personal growth becomes 'the results of changing
cultural interactions and locations',[81] and so Grania's initial experience of
the sea can be seen to develop her autonomy, the misogynist island to
foster her feminist awareness and her excursion to Galway to cause the
alienation that forces her back to Inishmaan and finally back to the sea and
its promise of liberation.[82]

Lawless's critique is directed at the values of a hidebound community,
and the novel continues her project of working out an identity that is
bound to the land but not necessarily to its people or the abstract idea of

a nation. It is significant that she does this primarily with reference to the west of Ireland, since the idealised West 'was an essential component of the late nineteenth-century construction of an Irish nationalism which, in its dependence on a Gaelic iconography, was to prove exclusive rather than inclusive'.[83] The West was seen as authentic, unspoiled by colonialism and untainted by Englishness, the 'true' Ireland which could serve as a model for the 'new' Ireland. Citing Karl Popper, Seán Ó Tuama remarks that 'when a culture is under severe strain it either completely rejects existing society or looks for a Utopia in the past or in the future'.[84] The Irish nineteenth-century utopia was usually placed in a mythical past and in regions where older and somehow 'genuine' lifestyles seemed to have survived. The conscious 'de-anglicising' of Ireland was grounded in a belief that it was possible to return to 'an essential, natural and historically continuous Irishness'[85] whose traces were visible in rural landscapes and cultures. A 'return', however, like the concepts 'genuine', 'real', 'pure' and 'authentic' that inform it, builds on the idea of a stable core and, by definition, a core cannot be fractured. The tendency to locate Irishness in ancient roots was therefore problematic for writers with other ethnic and religious backgrounds. While many Anglo-Irish and Protestant writers still wrote about rural areas, and some of them were driven by a desire to collect what could be salvaged from a dying tradition, there were also writers who attempted to balance the search for authenticity with descriptions of a landscape that could accommodate differences.

Lawless was obviously part of her period and its attitudes, and to a certain extent she joins the common nineteenth-century discourse of the 'almost-to-be-expected sense of the elusive, emotional – even intoxicating – difference distilled by the west of Ireland'.[86] She writes about Connaught:

> See, the Shannon is reached at last; is past; you are in no parti-coloured Ireland now, an Ireland of shreds and patches, a hybrid creature, bred within the Pale, at once the victim of a dozen incompatible theories and experiments of government. This is the real Ireland; the original one; the still more or less Irish-speaking one; an Ireland as it was from the beginning, or as little altered by the lapse of time as any country under the vagrant stars has yet contrived to be.[87]

Even so, she balances this romantic attitude with an emphasis on the disturbing features of the area. Although there is a relation between her view of the region as irrational and the 'instinctiveness, sexuality, and un-self-conscious sensuality of the primitive'[88] foregrounded in both nationalist and colonialist writing (though for opposite reasons), Lawless does not valorise the West because of a perceived simplicity in landscape and people. Her landscape is complex, and she is more concerned with the notion that the West is internally different than that it is different from, for instance, England.

As Jacqueline Belanger points out, the discourse of Celticism could also be appropriated 'to reconstruct a version of the "self" based on the "otherness" of the west'.[89] Lawless largely bypasses questions of cultural heritage and considers the West only as landscape, addressing such 'othering' strategies by emphasising that the region will affect what she ironically describes as 'the properly constituted mind' with 'a sense of discomfort', while for 'minds set in other moulds' the area 'responds to something within, as water responds to the needs of the water plant, or an echo to the voice that awakens it'.[90] Access to the West is a matter of mindset, then, not ethnic origin:

> May we not say that a prosaic pure-bred East Briton – the child of two incredulous Bible-reading parents – may in time grow positively Celtic in spirit if only he will surrender himself absolutely to these influences; if only he will fling away his miserable reason, and refuse from this day forward to disbelieve anything, especially anything that strikes him as absolutely impossible?
>
> And is not the converse at least equally true? May not a very Celt of the Celts – an O or a Mac into whose veins no minim of Saxon blood has ever entered since the Creation – become so un-Celtlike in his inner man, so be-Saxonised if one may use the phrase, in the atmosphere of caucuses and committee rooms; so appallingly practical, so depressingly hardheaded, nay – if the corruption be carried far enough – actually so logical, that at last, as a Celt, he cannot, strictly speaking, be said to have any existence at all?[91]

National identity depends on openness to influences and even will. The west of Ireland will remain out of reach for people like the party of tourists in *Grania* who enjoy 'the sense of discovery' a visit to Inishmaan provides (vol. 2, 175), and stare at Grania whom they find 'picturesque', although without the good and decent manners the 'poor creatures' of the West generally have (vol. 2, 177). But Grania has an intimate relationship with the island that such tourists can never attain, and when their visit is cut short because of the weather she is filled with 'a feeling of satisfaction in her own fierce sea and sky which had scared away these fine people so suddenly' (vol. 2, 178). The map that introduces the novel is of the Aran Islands alone, without any relation to mainland Ireland, England or any centre of which the islands could be the periphery, which further complicates the notion of the West as 'other'.[92]

Although the West can then neither function as the Same in terms of culture nor as the Other, Lawless still sees possibilities for the Anglo-Irish to construct an Irish identity for themselves with recourse to the western landscape. Grania, who is herself a foreigner, since her mother was born on the mainland, is able to establish a landscape identity which is more enabling than that of the other islanders, like the Daly family. It is not the land, but the rigidity of island society that shuts her out. In a sense, then, the novel *Grania* can be read as a microcosm of Ireland, where Inishmaan represents the threat of a new, culturally hegemonic nation-state, and Grania herself becomes a mirror of the increasingly displaced members of the Ascendancy.[93] Grania's link with the sixteenth-century Grace O'Malley, who was used as an allegory of Ireland in the *Aisling* poems, suggests that she, too, is a symbol of the country and, as such, her simultaneous insider and outsider status points towards the possibility of an Irish identity that would be inclusive rather than exclusive. Such an identity can be founded on nature, but not on a cultural heritage where the Anglo-Irish are figured as the enemy, Lawless suggests. According to Betty Webb Brewer, *Grania* freed Lawless from the necessity of addressing Irish politics,[94] but it could also be argued that the novel provided her with an opportunity to discuss central issues in Irish politics at the time, although in an indirect manner.

Thus, Lawless opposes both the native narrow-mindedness and the touristic appropriation of the West in favour of a, perhaps somewhat utopian, connection with the land which is neither that of the tourist nor that of the native, but the approach of:

> a being who does not fall strictly speaking into either one or other of these categories; who is not tied by the ties and shackled by the shackles of the resident, and who, on the other hand, does not believe in the possibility of exploring an entire tract of country, and plucking out the whole heart of its mystery within a space of twenty-four hours.[95]

This attitude to landscape leads to a conceptualisation of space that makes polarisation impossible, since it refuses both the resident's claim to territory and the reductive but conquering vision of the casual visitor. What Lawless proposes is 'the possibility of a space which does not replicate the exclusions of the Same and the Other', or, in other words, an *interspace*.[96] Whether geographically, socially or culturally defined, this concept of space allows the presence also of those who do not fit the prevailing systems.

*

The full implications but also the very real limitations of the interspace ideal can be seen in the last novel Lawless completed on her own, *The Book of Gilly: Four Months Out of a Life* (1906). The work clearly shows Lawless's belief in the healing powers of nature and landscape as a source of knowledge, and is one of the clearest examples of her vision of an elective geographical identity. Yet, while she valorises the conventionally feminine end of the nature–culture continuum, and to a certain extent robs ethnicity of its essentialist meanings, she is blind to class privilege.

Inishbeg, the small island the boy Gilly goes to, is introduced as a prehistoric place where humankind has yet to evolve, which draws attention to Ireland's potential to stimulate rebirth. England, in contrast, is figured as a 'machine', and Gilly's English tutor, Mr Griggs, stands for exactly the kind of education connected with this 'machine': an understanding of knowledge that is 'strictly practical, without loose fringes or metaphysical flummery'.[97] Griggs's opinion is presented as conventionally masculine and contrasted with the humanist lore represented by Gilly's friend Phil Acton, who has come to Inishbeg to recover from an illness. For Acton, science is inadequate: 'Rotten materialism! Rotten conceit! Rotten anything that could make a man suppose all earth, and sea, and sky were able to be summed up, packed away and settled by a handful of trumpery formula!' (253–4). While, a century earlier, Irish national character had been negatively compared with a Britishness that constructed itself in terms of progress and rationality, by the end of the nineteenth century the relationship was often reversed, and when the British national character was attacked as philistine, utilitarian and shallow, this benefited the construction of Irishness as spiritual and sensitive.[98] That Ireland can be the antidote to materialist thinking is suggested, for instance, by Yeats:

> In Ireland wherever the Gaelic tongue is still spoken, and to some little extent
> where it is not, the people live according to a tradition of life that existed
> before the world surrendered to the competition of merchants and to the
> vulgarity that has been founded upon it; and we who would keep the Gaelic
> tongue and Gaelic memories and Gaelic habits of our mind would keep
> them, as I think, that we may some day spread a tradition of life that would
> build up neither great wealth nor great poverty, that makes the arts a natural
> expression of life, that permits even common men to understand good art
> and high thinking and to have the fine manners these things can give.[99]

However, while Yeats emphasises the importance of customs and language,
Lawless resists this static view of culture and finds the cure in the land
itself, or perhaps in the cultural tradition of the early Celts for whom
'landscape *was* life', the site where 'the temporal and spiritual were always
in contact'.[100] In *The Book of Gilly,* personal development and 'self-
expansion' are the rewards promised by Phil Acton/Ireland (184), and
mystical communion with landscape or seascape gives access to deeper
knowledge. Echoing the lines in her article 'North Clare – Leaves from a
Diary', Lawless writes:

> Identity seemed to go floating about; to have lost its relationship, not only
> with every other identity, but even with itself. At such moments the entire
> scheme of things appeared to be in its essence not materially different from
> those pictures seen for a moment upon the bubbles which the tide scatters
> – pictures in which the eye beholds, or fancies that it beholds, the entire
> story of the sea; all its wonders and its terrors, its glories and its tragedies.
> (*The Book of Gilly*, 190).

Humanist knowledge and insights from emotional experiences are set
against rigid scientific explanations and valorised. But Lawless nevertheless
indicates that Gilly's future place as a cog in 'the machinery' to some extent
requires the mind-set represented by Griggs/England and, to be prepared
for a future as a leader, Gilly is shown the pleasures of ownership and the
power of class as the 'King of Inishbeg' (67).

At the end of the novel Gilly is to return to England and he goes to
tell his Irish friend Bride Kelly so. Her surprise makes him aware of his
difference from her – she racialises him, as it were – and he reacts with
indignation:

> ''Tisn't never Inglish ye are yourself, anyway?' the girl asked, with an
> astonishment that could hardly have been greater had it been suddenly
> broken to her that her small visitor was a Turk.

'Of *course* I'm not; I told you that long ago. Mummy is English, but fader and I are Irish – natuwally.' (262)

Gilly's grandmother was in fact not Irish, so neither was Gilly's father – if Irishness is defined in essential terms – but, where Gilly is concerned, Lawless presents race as unfixed and non-essential: as a matter of choice. Bride Kelly's ethnic identity is involuntary, however. Marked by her Hiberno-English dialect and her way of life she can never be other than Irish. Away from her country she would only become an exile: "Deed an' indeed, child, I never heard of no good coming to people through lavin' ould Ireland, 'cept 'twas to America maybe, an' then only because they couldn't help themselves', she says (275). To move between different national identities is an option only for members of the privileged classes. In Bride's case the solution is instead to firmly hold that Ireland is infinitely better than the alternatives: 'The further you gets from Ireland, the further you gets from dacency', she maintains (275). In the end the binary opposition between English and Irish, male and female, rational and spiritual, is thus partially dismantled through Gilly's hybrid identity but also upheld in Bride's position, albeit hierarchically reversed. For Gilly, closeness to nature is liberating, a way of expanding a consciousness that would otherwise have been fettered by the mind-numbing ideals of the 'machine-society', but Bride's organic bond with the land is rather a matter of confinement, similar to that of the Daly family in *Grania*. While Lawless is able to envisage the experience of Ireland as producing a more flexible concept of identity where the English and Anglo-Irish are concerned, she cannot see the same possibilities for the Gaelic-Irish, who are tied to the land in ways which allow few escape routes apart from death.

It can be argued, then, that, while Lawless manages to legitimise her place in Ireland by proposing an identity based on a geography in opposition to imperialist and nationalist discourses of control and definition, she thereby denies any possibility of a collective identity that could power political action, because political activity to a great extent 'depends on concepts of territoriality', as was the case during the Land War.[101] This is both the most radical and the most limiting aspect of her vision, since, on the one hand, the absence of a group identity precludes the logjam of sectarianism, on the other, social change is only really possible when many work to instigate it – which requires a sense of commonality. Lawless's vision of the interspace cannot really suggest how a community could be produced, unless it be through the love the land inspires:

> This is what you have panted for, have almost fallen sick for the lack of, not alone in less, but in admittedly far more attractive scenes. Already its atmosphere surrounds you; seems to be part of you, to have entered into the cockles of your heart and the marrow of your bones, or whatever other region of the body it is that is stirred, and not in man only, but in every sentient beast, by the touch of its mother-earth.[102]

Such love is not produced by cultural homogeneity or by a division of the land into yours and mine, but by an intense relationship between the individual and the landscape.

Chapter 4

Negotiating authority: history and biography

In Western culture uncertainty is generally perceived as a negative characteristic. Hesitation is a sign of weakness, while self-assurance is valued and a willingness to take a firm stand is regarded as a desirable quality. Indirectness is especially associated with women's language and is one of the elements that is said to make it less effective on the powerful/powerless scale, although more serviceable in a paradigm that valorises co-operation before competitiveness.[1] The issue of gender-based language differences is obviously deeply problematic, and any discussion couched in essentialist terms runs the risk of perpetuating stereotypes. Other aspects, such as class, ethnicity, sexual orientation, education, age, etc., also need to be considered and, more importantly, the instability of gender constructions makes terms like 'masculinity' and 'femininity' difficult to use. Nevertheless, certain modes are more readily connected with male than female language users, and the terms 'masculine' and 'feminine' are used to refer to such popular perceptions, not to gendered core identities.

Today, collaborative skills may be more valued than they were a few decades ago, but unassertive speech habits are still looked upon as 'credibility-robbing' problems that (mainly) women will have to solve to acquire power and influence. In other words, decisive and authoritative – that is, conventionally masculine – language continues to be privileged.[2] But powerlessness is not the only characteristic conveyed by indirect language, and ambivalence does not automatically engender distrust. The negotiations with the voice of authority in Emily Lawless's *Ireland* (1887) and *Maria Edgeworth* (1904) demonstrate how structures of indirectness may introduce dialogue into narrative history and literary biography, genres traditionally characterised by their public, authoritative tone. Text, subtext and narrative technique combine to question not only the social system Lawless belonged to but totalising ideology as such. By feminising the conventions of historiography and biography-writing she created a space for the woman writer in these male-dominated cultural fields.

The lack of assertiveness connected with the woman speaker is a prominent feature of women's literature as well. Women's texts are often marked by what has been described as a particularly feminine code of conduct, frequently represented in what could be termed literary politeness strategies or deliberately non-antagonistic approaches. When women's writing is evaluated and discussed in relation to a model that favours confidence and authority, it might therefore seem inferior to works that subscribe to such an ideal, which is one reason why many women's texts have been dismissed as second-rate. To escape judgement, women have sometimes resorted to male impersonation – the male pseudonym, the male narrator, the masculine style of public discourse – for their writing to be recognised, but such attempts to master 'the dominant and societal discourses' could in fact be 'self-effacing rather than empowering'.[3] As Susan Sniader Lanser notes, 'authorial voice has been so conventionally masculine that female authorship does not necessarily establish female voice'.[4] To write is in itself an assertive act and as such at odds with both historical and present-day definitions of femininity. Referring to Nancy Chodorow's understanding of gender, Carol J. Singley concludes that 'authorial aspiration, which seems to involve assertion or even aggression, contradicts female empathy and interdependence'.[5] These arguments veer quite far in the direction of essentialism and, as far as levels of linguistic assertiveness are concerned, it would seem as if women are caught in a double bind: if they use the conventionally male voice they are in danger of erasing themselves, and if they use what is perceived as feminine language they risk reinforcing prevalent gender stereotypes. It is therefore necessary to relate women's choice of narrative tone to the social and cultural conditions at the time of their writing, and to recognise that their stylistic manoeuvres might function as negotiations of inflexible gender constructions. As Monika Fludernik says, a feminist reinterpretation of unassertive discourse strategies 'reveals a tactics of deliberate, cooperative and interactive "public relations" management where a traditional perspective of female stereotyping inevitably tended to register only weakness, vagueness, rambling illogicality or even stupidity'.[6]

The conduct books of the early modern period establish a strong connection between women's chastity and silence, issuing injunctions against women speaking in public that go back to the Apostle Paul and beyond. With the increased importance of the middle class, silence and deference came to define women's linguistic behaviour. Women's public speech and writing was linked with sexual promiscuity and transgression of gender boundaries – a writing woman was seen as a loose woman, or no woman at all.[7] But prohibitions exist because there is already some resistance to what is proscribed, and the response of actual women to social dictates varies along the whole spectrum from compliance to defiance. The most common response is negotiation. Female writers from the Renaissance onwards have employed numerous strategies to be able to write and publish, and these tactics are integral parts of women's literary tradition. Many of the techniques exemplify the indirectness connected with women's speech habits and seem to be aimed at alleviating society's anxieties. Expressions of modesty, elaborate justifications, apologies, ambiguity and irony are only a few of the methods women have used to defend their presence on the literary scene. Textual authority is consequently diminished or concealed, in order not to exacerbate the provocation caused by the very act of writing. These devices constitute what Carol J. Singley and Susan Elizabeth Sweeney term 'anxious power'; that is, 'the various formal strategies with which [women] express their anxiety about the power conferred by reading and writing'.[8] In a cultural climate that privileges an authoritative tone, such tactics are easily interpreted as evidence of incompetence, especially since women writers themselves so willingly admit their ineptitude.

However, even though indirect expression may originally have been the result of internalised notions of inequality, it carries meanings beyond this relation to gender imbalance. According to postmodern theories, ambivalence is a powerful challenge to totalisation[9] and, in this light, women's ambiguity can be understood as a rejection of universal explanations. The element of uncertainty could indicate a reluctance to provide a final answer and the waiving of authority could be interpreted as a refusal to control both the material and its reception. The self-reflexive nature of much work by women draws attention to the author as producer, emphasising subjectivity and provisionality rather than universality, and making the reader a co-producer instead of a passive consumer. The operative word is 'doubleness' or, in Bakhtinian terms, *heteroglossia* and *dialogue:* 'an utterance that belongs, by its grammatical (syntactic) and compositional markers, to a single speaker, but that actually contains mixed within it two utterances, two speech manners, two styles, two "languages", two semantic and axiological belief systems'.[10] According to Bakhtin's theory all language is dialogic, and the speech genres he defines as 'monologic' are consequently monologues only because they create an illusion of authority linked to real or illusory power. Most discussions of Bakhtinian dialogue locate the phenomenon in the novel, as Bakhtin himself did, but, when the double voice occurs in conventionally monologic forms like narrative history or biography, it becomes particularly noticeable.

Bakhtin does not consider gender in his discussion, but the linguistic and narrative structures of uncertainty in women's writing correspond in many ways to his definition of the ambivalent word. Indirect language accommodates several contradictory meanings without unequivocally valuing one above the other – it is dialogic. The only explicit message is the rejection of single-voiced authority. As Laurie A. Finke says, 'language that is double-voiced calls into question the fiction of authoritative or monologic discourse' because a fragmented narrative technique reveals 'the messiness behind the illusion of unified narratives about the world by restoring information [. . .] previously marginalized and excluded by those narratives'.[11] A questioning attitude to monologue is precisely the effect conveyed through the unprocessed material in Lawless's history of Ireland and her biography of Maria Edgeworth.

To the extent that the voice of authority is also masculine, Lawless's dialogic strategies in *Ireland* and *Maria Edgeworth* mark her as woman. But they also define her as Irish, since they establish a connection between her writing and ancient Irish literature, where question-and-answer dialogue is the main structuring device. The *Acallam na Senórach – The Dialogue of the Ancients* – is an obvious example, but the Lives of Saints are equally dialogic, despite their postulated relation with the absolute authority of the word of God. In medieval hagiography, both in Latin and in Irish, the single authorial voice dissolves into open-ended dialogue where 'loose ends are left loose, contradictions are not resolved, and simmering tensions are allowed to boil over, leading into new episodes or opening up into altogether different lives or legend cycles'.[12] This lack of closure expresses the negotiations between spiritual and worldly, present and past, Christian and pre-Christian culture by incorporating alternative views. The technique also infuses the fixed form of the written text with the fluidity of oral literature, and so mitigates the anxieties of scribal authority. In an article about literary impersonation, Lawless gives the example of *The Rennes Dindsenchas,* a collection of stories explaining the origins of place-names in Ireland. Supplying one detailed explanation after another of the same name, apparently without hierarchical order, this work cannot satisfy 'a pedantic thirst after absolute accuracy',[13] and so the ultimate decision is left to the reader. Indeterminacy in this context becomes a conscious philosophical position that resists the limitations of an authoritative version, a balancing act that may well be what defined a text as 'literature' in medieval Ireland.[14] Emily Lawless's *Ireland* and *Maria Edgeworth* connect with this tradition. Despite the fact that history-writing and biography are public discourses expected to communicate confidence and authority, Lawless insists on conveying the uncertainty that surrounds any interpretation of the past.

*

Lawless's persistent representation of the implications of the past as elusive and indeterminate prefigures the insights of New-Historicism and the realisation that history is always also a matter of story-telling. Considered as a number of events in the past, history has no intrinsic meaning and an occurrence cannot be regarded as in itself favourable or unfavourable, since a change of perspective can reverse its significance. The meaning of history is a matter of emplotment, as Hayden White says,[15] and a number of factors – many, if not most, of them located in the present – determine what story the historian chooses to tell. This is no longer a particularly revolutionary insight. Especially where Irish history is concerned, it has long been recognised that history-writing functions as a means to further an agenda, which requires characters and incidents to be subordinated to the overall demands of plot.[16] The story format invites reader identification and encourages action and, in the turbulent political climate of nineteenth-century Ireland, writing history was almost a national pastime. The two basic plotlines are, first, the story of English oppression and Irish suffering put forward in, for instance, A. M. Sullivan's widely read *The Story of Ireland* (1867) and, second, the tale of benevolent English intervention and general Irish ineptitude presented in Standish O'Grady's much less appreciated *The Story of Ireland* (1893). As the title indicates, O'Grady's work was written in direct response to Sullivan's history and attempts to reverse its analysis of the past in every way. A story presupposes an ending, and the logical close of Sullivan's tale is liberation or Home Rule for Ireland, whereas O'Grady's story naturally leads up to continued Union with England.[17] What separates Emily Lawless's history of Ireland from these and other works emanating from either the nationalist or the unionist tradition is that Lawless is anxious to avoid political categorisation and to find a way of combining her love of Ireland with her doubts about the Irish people's ability to govern themselves. Her vision of Irish history corresponds closely to her image of the country itself as an *interspace* that cannot be described in rational terms: pluralist, complex and frequently confused. As a consequence, her plot needs to be indeterminate and the end of the story uncertain.

The desire for an uncertain ending has important implications for Lawless's style, since an open-ended plot cannot be transmitted in decisive, authoritative language, but other cultural developments are equally important, and her personal, unassertive tone can in many ways be regarded as a matter of gender negotiation. By the late nineteenth century, History was an established university discipline and, as such, male territory, but women's issues were also firmly on the agenda through the activities of the burgeoning Suffragette movement and the writings of the New Women. Although Lawless definitely did not see herself as a feminist, she was engaged in activities that were mainly encoded as male: entomology, cultural journalism, history and biography. The fact that she used a male narrator in most of her historical novels and some of her shorter works of historical fiction suggests, to some extent at least, that she regarded the Voice of History as essentially masculine.[18] The ideals assumed to be embedded in this male voice are negotiated in various ways in her production.

The nineteenth century saw a gradual professionalisation of history as an academic subject, even though this development was much stronger in France or Germany than in Britain, where history was still mostly perceived as an art.[19] Even so, English and Irish historians were of course influenced by continental developments, and in the years around 1887, when Lawless's history *Ireland* was published, both academics and general readers were engaged in debating the merits of narrative versus scientific approaches to history-writing. A common opinion was that attention to the scientific aspects of the subject made history boring, and that the true purpose of history was to convey the flavour of another time:

> There was a time when the Muse of History moved in the halls of monarchs with regal pomp and splendour, with retinue of cardinals and princes, with blare of heralds' trumpets and clank of knightly steel; [. . .] But now she has laid aside her royal robes; she has dismissed her splendid train; she has become clear, cold, prosaic, and precise.[20]

Though the article writer realises that times have changed, the implication is that Service to the Muse of History is better carried out by story-tellers than scholars influenced by the ideals of natural science. In another article, young historians are admonished not to forget the literary aspects of history-writing:

> After such a bout of scientific history as they have been enjoying for the past few years, it will do our young men no harm to be reminded, if only indirectly, that the subject has another side, that it is after all a form of literary composition, and that the historian's business is not only to collect his materials, but also to give them shape and proportion.[21]

There is no awareness in this article that the narrator might shape his material to carry a specific point of view, or that certain aspects might be obscured or lost in the interests of a coherent and pleasing tale. On the contrary, style and narrative flow are regarded as much more important than scrupulous research methods or ascertaining the reliability of historical evidence:

> While schoolmen wrangle over this method and that, over what the law may be and where to find the testimony, Gibbon and Macaulay will continue to be read with delight and profit by all who can understand good history and appreciate good literature.[22]

Good history and good literature are consequently considered germane to each other, and a good historian is the same as a good writer. In the historiographical debate, Lawless was firmly on the side of narrative history, and her description of William Edward Hartpole Lecky's monumental works of history as his 'permanent contributions to English literature' is an apt illustration of this attitude.[23] In a letter to Lecky about his *History of Ireland in the Eighteenth Century* she writes:

> I know that I for my part read the last volume almost without laying it down, and felt the interest of it as <u>story</u> breathlessly. This is a sort of praise that you I know hold in intense scorn, but that I cannot help! History is

and always will be to me a drama, & only interesting as a drama, & if I cannot get near enough to the actors to see their gestures & hear their words I do not care to know anything about them at all.[24]

It seems clear that Lawless expected – perhaps knew – that Lecky as a professional historian would take a more scientific approach to his subject. Her own preference for narrative is equally apparent. On the whole, she seems to have been more concerned with verisimilitude than strict historical accuracy. In 'Irish History Considered as a Pastime', she comments on a story about the son of Gerald the Great and Cardinal Wolsey:

> If the reader asks how far these utterances are or are not strictly historical, I confess that I am at a loss to reply. May one add that the matter is not of any profound consequence one way or other? Written down by contemporaries, they doubtless fitted well enough into the popular estimate of the men, or they would not have been told at all. Beyond this, who knows anything, with absolute certainty, about anybody? Let us be thankful if a few life-like fragments exist, and not scan their credentials too curiously. Certitude is not for this world, and certainly is not the peculiar prerogative of Ireland, or of Irish historians![25]

It is not only that historical accuracy is an impossible aspiration, but, at some level, Lawless suggests, it is not even necessary. In the article she discusses how to make history palatable for young readers, and she is convinced that it is the stories, not the facts, of the past that are needed.

A valorisation of narrative admittedly leaves a window open for women historians who would otherwise have been excluded as a result of the professionalisation of the subject. Women's involvement in history was frequently as popularisers of more academic work by male scholars and, in some ways, this might have fostered an attitude to history-as-story that lived on among women historians long into the twentieth century. Mary Hayden, for instance, appointed in 1911 as the first professor of modern Irish history at University College Dublin, regarded 'scientific history' with scepticism throughout her career.[26] Lawless's *Ireland* appeared in the Story of the Nations series, whose aim, according to William Linn, was to provide compressed, readable histories of countries and periods. The publishers, therefore, preferred writers who were not professional historians.[27] Thus Lawless was part of the tradition where women were regarded primarily as popularisers.

Nevertheless, for the nineteenth-century woman writer the problem remained that the authoritative voice of even popular narrative history ran counter to nineteenth-century ideals of femininity. Women reluctant to challenge the prevailing gender system outright would therefore need to obscure their function as interpreters, and Lawless transfers the responsibility of sense-making to the reader, saying in the Preface to her history *Ireland* that 'a good reader will read a great deal more into them than the mere words convey'.[28] Invitations to the reader to be the final judge, like such textual strategies as irony, allusions and digressions, may thus be seen as instances of the modesty topos identified in women's writing from the early modern period onwards. By insisting on her 'inadequacy' (417) and inability to make sense of the facts, Lawless ensures that she does not encroach too far on male territorial rights. This self-effacing attitude is present also in later editions of the work: 'The humbler and more restricted aim of this little book being rather to try to allure along the admittedly uninviting track of Irish history a few additional outside readers whom larger, more exhaustive, possibly more authentic, works might deter or alarm.'[29] The disappointing absence of women in her account of the past could be understood as another adjustment to the nineteenth-century gender order.

For readers who subscribe to the ideal of an assertive, authoritative manner of writing, Lawless's personal style is a serious flaw. While praising the impartiality of the account, the reviewer for the *Overland Monthly and Out West Magazine* is of the opinion that the 'literary style of the narrative is unfortunate' and asks for 'clearness' and 'smoothness'.[30] William Lecky, who read the history *Ireland* in proof, apparently regarded the style as too colloquial. Lawless acknowledged his criticism, but defended herself by saying that 'the publishers made such a strong point of its being as popularly written as possible that I had to throw the dignity of history to the winds'.[31] The publisher's requirements cannot fully explain Lawless's stylistic choices, however. William Linn lists a few peculiarities that he regards as flaws:

> She [Emily Lawless] also reveals an unfortunate fondness for whimsical, rather amateurish asides, which tend to destroy the tone of the work by interrupting the serious discussion of history with irrelevant, and often silly expressions of her personal feelings. [. . .] Sometimes her asides are self-deprecatory, at other times they merely reveal her lack of sophistication as a historian. Luckily this flaw only appears occasionally, and is far too

insignificant to detract markedly from the smooth, even flow of her narrative.[32]

In Linn's view, asides and personal comments are unfortunate mistakes, and he does not consider the possibility that they might be deliberately inserted for a specific purpose.

The personal tone of Lawless's history confronts and contrasts with the magisterial attitude displayed by most male historians at the time, and she questions both narrative and scientific history by giving credence and prominence to myth. The shaping and ordering activities of the historian exclude material and conceal prejudice, and she is sceptical of those ancient annals that purport to convey facts while featuring assertions such as 'there were giants in those days' (12). Instead, she prefers the legends, because they 'put forward no obtrusive pretensions to accuracy, and for that very reason are far truer in that larger sense in which all the genuine and spontaneous outgrowth of a country form part and parcel of its history' (13). This is the argument also in Standish O'Grady's *Early Bardic Literature, Ireland,* though O'Grady stresses that the tales are founded on historical facts. Yet, an important aspect of his plea for publishing the bardic texts is that their richness means that they cannot be fully understood at any one time: 'No men living, and no men to live, will ever so exhaust the meaning of any single tale as to render its publication unnecessary for the study of others.'[33] No interpretation is final, in other words, and a similar idea governs Lawless's attitude to historical sources. By continuously emphasising the fallibility of her own understanding of past events she manages to suggest that interpretative paradigms are suspect as such. Early in her work she emphasises that Ireland's geography encourages diversity, since the land itself guarantees that no group is wholly displaced when invaders attack: 'such wholesale exterminations [are], in fact, very rare, especially in a country which like Ireland seems specially laid out by kindly nature for the protection of a weaker race struggling in the grip of a stronger one' (6–7). Racial, religious or cultural purity is denied in favour of a version of the past where categories are mixed or at least juxtaposed. The underlying idea is that, since Ireland cannot be defined in either geographical or historical terms, the definition of the Irish people should be less pure – or, perhaps, inclusive enough to contain also unionist aristocrats like Lawless and her family.

Lawless was acutely aware that Irish historiography is to a great extent a matter of political manoeuvring, and in her Preface she cautiously touches upon this problem:

> Irish history is a long, dark road, with many blind alleys, many sudden turnings, many unaccountably crooked portions; a road which, if it has a few signposts to guide us, bristles with threatening notices, now upon the one side and now upon the other, the very ground underfoot being often full of unsuspected perils threatening to hurt the unwary. (ix)

The first paragraph mentions the word 'threatening' twice (ix), suggesting that to write the history of Ireland is to take a risk, and, although alluring to the 'genuine explorer' (ix), the uncertainties of the past are a 'serious impediment' (ix) to the historiographer. This imprecisely intimated political minefield is another reason for Lawless to downplay her role as expert and express her disinclination to attempt the role of guide 'even in the slightest and least responsible capacity' (ix):

> A history beset with such distracting problems, bristling with such thorny controversies, a history, above all, which has so much bearing on that portion of history which has still to be born, ought, it may be said, to be approached in the gravest and most authoritative fashion possible, or else not approached at all. (x)

However, Lawless makes 'no claim to authority' (x) and, instead of being written in 'the gravest and most authoritative fashion possible', her history uses a style that resembles fiction. Through her insistence on complexity she rejects both nationalist and unionist paradigms, preferring to highlight the contradictory and elusive nature of Irish history: it is a 'weltering tangle of confusion' (37), 'confused and baffling' (75), 'a confusion so penetrating and all-persuasive that the mind fairly refuses to grapple with it' (125), veiled in 'fog and misconception' (251), 'perplexing' (257) and characterised by 'puzzling contradictions and anomalies' (310). It cannot even be organised in any recognisable manner, because the usual division into periods based on the reigns of monarchs does not work in Ireland:

> One of the greatest difficulties to be faced in the study of Irish history, no matter upon what scale, is to discover any reasonable method of dividing our space. The habit of distributing all historical affairs into reigns is often misleading enough even in England; in Ireland it becomes simply ridiculous. (107)

The result is a narrative fundamentally different from the monologic account she paradoxically professes is necessary, couched in a mediatory style very different from, for instance, the direct exhortations to the reader in the Preface to John Mitchel's *History of Ireland* (1869):

> If the writer has succeeded – as he has earnestly desired to do – in arranging those facts in good order, and exhibiting the naked truth concerning English domination since the Treaty of Limerick, as our fathers saw it, and felt it; – if he has been enabled to picture, in some degree like life, the long agony of the Penal days, when the pride of the ancient Irish race was stung by daily, hourly humiliations, and their passions goaded to madness by brutal oppression; – and further, to picture the still more destructive devastations perpetrated upon our country in this enlightened nineteenth century; then it is hoped that every reader will draw for himself such general conclusions as the facts will warrant, without any declamatory appeals to patriotic resentment, or promptings to patriotic aspiration.[34]

While ostensibly inviting the reader to make the final decision, Mitchel leaves no room for doubt about the correct interpretation of the past. Lawless, on the other hand, constantly points out the problematic nature of Irish historiography and indicates the existence of a subtext by introducing seemingly irrelevant pieces of information, digressions and contradictory quotations. Such features make her text dialogic or double-voiced, challenging the totalisation of both past and contemporary history-writing at the same time as they negotiate the sexual and national politics of her time.

To some extent the dialogue is only superficial, of course, and identifying the dialogic elements in a work does not amount to saying that there is real exchange. What one critic celebrates as emancipatory heteroglossia, another might perceive as a cacophonic confusion where interaction breaks down. The privileged position of dialogue in literary criticism today makes it tempting to regard the identification of multivocality as an end in itself, without considering the 'questions about how – in concrete instances of dialogic exchange – conflicting agendas are negotiated and "footings" are rearranged'.[35] It is necessary to acknowledge that the effect – and functionality – of dialogue varies over time and between writers and that, in the last instance, it is the reader who decides whether dialogue is present at all. At least one reviewer denies the existence of dialogue in Lawless's history by pointing out that 'the fact that this story of a nation is dedicated to the earl of Dufferin is sufficiently indicative of her view of the Irish question to make explanation of the tone of the book equally unnecessary'.[36] The Earl of Dufferin, later Marquis of Dufferin and Ava, was Viceroy of India at the time when the history was written and consequently an important representative of British imperial power. He was also a strong supporter of Irish landlordism and opposed Home Rule, which he believed would be fatal to both England and Ireland.[37] Nevertheless, the same reviewer admits that Lawless has 'dealt very fairly' with the 'bulk of the Irish people',[38] so it seems that her text is open-ended enough to at least partially off-set the implications of the dedication. Even so, there are instances when dialogic exchange is excluded, as when Lawless comments on the attacks on the Ulster settlers in 1641:

> Nothing that has happened within living memory can be even approximately compared to it, though, perhaps, those who are old enough to remember the sensations awakened by the news of the Indian Mutiny will be able most nearly to realize the wrath and passionate desire of revenge which filled every Protestant breast. (251)

Lawless's position is easily inferred, since the feelings she claims to be able to understand are only those of the attacked, and she seems blind to the ironic circumstance that both the Irish revolt of 1641 and the sepoy rising turned on representatives of the same imperial power and had their roots in a similar resentment of English rule. On other occasions her comments may be obliquely worded but will cause no trouble for the initiated, as when she describes how the Tuatha-da-Danaans[39] resorted to guerrilla tactics 'as another defeated race did upon their conquerors in later days' (9). But even though the indirect reference to English-Irish frictions is quite clear to the informed reader, it is sufficiently unspecific to leave room for other interpretations. The same is true about Lawless's use of irony: to a certain degree it guides the reader's responses, but the final explanation remains unexpressed. The opening quotation of the history introduces the double voice of irony particularly effectively, since it contains a challenge to the single voice of authority:

> 'It seems to be certain,' says the Abbé McGecghehan,[40] 'that Ireland continued uninhabited from the Creation to the Deluge.' With this assurance to help us on our onward way I may venture to supplement it

by saying that little is known about the first, or even about the second, third and fourth succession of settlers in Ireland. (2)

As a Darwinist, Lawless could hardly have accepted MacGeoghegan's Biblical interpretation of the past, but, although the absolutes of Church language and the fundamentalist conceptions of history are subtly rejected by her irony, they are also allowed to stand unopposed. The text becomes dialogic, since it 'refuses to synthesize and thus erase opposition',[41] and so Lawless is able to acknowledge the fundamental uncertainty and plurality of Ireland's past.

Thus 'truth', for Lawless, does not reside in authoritative accounts, despite her call for a definitive history of Ireland in the Preface. She was certainly guided by the publishers – as her mother explains in a letter to William Lecky, 'the chief point especially for the American public was to avoid any appearance of bias or special pleading'[42] – but her desire to produce an objective account of the past is also both a result of her scholarly beliefs and a political necessity. She greatly admired Lecky, whom she regarded as one of the few historians who managed to be fair to both sides:

> In his 'History of the Eighteenth Century' Mr. Lecky has done for the Ireland of one century what it is much desired some one would hasten to do for the Ireland of all. He has broken down a barrier of prejudice so solid and of such long standing that it seemed to be invulnerable, and has proved that it is actually possible to be just in two directions at once – a feat no previous historian of Ireland can be said to have even attempted. (*Ireland*, 300)

In her reminiscence of Lecky she writes that 'a power of entering into, and even to some extent of sympathising with, an antagonistic point of view is one of the chief requisites for understanding it', and she attacks James Anthony Froude for dedicating 'his unique gifts of style and persuasion to the service, not of truth, but of partisanship; to a deliberate, or what looks like a deliberate, falsifying of the records; to the darkening and confusing of what was already only too dark and tangled'.[43] As Lawless sees it, political bias destroys both the truth and the reader's enjoyment of the historical text:

> Personally I think that we enjoy this *rôle* of historic looker-on best when we have no particular purpose of our own to forward at the time; no special

little task in hand; no pet theory, which must be supported at any cost, and after which we go burrowing blindly through the past, as moles burrow through the choicest seed-beds. Here, as elsewhere, the impersonal attitude brings its own reward.[44]

The focus of attention should not be on the struggle between opposing political creeds because, if the opposition between, for instance, nationalist and unionist value systems is still recognised as valid, the hierarchy can be reversed again and again, but reconciliation remains as far away as ever. Therefore, the most important lesson Lawless attempts to teach is that almost every conflict in Ireland has been about land. The Irish problem is agrarian, not sectarian, in nature, she argues in *Ireland:*

> Could the plantations of James the First's time have been formed exclusively of English or Scotch Roman Catholics, we have no reason, and certainly no right to conclude that the event would have been in any way different, or that the number of those slaughtered would have been reduced by even a single victim. (252)

Battles over land have practical solutions, but when questions of cultural and religious identity are brought into the equation the problem is no longer practical but ethical, moral and ideological. When identity is defined in essential terms it becomes impossible to be both 'us' and 'them' or to be 'just in two directions at once' (300). That Lawless's attempts at impartiality were quite successful is indicated by the reviewers who comment that 'the author's sympathies, if we may be permitted to use what looks like a Hibernicism, are on both sides',[45] or note that in 'a somewhat hasty reading we have not noticed a line which would show whether Miss Emily Lawless is an Englishwoman or an Irishwoman, a Protestant or a Roman Catholic'.[46] A less favourable interpretation of her neutrality is William Linn's contention that Lawless avoided taking sides so as not to offend either members of her own class or the Irish reading public.[47] Linn's argument, however, presupposes a strict polarity in Irish affairs that does not allow for the possibility that Lawless might truly represent a third position. What the commentators do not seem to recognise is that it was vital for Lawless to imagine Ireland as a country where it would no longer be possible to distinguish between Protestants and Catholics. One reviewer expects that some readers will be disappointed, since Lawless allotted 'only a few pages to current politics',[48] but it is truer to say that the whole book is about the present. Despite the absence of openly partisan statements, Emily Lawless's account of the past is a clear example of how history-writing is always governed by current needs.

Perhaps the greatest irony is that Lawless's history was published in the series Story of the Nations, since the work is governed by the idea that Ireland is not and has never been a nation. This view is obviously closely connected to the political developments at the time when the history was written. Published in 1887, it must have been composed in the years leading up to William E. Gladstone's first Home Rule Bill in 1886, when the Land League was intensely active, Charles Stewart Parnell emerged as a possible future leader of the country and the Protestant landowning classes were under considerable pressure. It was important for Lawless to show, therefore, the historical reasons why the country was unfit to govern itself, and she repeatedly comes back to Ireland's character as a tribal society which 'can hardly be said to have had any corporate existence' (95). A strong ruler might have saved the country at any given time in the past, but the myriad of self-governing septs, clans and tribes meant that the 'theory of life' remained 'purely local' (30), despite the fact that 'Ireland was pining, as it had always pined, as it continued afterwards to pine, for a settled government; for a strong central rule of some sort' (73). The problem, as Lawless presents it, was that, owing to a history of conquests and foreign rule, the Irish people had developed a local rather than a national mentality, which made it unlikely that a native Irish government could succeed. In her analysis, the only options are an uncertain future in a Catholic nationalist Ireland where there may not even be a place for an Anglo-Irish aristocrat like herself, or continued union with England according to a system whose worst features are at least already known. Although Lawless never explicitly rejects Home Rule, and is careful to keep her narrative open-ended most of the time, she seems in the end to have preferred the evil she knew (414–16).

*

Initially it would seem as if Lawless is more willing to take charge of her material in her biography of Maria Edgeworth than in her history, since she opens the biography by denouncing the extant accounts of the writer's life and works as biased. Edgeworth's previous biographers had been

English, and thus incapable of understanding 'the more purely Irish side of her writings, as well as the influence which those writings have exercised in Ireland itself'.[49] In particular Lawless attacks Helen Zimmern's *Maria Edgeworth* (1883), where the lack of interest in Irish matters 'may almost be said to go to the length of antipathy' (2). This confrontational beginning should logically introduce a completely revised picture of Edgeworth's literary career, and Lawless certainly sets out to show Edgeworth as an Irish writer first of all, deploring the fact that the author spent almost the whole of her childhood outside Ireland. Both Zimmern and Augustus John Hare in his *Life and Letters of Maria Edgeworth* (1894) maintain that Edgeworth's English upbringing made her better suited to describe her countrymen dispassionately. However, rather than rejecting Hare's and Zimmern's claims completely, Lawless's text initiates a dialogue:

> The theory that Miss Edgeworth had gained, rather than lost, by her own acquaintance with that country having been so long postponed, is one which I have myself already disputed. At the same time, honesty forces the avowal that the idea of an Ireland visited for the first time in mature years by an Irishman or half-Irishman, was evidently one which had stamped itself strongly upon her consciousness, and so far the opposite theory gains support. (136)

Lawless's reference to earlier Edgeworth biographers as 'able pilgrims' (1) and her repetition of phrases like 'in the opinion of her present biographer' (3) ensure that her corrections remain personal views and never take on the appearance of facts. In contrast to most life-writers at the turn of the last century, she refrains from posing as an authority on her subject and instead juxtaposes her arguments with those of other scholars, indicating that a single version of 'truth' is unattainable.

Maria Edgeworth is an uneven text. Like the history *Ireland*, it is written in a subjective voice that conveys as much information about Lawless as about Edgeworth or her country. The biography was consequently received with a mixture of praise and disapproval.[50] *The Irish Book Lover* describes it as an unsuccessful work, 'lacking in the chief qualities of literary biography'.[51] The *Bookman* reviewer wonders why it has 'less hold upon the reader than many biographies in the same series of inferior persons by inferior hands', finding the answer in the dearth of quoted material, since in his opinion Edgeworth's life was not sufficiently interesting to provide matter for a conventional narrative biography.[52] The reviewer in the *Times Literary Supplement* agrees, claiming that the quotations included are too few, and ill-chosen to boot, and maintains that Lawless fails to convince the reader of Edgeworth's importance.[53] The *Atlantic Monthly* commentator, on the other hand, admires the biographical sections of the book but finds the literary criticism deficient,[54] while the *Oxford Magazine* review states that 'no one can read Miss Lawless's pages without keen interest'.[55] In William Linn's opinion, *Maria Edgeworth* does not measure up to Lawless's earlier works and reveals that she had only a limited understanding of biographical techniques.[56] Thus, his verdict is that 'the result is more in order of a literary portrait than a biography'.[57] It seems clear that a rather fixed notion of what a biography ought to be like lies behind his conclusion.

A major reason for the contradictory responses to *Maria Edgeworth* is the dialogic quality of Lawless's writing. The nineteenth-century model of biographical scholarship, as represented by Sir Leslie Stephen, conceived of the biographer as the expert and the biographee as the object, to be described and explained. In an 1892 article in *Macmillan's Magazine*, George Saintsbury declares that the best biography is the kind where all material is interpreted by the biographer:

> All biography is obviously and naturally divided into two kinds. There is the biography pure and simple, in which the whole of the materials is passed through the alembic of the biographer, and in which few if any of these materials appear except in an altered and digested condition. This, though apparently the oldest, is artistically the most perfect kind.[58]

Saintsbury's ideal is consequently a biographer completely in command of the material and its presentation. The second type of biography he describes is what he calls 'applied' or 'mixed' biography, where letters, diary extracts and anecdotes are interspersed in the narrative. Such mixed biographies were the main kind written at the time of Saintsbury's article, and he argues for an approach to the material that will result in a seamless narrative. His primary model is John Gibson Lockhart's biography of Sir Walter Scott:

> Here then we have something like the type and standard example of the elaborate biography of the composite kind, the kind which not stinting itself of any possible sizing allowable to the biographer, admitting great portions of original matter, and permitting the subject to a great extent to

illustrate himself, keeps a perpetual regulating hand on these materials, adjusts the connecting links of narrative and comment to one consistent plan of exposition, and so presents the subject 'in the round', on all sides, in all lights, doing this not merely by ingenious management in the original part, but by severe and masterly selection in that which is not original.[59]

It seems clear that a common opinion was that the biographer should exercise control. Lawless, however, evades these principles. She uses quotations in a way that allows Maria Edgeworth to speak for herself, without keeping the 'regulating hand' on this material that Saintsbury recommends, and she employs a number of stylistic negotiations that counter the establishment of an authoritative voice.

According to J. Hillis Miller there are four different ways to read the biography of a writer: for what it has to tell about the life and works of its subject, for its expression of prevailing presuppositions about the nature and function of literature, for what it reveals about the biographer and, when the biographer is also a writer of fiction, as a semi-fictional work, the subject of the biography understood as the protagonist of a novel.[60] There is also a fifth way: a biography may be read for what it says about the genre itself at a certain period. At the end of the nineteenth and the beginning of the twentieth centuries the codes of biographical writing are probably best illustrated by the work of Sir Leslie Stephen. He is the most frequently represented author in the series *English Men of Letters*, where, ironically, Lawless's *Maria Edgeworth* also appeared,[61] with three volumes in the first and two volumes in the second set. It seems reasonable to assume, therefore, that Stephen's style is eminently germane to contemporary ideals. As the editor of the first twenty-six volumes of the *Dictionary of National Biography* Stephen was in a position to impose his views on others. For instance, he required contributors to the dictionary to refrain from eulogising their subjects and be restrictive about what they included. The literary critic and the biographer should approach their tasks dispassionately and scientifically so as to escape personal bias, and their business was to pass judgement on, above all, the moral content of the work and, by extension, the moral qualities of the writer. A good novel, according to this set of assumptions, is formally unified and teaches sound morals, whereas a good biography shows the relation between the works and the moral standards of an author.[62]

'Unity' is the catch-word. Stephen's attitude in works such as *Pope* (1880), *Swift* (1882) and *George Eliot* (1902) is confident, authoritative and instructive, his subjectivity elevated to a theory of literary value. Speaking at the beginning of *George Eliot* is the critic-as-scientist: 'It is proper, however, at the present day to begin from the physical "environment" of the organism whose history we are to study'.[63] The sentence aptly sums up Stephen's opinion and method: the author's life is an object to be scrutinised by a detached observer who is also the spokesman for an intellectually and culturally united group – 'we'. Quotations and references are woven into the text, enclosed by quotation marks, but the sources are rarely acknowledged, as if Stephen's renditions are sufficient or the reader's familiarity with the originals can be taken for granted.[64] The end-product is a seamless narrative. In relation to such a norm the uncertain voice in so much of women's writing is automatically disqualifying. Besides Lawless, the only woman biographer in the *English Men of Letters* series is Margaret (Mrs) Oliphant.[65]

Any text is generated in relation to previous and contemporary 'texts' of social conditions, cultural practices and literary traditions, and thus the conventions exemplified by Leslie Stephen's work function as intertexts in Emily Lawless's biography.[66] This is not to say that Lawless intended to attack Stephen in any way – on the contrary, she thought very highly of his work and suggested in a letter to Mr Macmillan that he should write a biography of Margaret Oliphant for the *English Men of Letters* series[67] – but in clear contrast to the confidence of Stephen's manner, *Maria Edgeworth* is intensely personal and thoroughly double- or even multi-voiced. To some extent, the personal tone may have corresponded to Lawless's ideal of biography-writing. In a letter to Sir Alfred Lyall, she praises Lyall's biography of Tennyson, saying: 'I have been reading your "Tennyson" with such delight & interest. Your personality seems to me to be stamped on every page of it, nearly as much if not quite as much as his, so that as I read I hardly know which poet is most in my thoughts'.[68] Thus, in her own text, Lawless uses the personal 'I' but rarely the inclusive 'we', and her style is close to the spoken word, fast-moving, meandering and immediate, full of dashes and exclamation marks. She does not monologically incorporate quotations in her narrative but allows Edgeworth to speak for herself in long passages from letters and fiction, sometimes without commentary. She is frequently ironic and expresses both likes and dislikes through understatements. The technique draws attention to the presence of a subtext, as when the Edgeworth family see a murdered man by the wayside and Lawless refers to the episode as one of the 'pleasing incidents' of the 1798 rebellion (69). The ironic description is certainly intended to invoke the opposite idea, but, as with all instances of irony, it is double-voiced and allows at least the possibility of a literal interpretation. Hence, the reader is invited to decide the final meaning of the passage.

Self-reflexive remarks disturb the flow of the narrative and departures from the main story give the impression that the text is unplanned, as when Lawless unchronologically mentions Maria Edgeworth's first stepmother Honora Sneyd: 'This, however, is wild anticipation!' (4).[69] A several-pages-long description of Mary Martin of Ballinahinch and her fate is concluded with the self-reproach: 'This, it is as well, however, to remember, is a biography, not of Mary Martin, but of Maria Edgeworth!' (190), thus emphasising the irrelevance of the section. Similar digressions can be found in folkloric practice such as Irish storytelling, where they function as comments, explanations, emotional expressions or personal reflections and asides, ensuring that the narrator is present in the tale. The storyteller is thus 'not a mere instrument through which oral tradition is transmitted anonymously but rather a living, thinking, feeling being whose performance is imbued with her humanity'.[70] By drawing attention to her digressions Lawless underscores the element of orality in her work at the same time as she foregrounds its lack of unity and her own subjectivity. The result is a fractured text that constantly undercuts the conventional authority of the author.

As Lawless possessed a rich vocabulary and was able to use registers ranging from the Irish brogue of *Hurrish* (1886) to the sixteenth-century idiom of *With Essex in Ireland* (1890) and the objective-scientific style of some of her articles on natural science, the personal tone of *Maria Edgeworth* must be seen as a deliberate choice. Discussing Mary Wollstonecraft's *A Vindication of the Rights of Woman*, Laurie A. Finke suggests that dialogic rhetorical strategies undermine the power of patriarchy:

> Central to her [Wollstonecraft's] critique of patriarchal culture is her challenge of a rhetoric that can so neatly dispose of contradictions by creating rigid dichotomies, often in the service of oppression. All such oppositions imply the valorization of one term to the exclusion of the

other; the powerful are privileged over the powerless, objective knowledge over the subjective passion, reason over emotion, and male over female.[71]

Lawless's dialogic writing would then 'counter the oppressive power of this confrontational rhetoric by conflating oppositions, collapsing one term into the other'.[72] If confrontation, and thus dichotomy, is removed, there is no longer a system whereby hierarchies can be established or reversed. Diane P. Freedman uses the term 'female mode' for such non-combative writing and argues that:

> Writers in the female mode use language not to gain power but to create intimacy [. . .] intimacy often achieved through self-reflexive statements on the why and how of their practice. Such self-conscious or metadiscursive comments commonly announce the substitution of unconventional or multiple genres for the traditional essay, argue for personal over fixed forms.[73]

It is in non-fictional writing that the effects of mixing genres or using a personal style are most obvious, since the rhetorical norm is the authoritative statement. Dialogue disposes of the notion of a hierarchical relationship altogether. Thus, the style of *Maria Edgeworth* is not an expression of opposition and confrontation, which would entail clear-cut positioning, but a constant negotiation with power, authority and control – on the levels of word, sentence and narrative.

On the word level, Lawless's use of the first person singular challenges the conventions of biography-writing by exhibiting her subjectivity. In the late twentieth-century advice literature studied by Deborah Cameron, women are frequently encouraged to use so-called 'I-language' to assert themselves.[74] But although 'I' certainly connotes supremacy, it also implies the personal as opposed to the universal, and it may even be that I-language is received differently when used by male or female speakers. As much as the choice of words, it is the status of the speaker that determines the force and reliability of the message. The nature of the narrating 'I' governs the credibility of a text in a similar way. In Leslie Stephen's *George Eliot,* for example, deliberately obscure information constructs a narrator of exceptional erudition: 'She is introduced to the daughter of the *Religion of the Universe,* and perhaps few readers will be able to say offhand that the phrase means the religion of Mr. Robert Fellowes.'[75] As the remark is to demonstrate, Stephen is among the chosen few who is well-read enough

to recognise the phrase, and when he uses the personal 'I' he consequently claims the authority of superior knowledge. This means that modifying expressions do not really diminish the force of his pronouncements: 'This, I think, explains the rather painful impression which is made by *Middlemarch*.'[76] Stephen's 'I think' qualifies the explanation he supplies for his verdict, but the opinion itself is presented as unquestionable fact, and so his use of 'I' merely reinforces his position as cultural arbiter.

The voice constructed in Lawless's text, in contrast, is permeated by the discourses generally available to women at the end of the nineteenth and beginning of the twentieth centuries: the confessional, the private letter, the familial anecdote, the informal conversation. When used by such a narrator, I-language and other signs of the author's presence signal intimacy and, above all, subjective choice, as when Lawless declares: 'For strictly personal reasons the most interesting part of that expedition to her present biographer lies in the fact of Miss Edgeworth having on this occasion made acquaintance with the Martins of Ballinahinch' (184–85) or when she says in relation to Edgeworth's *Tales of Fashionable Life*: 'As a matter of preference I will not pretend to follow her in this new departure with the same interest as in the preceding one' (98). The inclusion of opposing views emphasises that the personal voice expresses only one of a number of available positions:

> That she had sustained no slight loss in having spent the irrecoverable years of childhood and early youth in what were not the scenes she was destined to commemorate, I have already stated to be my opinion. This is a point upon which I am so clearly at variance with her previous biographers, that it evidently is one which admits of considerable divergence of opinion. (48)

The dialogue with other views reduces the authority of the account and, although Lawless claims the right of interpretation, she accentuates the inescapable subjectivity it entails.

The dialogic attitude is also embodied in Lawless's stylistic devices of uncertainty, and functions as a challenge to the monologue of authority on the sentence level. Thus Frances Edgeworth's view that Maria Edgeworth was deeply in love with the Swedish chevalier Edelcrantz is rejected in a manner that fully admits the possibility of another truth: 'Unquestionably Mrs Edgeworth was in a position to know the actual facts, yet I find a certain amount of difficulty in accepting that assertion' (110).[77] Critical judgements are similarly modified, as when Lawless does 'not find it easy to discover anything very favourable to say' (132) about *Vivian* or *The Modern Griselda,* or she finds it 'difficult to believe that any devout reader of Miss Edgeworth can fail to regret that she should have expended so much of her time upon what was for her – I will not assert for *every one* – distinctly the wrong side of the Channel' (132). Sometimes she defers to the opinion of more influential judges, as when she refers to Macaulay's view of *The Absentee:*

> Every one, it is to be hoped, has read or heard of Lord Macaulay's solemn declaration that the scene in which Lord Colambre discovers himself to his father's tenants, and discomfits the demon agent, has had no parallel in literature since the opening of the twenty-second book of the *Odyssey!* Humbler admirers might hardly perhaps have risen unaided to quite such lofty heights of panegyric as these. Still, when the vast, the almost immeasurable difference, between a new and a merely old novel has been discounted, the result can hardly fail to redound to the permanent distinction of its author. (133)

Lawless prefers *Castle Rackrent* to *The Absentee,* but, by reserving the role of 'humble admirer' for herself, she implies that she belongs to a cultural community where the social status of the critic is of great importance. The hesitation displayed in her ironic disagreement with Macaulay – 'might hardly perhaps have risen unaided' – indicates that she speaks from below, negotiating rather than rejecting his opinion. Even apparently confrontational remarks are modified, as when Lawless's scathing criticism of a bigoted review of Richard Lovell Edgeworth's *Memoir* is alleviated by her recognition of the cultural limitations of another time:

> Studying this attractive production, and reflecting, moreover, upon its evident animus, it is not easy for a biographer to set bounds to his or her indignation. We must, however, in fairness remember that the inquisitorial note, which to the taste of to-day reads like the worst and most gratuitous form of impertinence, was, at the time it was penned, indeed long afterwards, the rule rather than the exception, on the part of critics who considered themselves to be the guardians, not of religion only, but of morality and decency. (154)

The final outcome is not a compromise, nor is it the resolution of a dialectic process, but the unresolved dialogue of juxtaposed views.

Part of the attraction of reading a biography is that it appears to give access to the private life of a public figure, but Lawless's strategies destabilise the surface text and challenge the voice of authority on the narrative level as well. The biographer's ubiquitous presence shatters the illusion of the work as a transmission of past reality. Reflections on the art of biography cause further disruptions, and by commenting on her practice Lawless highlights her role as producer: 'even the most patient of biographers' might tire of chronicling the succession of 'mothers' in the Edgeworth household (68), 'even a partial biographer must be frank' (211). Before describing Maria Edgeworth's inner feelings, Lawless creates distance by drawing attention to her own activities:

> To delve into the more intimate recesses of one's subject is frequently held to be a prerogative of biographers. While a little doubtful as to there having been any particular recesses in this case to delve into, I need not hesitate to express my conviction that Scott – the man, no less than the author – stood for a good deal more in Miss Edgeworth's eyes than did ever that very shadowy personage, M. Edelcrantz. (180)

The comment underscores the fundamental inaccessibility of another's mind, and the force of Lawless's conviction is weakened, since it is presented as an interpretation, not a certainty.

Further emphasising her lack of authority, Lawless creates the illusion that she is not in control of the people whose lives she describes but is controlled by them: 'Mr. Day is one of those incredibly erratic mortals, dear to the student of human nature, who, when they cross the path of a biographer, are apt to turn him aside for a while from his proper business' (10). Forces outside the text govern the outcome, and she has to forgo quotation because she has already included 'all the extracts which the scale of this book will admit of' (141). Yet the material itself compels her to break this rule: 'After saying that no more letters of Miss Edgeworth were to find place in this volume, I find myself irresistibly drawn into adding two more' (202). The sources themselves, it is implied, have the power to determine the course of the narrative. Lawless admired Edgeworth's letter-writing skills very much and wrote to Mr Macmillan:

> I have been on a visit recently at Oxford with Mrs Butler who is 'own niece', odd to say, of Miss Edgeworth, & both from her & Prof. Edgeworth I heard a great many new details, & what was more important was given various new letters of hers, not only never published, but never even printed, some of which I propose to use, & I think you will consider them, as I do, about the best she has ever written. Personally I place her very high

as a letter-writer, as one of the very best, if not the best woman letter-writer in the language, far better in this respect than either George Eliot or Jane Austin [*sic*], though her books of course rank for the most part considerably lower than theirs.[78]

The prominent place of 'the archive' is connected to the idea that the past is irrecoverable except as text, and Lawless maintains that documents from the past 'are extraordinarily living, far more so, I think than the same materials after they have been worked over by even the best of historians'.[79]

Though highly critical of translators who allow their historical narratives to be contaminated by modernity,[80] Lawless situates her biography in time by relating events in Maria Edgeworth's life to the present. Clifton is described as a place 'in those days boasting of a reputation as a health resort, which it seems in our own to have quite lost', and the Edgeworth family's journey to the town is seen as 'no light undertaking, as will readily be perceived when we consider the size of that enormous family party, the indifferent travelling arrangements attainable, and the distance, little now, but how formidable then!' (60). Anachronisms reinforce the understanding that the past can only ever be approached from the writer's position in the present: 'She "sat lightly", as we nowadays put it, to life in general, including – more particularly including – her own pretensions as an authoress' (165). The perspective of the early twentieth century means that a unified picture of the past never emerges. While desirable in fiction, where Lawless argues for 'carefully preserved atmosphere',[81] the illusion of a coherent truth is no more sustained in her biography than in her history, since it would mask the complexities of life.

Lawless makes perfectly clear that she is writing to a specific agenda, thus qualifying her 'truth' by making her intentions apparent. Her main undertaking is to establish Maria Edgeworth's central role in Irish literature. As an Ascendancy writer, Edgeworth's status is closely related to Lawless's own and, arguing for the 'Irishness' of Edgeworth's writing, Lawless is also claiming a place for her own work. But this project is somewhat problematic at a time when 'the words "Irish books", "Irish writers"', are 'surrounded by a certain amount of ambiguity' (127). As in her history and her fiction, Lawless is reluctant to address the political issues involved and avoids answering the question why so much of Irish literature is in English and so comparatively few Irish-born writers have written about Ireland:

> Considerations of geography, of history, of religion, all are entangled in it;
> the relations of two conflicting, and not very sympathetic races, and the
> further consideration of how far one such race may have a stunting and a
> deteriorating influence upon another – these, and various other points,
> would have to be gone over and debated, more or less in detail.
>
>   Want of space – *as well as other considerations* – forbid the interpolation
> of any similar discussions at the present moment. (128, my emphasis)

The problem is acknowledged, but there is no synthesis. Instead, the
dialogic presence of contradictory opinions enables Lawless to speak in
two voices. This makes her work appear apolitical, but the incorporation
of differences is in fact a profoundly political act that recognises
suppression as the unpleasant corollary of consensus. Just as she does when
she pleads for the historian to be 'just in two directions at once', (*Ireland*,
300) Lawless indicates through her double voice that the reversal of one
hierarchy only serves to establish another, and introduces a system that
builds on dialogue instead of binary opposition.

  This unwillingness to take a stand causes certain problems for feminist
interpretations, especially as Lawless cannot be seen as a representative of
the early twentieth-century women's struggle, since she was uninterested
in the vote and rejected Suffragette methods.[82] Even so, her other main
objective in the biography, according to Marilyn Butler, is to depict Maria
Edgeworth as 'attractively feminine', continuing the myth that she was
subdued by her father.[83] Lawless certainly creates a story of fatherly
domination and condemns Richard Lovell Edgeworth's influence not only
on Maria Edgeworth's writing, but also on her personality:

> Wherever, in her case, the didactic impulse is seen to distinctly overpower
> the creative one; wherever we find Utility lauded to the skies as the only
> guide of an otherwise foundering humanity; above all, wherever we find an
> enormous emphasis laid upon the necessity at all times and places of a due
> subordination of the feminine to the masculine judgment, – there we may
> feel sure that we are upon his track, and that such sentiments were uttered
> primarily with a view to the approbation of the domestic critic. (18)

In a letter to Lawless, George Tyrrell comments on Lawless's critical views
of Edgeworth's father. While conceding that Richard Lovell Edgeworth
was 'impossible', Tyrrell suggests the more forgiving interpretation that, at
the time, '[m]en *could* not say what they meant or were, but only what
they *ought* to mean and be'.[84] Lawless did not see Lovell Edgeworth as a

product of his time, however, but regarded his – in her opinion – negative impact on his daughter's work as a matter of patriarchal oppression. Not until after her father's death, Lawless maintains, 'did the natural and spontaneous woman rise to the surface' (206).[85] But her re-endorsement of conventional femininity at the end of the book appears to contradict the attacks on repressive patriarchy:

> It has been the woman that has been desired to be shown in them, rather than the author, the wit, the moralist, or anything else of the sort; an exceptionally pleasant woman, nay, an exceptionally pleasant Irishwoman; one whom few people ever grew to know, without also growing to like, and whom few ever found themselves brought into even accidental contact with, without being in some way or other the better for it. That, as regards the more obvious and unavoidable relationships of life – as sister, friend, employer, daughter – that in all these respects she was as little open to reproach as it has often been given to humanity to attain to, this will, I think, without any great difficulty be conceded. (213)

In her final passage – the last word, so to speak – Lawless celebrates both Maria Edgeworth's conventionally masculine accomplishments as writer and employer and her feminine roles as daughter and sister. Although the dialogic arrangement precludes easy labelling, this indicates a more complex feminism that has moved beyond mere confrontation and questions the stability of gender constructions as such. There is no synthesis, because dialogue has the potential to collapse a binary system without establishing new, equally confining definitions.

James M. Cahalan singles out *Maria Edgeworth* as a 'major feminist or proto-feminist work' that sheds light on Lawless's views of gender as well as on her place in the Irish literary tradition.[86] As an Ascendancy woman with strong feelings for her country, says Cahalan, Lawless saw Edgeworth as her literary mother. There are certainly indications that point to this, but there are more important connections between the writers than accidents of birth. Since double-voiced narration is a prominent feature of Maria Edgeworth's *Castle Rackrent,* and other varieties of dialogic writing are present in *The Absentee, Ormond* and *Ennui,* Edgeworth and Lawless are linked by their literary attitudes of negotiation, not simply by class privilege or 'Englishness'.

'In fiction, as in poetry', says Emily Lawless, 'we all to a great degree find what we bring' (141), and the same is true about biography. If Lawless's *Maria Edgeworth* is approached from an aesthetic perspective that privileges sequence, shape and finality, the verdict will inevitably be that it is an unstructured, uncertain text that suggests that Lawless had internalised her society's definition of femininity. From a feminist – or an Irish-nationalist – perspective, the danger is that the strategy will result in paralysing relativism, and that by refusing to fight (English) patriarchy on its own terms Lawless might effect nothing more than an expression of her own marginality. It is true that she constantly relates her voice to the dominant code, and, as far as a linguistic model of authority continues to be valorised, marginalisation is a very real threat. But by privatising a public form of discourse, Lawless also subverts masculine language from within. Through her use of the first person singular she manifests her right to a subject position in a literary culture predominantly populated by men, neither subordinating her voice to the prevailing ideal nor appropriating patriarchal rhetoric but opening a space for self-affirmation in the official genre of biography, just as she does in her history. Securing a position for herself as writer and Maria Edgeworth as subject – and for them both as Irishwomen – in the masculine territory of the *English Men of Letters* series Lawless rejects constricting definitions of femininity at the same time as she celebrates the conventionally feminine through her stylistic negotiations. Like the linguistic and narrative strategies in the history *Ireland*, this creates a double-voiced text that cannot be contained in, or explained by, any absolute paradigm. Her dialogic technique is more than a simple reversal of a patriarchal or political order: it is an acknowledgement of the complexities of gender, of national identity, of truth that destabilises the whole system.

Chapter 5

Dialogues with the past: historical fiction

In her history, as in her biography of Maria Edgeworth, Lawless negotiates the authoritarian voices of national and sexual politics of her time through stylistic strategies that make her work dialogic. In her fictional treatment of the past, the dialogue is often embedded in the narrative technique itself, since most of her historical novels were written in a first-person male voice.[1] Such cross-gendered writing, whether as the use of female voices by male writers or the reverse, calls for a reading paradigm that recognises the importance of men's and women's roles in society and relates the conditions of the writers to both the ideas expressed in the work and the narrative devices used to express them. Discussing male eighteenth-century authors, James Carson argues that female impersonation can be a liberating strategy for men, a parallel to the cross-dressing of medieval carnival. As 'mere women', male writers are able to dissociate themselves from the social elite they actually belong to and protest against the system without taking responsibility for their criticisms.[2] This licence is achieved regardless of the credibility of the female narrator – in fact, an unreliable narrator offers even greater liberty. Women's use of men's voices, in contrast, usually allows women writers to speak out by providing them with imaginative access to the elite. As Carla Caplan says, this saves them from 'being caught in such devalued discourses as "girl talk" or "gossip", by being caught in a "hen party" of supposed meaninglessness'.[3] Cross-gendered writing gives women writers entrance to the public sphere and a privileged audience. As far as narrative technique 'embodies the social, economic, and literary conditions under which it has been produced',[4] in Susan Sniader Lanser's words, women's adoption of a male voice can thus be understood as an attempt to achieve textual authority. The use of the male voice may function as an exploitation of the gender system that enables women to overcome social limitations and tackle traditionally male subjects. But women do not silence their female voices simply to let male voices speak *for* them – the familiar equation of masculinity with power is incomplete as an explanation. As becomes evident in Lawless's first cross-gendered novel, *A Millionaire's Cousin*, and even more clearly in the historical novel, *With Essex in Ireland* (1890), an important aspect is also the interrogation of gendered identity as such.

The ambiguous effects of using the voice of the other gender is due to the internal duality of a cross-gendered narrative. As Carson suggests, a 'mask indicative of radical otherness, such as a gender difference between author and narrator, may also serve to highlight the conflict of perspectives within an individual utterance'.[5] The female signature leads the reader in one direction while the male narrative voice may indicate the opposite. In the case of Emily Lawless, essential questions are to what extent the choice of narrative perspective can be connected to the feminine ideals of her time and whether the appropriation of a man's voice eventually challenges or re-establishes conventional gender roles. William Linn uses the term 'simulated authenticity' to describe Lawless's technique in the historical novels, which gives the impression that he sees the male voice as somehow more authentic where topics like war and rebellion are concerned.[6] On the other hand, Linn also contends that Lawless understood the realities of Irish life in a masculine way, which indicates that the male voice she employs should have been a logical effect of her personal characteristics.[7] Since most of Lawless's cross-gendered works are concerned with history, it would seem as if an important consideration is that the male voice provides the authority necessary to speak about matters located in the male cultural domain. This is contradicted to some extent, however, by the circumstance that the narrator in her most celebrated cross-gendered novel *With Essex in Ireland* is clearly unreliable. As a result, there is an ironic distance between author and narrator instead of the identification which would be logical if Lawless used the masculine voice solely to provide more authority for herself.

With Essex in Ireland purports to be a journal of the English campaign to subdue the rebellion of Hugh O'Neill, Earl of Tyrone, written by the fictional secretary to Robert Devereux, second Earl of Essex.[8] The historical background is that Essex set out for Ireland in March 1599. Together with the troops already in Ireland, his force numbered 16,000 foot and 1,300 horse, and English spies established that Tyrone's army was of almost exactly the same size – 17,997 men.[9] Had Essex immediately moved against Tyrone, he might have been victorious, but instead he first marched south against the rebels in Leinster and Munster, then west to Athlone and back. Fever and dysentery depleted his forces and when he finally turned north on 25 July 1599 his army had shrunk considerably. The weather was apparently appalling throughout the summer of 1599, and the English army was little prepared for the type of guerrilla warfare the Irish excelled in. On 7 September Essex met to parley with Tyrone at the ford of Bellaclynth and a six-week ceasefire was agreed, the truce to be renewed every six weeks until May 1600 unless either of the parties decided to open hostilities again. There were no witnesses to the agreement, however, and thus Essex's decision could be construed as treasonable. Elizabeth I refused to accept the terms of the truce and, to defend himself and diminish the influence of his enemies over the Queen, Essex returned to England on 24 September 1599. He was immediately placed under house arrest and, following an attempted *coup d'état* in 1601, he was executed on 25 February the same year. Lawless's novel deals with the Irish campaign and ends when Essex takes his ship back to England.

As the *Pall Mall Gazette* review indicates, *With Essex in Ireland* was believed, at least by some readers, to be a genuine sixteenth-century text: 'This brilliant sketch is not, as more than one reviewer fancies, an MS. of the sixteenth century discovered by its London publishers and edited by the author of "Hurrish".' [10] The most notable reader to take the novel as an authentic document is probably William E. Gladstone.[11] A note in the copy of the novel in Marsh's Library, Dublin, says:

> W. E. Gladstone M. P. was completely taken in by this book for on June 6th 1890 he writes to Emily's publisher
>
> 'Dear Sirs, I have read with great interest the "With Essex in Ireland", which you were so good as to send me. Both as regards Essex himself, and in the respect of Ireland, it seems to me to constitute a valuable addition to the store of our historical information.
>
> Yours very faithfully
> W. E. Gladstone'[12]

Alhough the novelistic features of *With Essex in Ireland* are apparent, the work as a whole is a highly accomplished pastiche of Elizabethan style. Lady Gregory found it 'very good' in 'its reproduction of the writing – of the style – of that time'[13] and most reviewers comment on Lawless's successful recreation of sixteenth-century language:

> The charm that lies on the pages of Sir Philip Sidney is reproduced here, seemingly without an effort, as it is without a lapse. We read the very dialect of Shakespeare's time, and we have no sense that this is the work of a modern writer, save from the fine art which has removed the worst blemishes in the expression of sixteenth-century English thought, and preserved clearness and simplicity against which Elizabethan authors too often sinned.[14]

The narrator Henry Harvey is primarily constructed through his use of language, and he consistently represents Elizabethan ideology, particularly as regards views about women and the Irish people. Before the beginning of the narrative proper the fictional editor Oliver Maddox draws attention to Harvey's partiality and distances himself from portions of the account that he feels to be contrary 'both to Religion and Firm Reason'.[15] It is consequently made clear that Harvey's version of events is not to be completely trusted and may even break the rules of common sense.

Harvey's conviction that English and male supremacy is the natural social order makes him a credible sixteenth-century character, and in Lawless's view such consistency is necessary. Discussing translations of ancient texts, she writes:

> Let him [the author] only allow himself to be betrayed into any touch of modernity – hateful word! – let him employ but a single syllable that recalls to-day in any of its hundredfold aspects; to-day's newspaper, to-day's novel, to-day's anything; nay, let him merely allow us to perceive that he is aware of being himself a man of to-day, and the spell is broken! Illusion spreads its wings and flies. Our carefully preserved atmosphere shudders around us like a badly shifted transformation scene. We discover in a moment that it is no longer our archaic author, but quite another sort of person who is addressing us.[16]

This insistence on stylistic realism in translations indicates that Lawless would also regard it as vital to be true to the period both in terms of language and ideas where historical fiction is concerned. Her cross-gendered technique is thus historically motivated, since writing about war would have been next to impossible for a sixteenth-century woman and a nineteenth-century perspective would shatter the illusion. But contemporary limitations also come into play, because, as Lanser says, just like a 'female personal narrator risks the reader's resistance if the act of telling, the story she tells, or the self she constructs through telling it transgresses the limits of the acceptably feminine',[17] a female writer risks social censure if she deals with themes considered inappropriate for a woman. By using a male voice rather than a third-person perspective and, moreover, framing the narrative by constructing a fictional editor of the text, Lawless obscures her own role as author, which enables her to transcend nineteenth-century gender boundaries. Hence, prevalent definitions of gender are interrogated through the writing strategy itself.

With Essex in Ireland is partly an instance of nationalist expression couched in the voice of the oppressor, partly an exploration of the consequences of hybridity in a social system based on rigid demarcations. The novel is structured around the clash between an Ireland where 'all rules elsewhere laid down for a man's guidance seem to be as it were reversed and made invalid' (70–1) and the elaborate hierarchical system of Elizabethan England, as understood by Henry Harvey:

> For as Porphyry shows that there is a scale of creatures rising through the lower animals to ourselves, and through us to the Heavenly Essences, or Angels, so it had always seemed to me natural to regard these native Irish as intermediate betwixt us and the lower animals, having the outward form of man, but in all higher matters no share of his heritage. A mode of regarding the matter which I now perceive may be carried too far, and might even lead to a foolish and heady arrogance, seeing that they are in truth humans like ourselves, as are also the Red Americans, and other lowly races. (167)

Lawless problematises the concept of hierarchy by showing how categorical definitions lead to oppositions that may be reversed but never reconciled, just as she does in her history when she attempts to minimise the importance of sectarianism. Her alternative is the disintegration of categories signified by Ireland, a world order based on negotiation, compromise and fluctuating gender definitions – or, in other words, an *interspace*. As an English soldier formed by the Elizabethan world-view but susceptible to the influence of his Irish environment, Essex, as Lawless depicts him, incarnates the conflict between the two systems.

Initially, the narrator Harvey presents Essex as more than a man, with powers that 'exceed those of all men, upon sea no less than on land' (5). Expected to be Ireland's saviour, the Lord Lieutenant is received by the English loyalists 'as though a very King or God had come amongst them'

(11). He is polite, noble and wise, disgusted by the barbaric aspects of war and incapable of deceit. His rejection of brutality and his reluctance to use such weapons as famine against the Irish mean that his manliness is compromised, however. Upset after some of his men pour out a sack-full of heads on the ground before him he says 'why I ask you Hal, should I – saving for some womanish weakness or folly that I carry from my mother – feel thus perturbed and sickened by what other men heed not?' (182). To be a man is to perform atrocities without being affected, to 'learn to stomach it, and say naught; so that by degrees, the habit coming with practice, he will learn to see unmoved things which at first sight made his very soul to heave and sicken' (72). At least one critic found Lawless's portrait of Essex too sympathetic and the reluctance to make use of starvation as a weapon she makes him express (243–4) as a grave error on her part, since Essex actually advocated starving the people as a military strategy. In the reviewer's opinion, 'Essex is whitewashed, for no artistic purpose, but apparently from a mere sentimental liking for whitewash'.[18] Another commentator notes that 'Essex is sicklied o'er with the pale cast of thought, and altogether more of a Hamlet than actual history would lead us to surmise he was' and continues to wonder how far 'Elizabeth or her spoiled and punished favourite would recognise this portrait of the Earl of Essex'.[19] Such comparisons with accepted history draw attention to the question of whether it is the historical person or the fictional character that is represented in a historical novel. Lawless's Essex is placed in a documented historical situation, but his personal characteristics are imagined by the author. Her portrayal of Essex as uncomfortable with the gruesome aspects of war may be historically inaccurate, but it is fundamental to the interrogation of national and gender identity that runs through the work.

Essex's main contrast in the novel is the war-hungry youth Frank Gardner, who exemplifies a heroic masculinity untainted by any doubts. For Frank, battle prowess is the primary sign of manliness:

> Women are fair, and I their humble servant yet a *Man* is a *Man*, and it were a poor tribute to his manhood if all his thoughts must needs run upon what he has left behind him, so that he can spare none for that which lies before, and on which his manhood chiefly depends! (63–4).

This hero-model is rejected when Frank dies, early in the campaign in a completely unimportant and unnecessary skirmish. Frank's efforts to live up to a conventional masculine ideal end in disaster, which further reinforces the critique of inflexible gender constructions that permeates the novel. The one who survives to tell the story is Henry Harvey, whose less active military role enables him to combine his society's patronising view of women with an acceptance of his own feminine side.

Harvey is a lovesick poet with a melancholic disposition, 'being rather given to the ways of peace than of war' (48). He idolises Essex and is convinced of the justice of the cause, but his conviction as to the methods is weakened in a conversation he has with Mistress Agatha Usher in the grounds of Dublin Castle. When a woman's voice is introduced into the narrative this consequently contributes to challenging the certainties of Harvey's world-view. As Lia Mills has noticed, the only Irish people who speak directly to Harvey in the novel are women, and the only occasion when he himself takes direct action is when he saves a woman and her child from being shot by the English soldiers.[20] However, although Harvey is deeply moved by the story Agatha tells, he is able to persuade himself that he is affected by her sex, not by the insights she gives him:

> I marvelled how the troubles of one who was after all but a Froward Rebel and doubtless a Papist to boot, should have so overcome me. Soon however I perceived that it was not his story, albeit a piteous one, but the manner and look of sweet Mistress Agatha, and the fashion in which she did tell of her cousin's grief. (32)

In Harvey's view, women influence men by what they are, not by what they say, and, when women's opinions matter at all, it is in the personal realm. Worrying about how to deliver the news of Frank Gardner's death to the boy's mother, Harvey asks a Mistress Butler for help, reflecting:

> for that sex – when, departing from its usual custom, it doth think at all – can often I have before now found do so with as much purposefulness as we ourselves. Nay it sometimes happens that their minds, being doubtless less cumbered with large and weighty matters, do bring forth thoughts that our solider ones had perchance scarce lighted on. (104–5)

Harvey's acknowledgement of women's understanding does not contradict his view of men as superior, since he describes thought as an unusual activity for women and their suggestions as valuable only in the private sphere. Lawless shows how the gender ideology of his culture firmly controls his narrative, in apparent opposition to the feminine characteristics she also makes him display.

Harvey's encounters with Agatha Usher and Mistress Butler are used to highlight the difference between the military methods of men and women's strategies. Mistress Agatha does not question English rule, but criticises the cruelty of the rulers. She advocates information and an appeal to the Queen's humane feelings on the grounds that, if the Queen knew what was being done in her name in Ireland, 'she would give commandment to those that are set to execute her will and pleasure that they exercise a nicer discernment', (28) so that only those truly guilty would be punished. Mistress Butler's situation is an even clearer example of compromise: as a dependant of the Earl of Ormonde, she has to accept the protection of the very man who beheaded one of her relatives. Her unemotional comment on her plight is that

> it is in the endurance of such woes as these that the strength and courage of we women is mainly shewn. For both by nature, and circumstances we are oft forced to bear, aye and seemingly to bear willingly, the presence of those who have wrought us some deadly injury. (107)

By choice or necessity, women are shown to replace confrontation with negotiation and, even though their circumstances sometimes breed resentment, there is at least hope of reconciliation. Essex's – and Ireland's – tragedy, the novel suggests, is that the unconditional divisions governing Elizabethan thought preclude such solutions. As a sixteenth-century man and a representative of a colonising force, Essex is bound by a system of absolutes that makes his attempt to attain reconciliation through a treaty with Tyrone an instance of treason.

The view that compassion and empathy are female characteristics does not belong only to the sixteenth-century world. As Eve Patten suggests, Lawless also addresses late Victorian anxieties regarding Britain's colonial enterprise by making Essex's gradual feminisation an important reason for his failure. In the final decades of the nineteenth century, Patten says, 'political commentary began to posit that "manliness" was signified by the muscular act of imperial conquest, and that weak or reticent rule, equated with supposedly womanly attributes, represented the collapse of national backbone'.[21] The debate frequently returned to the role of force in imperial administration and invoked the familiar dichotomy between active masculinity and passive femininity. At the same time, the woman question occupied a prominent place on the agenda in Britain and Ireland, and at a time when women are in the ascendancy the privileging of conventionally male characteristics is no longer automatic. By upgrading the feminine, Lawless's text demonstrates that, even though Essex is a failed imperialist because of his womanly traits, this is in fact what makes him an honourable man. In a society troubled by feminist awakenings this valorisation of femininity is obviously not universally acceptable, and a contemporary review of the novel offers a culturally more palatable interpretation that focuses on Essex's exemplary masculinity: 'The book suggests that the English wished Essex to break truce with Tyrone, and it plainly, and possibly truthfully, infers that it was Essex's uprightness and straightforward *manliness* [my emphasis] which caused his own fall.'[22] The hybridity embodied by Essex and manifested in the narrative technique challenges both the absolute gender boundaries of the Elizabethan world and late nineteenth-century sexual politics.

Hence, Lawless's critique of English rule in Ireland is not aimed at Essex. On the contrary, her oblique references to the methods of his successor Mountjoy indicate that the Irish would have fared better if Essex had remained as Lord Lieutenant.[23] The target is rather Elizabeth I and the unreasonable demands of the office:

> For the man who undertakes to hold it must be pitiless as Nero, yet must no trace of blood be found on his hands. He must give ear to all petitioners, and promise to redress all wrongs, yet must he do nothing, and perform nothing, for that were to bring upon himself the reproach of highmindedness. He must know every wound and bleeding sore with which this wretched country bleeds to death, yet must be content to staunch none of them, for that were costly, and money is of all things that which her Majesty least loves to see shed in Ireland. (238)

In terms of gender, Elizabeth I is a hybrid, an anomaly in a sixteenth-century universe built on a divinely ordained order that subjects women to men. Lawless's references to her serve to foreground both sixteenth- and nineteenth-century gender anxieties. Essex's situation is complicated and exacerbated by his role as the representative of a woman ruler, and he is shown as clearly resenting the necessity to obey his Queen: 'We must all do her pleasure, be it for our own banning, or even for hers also' (130). As a woman Elizabeth is inferior to the men she governs. Her rule can therefore be accepted only because it is God-given and she herself is sexless – 'ever accounted a Goddess, rather than a Queen or Woman' (46). Lawless obviously recognised that the contemporary emphasis on Elizabeth's virginity and divine status was a means to conceal her femininity and a reflection of her culture's failure to accommodate the idea of female power. But the common identification of Ireland with the earth mother or goddess Ériu and her analogues creates an uncomfortable link of divine origin between the country and Elizabeth. The association is strengthened by the connection between the Virgin Queen and the kind of colonialist discourse where Ireland is perceived 'as a virgin inviting penetration by virile explorers'.[24] To justify English rule, it becomes necessary to emphasise Ireland's difference from Elizabeth by downplaying such similarities while at the same time maintaining the basically feminine nature of the country. These complexities are integrated in Lawless's characterisation of Essex, who sees Ireland as:

> a woman, one who was froward, and had done many things contrary to order and reasonableness, being led away by those that would betray her to her own undoing, and yet withal not without much faithfulness of nature, who, were her affections once secured, might follow him whom she loved to the world's end. (9)

Suppressing the divine and virginal connotations, Essex figures the country as a rebellious woman who – unlike Elizabeth – can be mastered. Thus, the main justification for his attempted conquest is that Ireland needs a man's guidance to be set right again. The desire to sexualise space is often a strategy of confinement and, as Catherine Nash notes, the image was common enough in the early modern period, when

> Ireland, like other colonies or potential colonies, was figured as female in ways which naturalised colonial penetration and regulation. As mysterious and unknown territory she must be explored and made known; as wanton woman she evokes disgust and must be tamed.[25]

Ireland is spatially incoherent, and Essex's problems are to a great extent presented as the effects of his failure to create a controllable image of the land. The wish to enclose space by figuring it as a woman also contains its opposite: the fear that perhaps neither woman nor space can be that easily controlled. As Sue Best expresses it:

feminising space seems to suggest, on the one hand, the production of a safe, familiar, clearly defined entity, which, because it is female, should be appropriately docile or able to be dominated. But, on the other hand, this very same production also underscores an anxiety about this 'entity' and the precariousness of its boundedness.[26]

While Essex, in line with the imperialist values that legitimise his venture, conceives of Ireland's femininity in negative terms, Ireland is also feminised by Lawless/the narrator to show that the country's resistance greatly depends on its status as 'mysterious, unknowable, beyond language and rationality, and feminine'.[27] Essex and his followers expect a landscape that can be mapped, traversed and penetrated, but what they find is a metaphysical landscape where fog (145–6, 287) and impenetrable forests (82–3, 116, 169) obscure the view, trees and streams communicate with them (96–7, 100) and supernatural beings and forces affect both their sanity and their actions (141–50, 246–53). The idea that it was the irrational nature of Ireland that eventually led to Essex's failure has been very persistent. In his 1928 study, *Elizabeth and Essex: A Tragic History,* Lytton Strachey writes:

> Essex marched into Leinster, confident that nothing could resist him – and nothing could. But he was encountered by something more dangerous than resistance – by the soft, insidious, undermining atmosphere of that paradoxical country which, a quarter of a century earlier, had brought his father to despair and death.
>
> The strange air engulfed him. The strange land – charming, savage, mythical – lured him on with indulgent ease. He moved, triumphant, through a new peculiar universe of the unimagined and the unreal. Who or what were these people, with their mantles and their nakedness, their long locks of hair hanging over their faces, their wild battle-cries and gruesome wailings, their kerns and their gallowglass, their jesters and their bards? Who were their ancestors? Scythians? Or Spaniards? Or Gauls? What state of society was this, where chiefs jostled with gypsies, where ragged women lay all day long laughing in the hedgerows, where ragged men gambled away among each other their very rags, their very forelocks, their very [. . .] parts more precious still, where wizards flew on whirlwinds, and rats were rhymed into dissolution? All was vague, contradictory, and unaccountable; and the Lord Deputy, advancing further and further into the green wilderness, began – like so many others before and after him – to catch the surrounding infection, to lose the solid sense of things, and to grow confused over what was fancy and what was fact.[28]

In Lawless's novel, it is particularly the forests that represent the threat of the unknown, and the narrator Henry Harvey holds it

> part of true policy and sound wisdom to cut down these same traitor-harbouring trees wherever and wheresoever they can be got at; seeing that it is better plainly to have a naked land and obedience, than a well-covered one filled with such godless Runagates and Haltersacks. (169)

'A naked land' allows for the conquering gaze, but an elusive and incomprehensible landscape affects the senses instead. A near-encounter with a woman in the forest outside Kilkenny makes Henry Harvey modify his opinion about the righteousness of the campaign:

> We had not gone more than a mile before we heard a sound as of singing, which at first I wondered at, asking myself whether it could be Magical, it seeming to proceed less from a level with ourselves than to be rising up out of the ground below. Nor was it like any singing I had ever heard before, being a strange and gentle cadence, sad and at the same time cheerful, such as rustical folks pretend the fairy or elfin music to be. (111)

Deep within the forest, Harvey is more predisposed for a meeting with supernatural creatures than with outlaws, which is, of course, the case. When he finally finds the source of the music, it turns out to be a young mother singing to her child. His companion gets ready to shoot, but, suddenly furious, Harvey stops him: '"Rebel me no rebels, rascal!" quoth I. "They are women and infants, and are doing no harm to mortal man"' (115). In the forest, Harvey no longer thinks like the Queen's representative, engaged on a mission to wipe out Irish resistance, but thinks instead 'of the hard lot of those who, without fault of their own, are set in the midst of cruel warfare, and beset with many pangs and perils, which they, being weak and helpless, can by no means hinder or avert' (114–15). The forest becomes a landscape of Irishness and of femininity, with the power to subvert both conventionally English and masculine attitudes. In this landscape it becomes impossible to retain the initial categorisation of people in terms of friends and foes.

Thus Essex and his followers are gradually feminised – or hibernicised – by their exposure to Irish geography and culture. Essex's gender identity is destabilised on the one hand by a desexualised Queen who requires him to exercise the masculine attributes of violence and force but deprives him of his masculinity by her position as his superior, on the other by a feminine Ireland that awakens his sensitivity and his irrational side but remains thoroughly elusive and incomprehensible. The novel transposes Essex's ability to 'see two sides of a question'[29] into a paralysing gender conflict that makes him insufficiently male to conquer, yet not female enough to side with the Irish. His only option is to go home to England where execution awaits him since he no longer fits the system he set out to defend.

There were obviously critics who took exception to the framing of *With Essex in Ireland* as an authentic chronicle. In 'A Note on the Ethics of Literary Forgery', Lawless responds to such criticism, not only in relation to the novel, but even more passionately in connection with the short story 'The Builder of the Round Towers: A Chronicle of the Eighth Century':

> Before allowing our vagrant pens to take any further liberties with kings, queens, bards, chiefs, culdees – with any one that belongs to the past, but especially with *saints* – let us ascertain how far such liberties are permissible, and how far they are not; what in short is to be regarded as honest cheating, and what as dishonest. Where such an authoritative tribunal is to be found, and who the literary Cæsar is that we are to get to preside over it, I confess that I do not at the present moment perceive. Doubtless, however, it might be found, and then all our woes would be at an end. Henceforward it would only have to speak, and we should obey. I appeal unto Cæsar![30]

On the surface, 'The Builder of the Round Towers' tells the story of how the imaginary monk Fechin, subsequently canonised as a saint, brings the technology of building round towers to Ireland.[31] The underlying theme, however, is the power of voice. The repeated descriptions of how Fechin's voice allows him to perform miracles and defeat enemies make the story a symbolic comment on the importance of being heard and, hence, on authorship and cross-gendered narration as a strategy. St Fechin's great voice enables him to transform his culture. Access to a voice that ensures that the speaker/writer is being listened to opens the possibility of influencing cultural developments.

The cross-gendered narration Lawless uses in *With Essex in Ireland* partly conceals her own role as author as well as her nineteenth-century perspective, but in the process the voices of both women and the Irish are almost completely silenced. The power of the word – emblematised as

Harvey's control of the narrative – belongs to men. This means that Irish nationalist or feminist questions can only be treated inversely, by making the subjectivity of the narrator so obvious that a contradictory view is ironically installed. But since Harvey is presented as a sympathetic character and his bigotry placed in the context of the Elizabethan world-view, his attitudes are made understandable even if they are not condoned. The gap between author and narrator created by the cross-gendered technique and by the construction of Harvey as an unreliable narrator enables Lawless to dissociate herself from the ideological system Harvey belongs to at the same time as she manages to explain the cultural circumstances that produced his prejudice: she speaks in two voices.

*

With Essex in Ireland is an example of unresolved dialogue, where the binary oppositions underwriting rigid gender definitions and national loyalties are interrogated but not reversed. A similar scrutiny of rigid positioning characterises the short story 'A Bardic Chronicle' (1891), a narrative that mimics the style of medieval bardic literature. The young Flann MacFlathri is taken prisoner by the men of East Ossory and decides that his best chance of survival is to become *fuidhar,* or stranger man, to the tanist – the heir-elect – of the clan. He pledges allegiance to the leader of his own clan's worst enemies, in other words. His psychological bond with the tanist is an example of what is now termed the Stockholm Syndrome, the mixture of love and hate felt by hostages for their captors. Even in the extreme situation of captivity, people do not fall into neat categories of friends and foes, and after the tanist has defended him against another clansman Flann's feelings become utterly confused:

> For that word of his, and because of the blow that he had struck that day, Flann had loved him, and forgave him his ill-usage and his hard service, and his love had come up warm and strong through his hate, so that the two had mingled, and he knew not sometimes which was which.[32]

As a result of his mixed feelings for his captor Flann also becomes confused about where his real loyalty lies. When at the end of the story he has the opportunity to assist the enemies of East Ossory, he warns the tanist instead, with a bloody battle as the result. The tanist, far from showing any gratitude, kills Flann on the off-chance that he might have intended betrayal, and Flann himself is equally uncertain about his motives: 'whether he had done well or whether he had done ill he wist not – neither what was well or what was ill, for all was dark and clouded' (656). The combination of political opportunism and coincidence that determines Flann's fate challenges the ideal of the hero-martyr and, when Flann is asked why he acted like he did, his answer is 'Flann does not know' (657). There is no resolution.

In nineteenth-century Ireland, where antiquarian activity was often co-opted into the nationalist project, the version constructed of the past legitimised the political positions of the time. In a similar fashion, an attachment to ancient literary traditions gave a semblance of authenticity. The first lines of Lawless's story certainly suggest that the bards authorise her tale: 'The bards of Erinn relate that the men of East Ossory took captive Flann, who was the son of Flathri, the grandson of Tordhelfach' (645). But Flann's story, with its blurred boundaries between right and wrong, cannot legitimise anything, and although Lawless writes herself into the tradition of bardic literature she also distances herself from it, indicating that the bards, too, only provide a subjective version of truth. A few pages later the bards are drawn in to quite unnecessarily provide authority for the moon rising: 'about eight o'clock in the evening the moon, the bards say, began to rise' (646). The sheer meaninglessness of the reference draws attention to the contrived nature of such bardic authentication.

To some extent, then, 'A Bardic Chronicle' can be read as a critique of inflexible political positioning. The idea that the choices of an individual have more to do with self-preservation than abstract allegiance to a cause recurs in Lawless's second historical novel, *Maelcho: A Sixteenth Century Narrative* (1894). The work is set during the Desmond rebellion in Munster (1569–73, 1579–83), when James Fitzmaurice Fitzgerald, Captain General of the forces of Gerald, 14th Earl of Desmond, led a revolt against Tudor centralisation. The events in *Maelcho* mainly take place during the second phase of the revolt, when Fitzmaurice was aided by a force sent by Pope Gregory XIII and proclaimed holy war. The foreign help raised Irish hopes, but Fitzmaurice was killed in a local skirmish later in 1579 and so the rebels lost their leader even before the struggle had properly begun. Though resistance continued, and the Earl of Desmond was still at large, the representatives of English power, the

Lord General Ormonde and Sir William Pelham, initiated a scorched earth and famine policy that led to enormous suffering for the Irish peasants. The rebellion finally ended when the Earl of Desmond was killed on 11 November 1583. His head was sent to Queen Elizabeth, who had it put up on London Bridge.

The first part of Lawless's work is a rather straightforward 'strange country'[33] narrative, mostly concerned with the experiences of the young, Anglo-Irish Hugh Gaynard, a fictional character placed at the centre of the events of the Desmond uprising. The narrative follows the historical course of the rebellion very closely and quotations from State Papers and other documentary material constitute a large part of the text. The novel should not be regarded as a history of the rebellion, however, and the meanings of events and the experiences and emotions of the characters are clearly shaped by Lawless.

Maelcho contains echoes of Maria Edgeworth's *The Absentee* and *Ennui,* but, while Edgeworth shows how her Anglo-Irish characters change and learn to appreciate Irish life, Hugh Gaynard's lack of imagination and ambition makes him blind and deaf to both Irish culture and Irish suffering. The Ireland he encounters is both spatially and socially incomprehensible. When he flees his uncle's castle during a raid at the beginning of the story, Hugh leaves what he thinks of as the rational world behind, and he does not find it again until he becomes a soldier in Sir Nicholas Maltby's army at the end, once more an Englishman. His first experience of Celtic Ireland is as a prisoner of the O'Flahertys, the rulers of Connemara at the time. Like Flann MacFlathri in 'A Bardic Chronicle' he takes a very pragmatic view of his situation and reflects that to 'decline such alleviations as came in one's way, simply because they carried a certain taint of disloyalty about them, would be the act, he told himself, of a fool'.[34]

The description of the O'Flaherty clan is indistinguishable from nineteenth-century tales of Native Americans or the stories sent home by missionaries in Africa or India, especially in the light of the comment that Hugh had picked up his knowledge of Irish from the family's servants, 'as Anglo-Indian [children] pick up Hindustanee to-day' (19). To some extent it seems as if Lawless is pitting English, masculine common sense against native, feminine superstition and irrationality, privileging the former qualities. But this is gainsaid by the frequent ironic asides on English perceptions of Ireland and the importance placed on traditionally feminine qualities. Every time Hugh gets into a troublesome situation he is protected by a woman or a feminised man. During his stay with the O'Flahertys his defender is the woman Beara, who clearly disturbs the equation of female body and conventional feminine nature through her tall, masculine body and her 'air of one who expects instant obedience' (17).[35] According to Pierre Bourdieu, body language, understood as the body's 'social physiognomy', is shaped by and expresses the individual's relationship to society through 'the space one claims with one's body in physical space, through a bearing and gestures that are self-assured or reserved, expansive or constricted ("presence" or "insignificance")'.[36] Men are generally 'present,' whereas women are 'insignificant'. Since Lawless's Beara takes up so much space through her tall body and commanding posture, she is seen as 'not a mere woman at all in tribal estimation, nay, in her father's and brother's absence, [she] was the virtual leader of the encampment and arbitress of all points of dispute' (67). Because Beara is intensely 'present', she cannot be defined in ordinary gender terms, despite her sometimes feminine behaviour.

While Beara transcends her femininity through her body, Maelcho the seanachie transcends his masculinity through his actions. When Hugh escapes to the camp of Sir James Fitzmaurice of Desmond he is cared for by Maelcho, who, despite his reputation of being a fierce warrior, is introduced as a kind and loving nursemaid to Fitzmaurice's daughters. Hugh's final protector is the English officer Fenwick, a son of the Italian Renaissance who 'possessed all the mental nimbleness, the personal distinction, the curious, flowerlike grace and attractiveness, which marked the type', as well as 'its sensitiveness of organisation, verging upon effeminacy' (256). Although Maelcho and Fenwick readily use violence, their personal characteristics are feminine. Like national identity, gender identity is shown to be fundamentally unstable in the novel.

As in her depiction of Henry Harvey in *With Essex in Ireland,* Lawless is careful to show, and even didactically mentions, that Hugh is a product of his time: 'too practical a person to be superior to his century' (66). His views of the O'Flahertys are the views expected of a 'young Anglo-Irishman, brought up to regard himself as a sort of Heaven-descended being, lord of a whole world of serfs and inferiors' (64–5). To be credible as a sixteenth-century character, Hugh must display the prejudices of the period. The narrative itself, on the other hand, is firmly situated in Lawless's own time, in apparent opposition to her declaration in 'The

Ethics of Literary Forgery', where she denounces anachronism. Intrusive authorial comments draw attention to the distance between author and characters and install the idea that the past is inaccessible except as interpretation. By foregrounding the author's presence and thus her subjectivity, these comments emphasise the fundamental unavailability of the past as past, and this is further underscored by the inclusion of long excerpts from letters and State Papers, the documental traces that are all that is left. Rather than producing a seamless picture of the past, *Maelcho* recreates the past as 'noise', to use Laurie Finke's term, showing that the past we can access from our positions in the present is a tangled web of voices, stories and interpretations that frequently oppose each other.[37] The result is a rather contradictory text that at least the *Atheneum* reviewer regards as evidence of Lawless's objectivity: 'There is no attempt to extenuate the inherent weaknesses of the Celtic character any more than to palliate the brutal savagery of the English soldiery. "Maelcho", in this respect, is a standing rebuke to those critics who deny to women the attribute of impartiality.'[38] The idea that weakness was inherent in the Celts was so widespread at the time that it was seen rather as a fact than an opinion.

As in *With Essex in Ireland*, the forest plays an immensely important role in *Maelcho*. Both these works are set in the sixteenth century, when forests still covered large parts of Ireland, and in both novels the woods represent the country. In this, Lawless attaches to a 'long, rich, and pagan tradition that imagined forests as the primal birthplace of nations'.[39] Trees, and especially oaks, were immensely important in early Irish culture. One explanation of the word 'druid', for instance, is that it means 'the man by the sacred oak tree who knew the truth',[40] and at least eight letters of the old ogham script are named after trees: B is associated with the birch tree, D with the oak, and other letters are linked with the alder, willow, hazel, pine, ash and yew trees. In the Middle Ages scholars tried to find a tree correspondent to the rest of the twenty letters, so that ogham became a real tree alphabet. The old Irish manuscript 'Auraicept na nÉces' (The Scholar's Primer) contains the following instruction for reading this script: 'Ogham is climbed as a tree is climbed; by treading on the root of the tree first with one's right hand before one and one's left hand last. After that it is across it and against it and through it and around it (one goes).'[41]

Despite the important place of trees in Celtic culture, the wood symbol never gained any particular purchase in nineteenth-century Irish thought. In the seventeenth century Ireland was already one of Europe's least forested countries, partly because what Daniel Corkery calls 'land pirates' sold off the timber to the ship-building and mining industries,[42] partly because the English army cut down the forests to prevent the Irish from hiding there. The Gaelic poem 'Cill Chais' is a beautiful evocation of the lost woods:

> Now what will we do for timber,
> with the last of the woods laid low?
> [. . .]
> No hazel nor holly nor berry
> But boulders and bare stone heaps,
> Not a branch in our neighbourly haggard,
> And the game all scattered and gone.[43]

A central component of tree worship is the consolation it offers for our mortality through the yearly cycle of death and rebirth,[44] but in the Irish forests this vegetation cycle was arrested. While the decrease of woodland led to its veneration in other European countries, such as Germany, in Ireland the forests were irretrievably lost, and any symbolic use of woods would have to take account of this. In one way, the absence of actual forests is liberating, since the woodland can then become solely a landscape of imagination, rather like the mythical Ireland of the past. Because it no longer exists, the forest can be imbued with all kinds of meaning. However, from a nineteenth-century perspective, the loss of woodland would necessarily have to be a part of the symbolic meaning and, in contrast to the appropriation of the west of Ireland as a place where the nation's roots could be reclaimed, the forest symbol involves the sense that a return to the past is impossible. There is no real Irish romance of the woods.

Nevertheless, the forest is an important symbol in other European literatures, and this influences how it can function also in Irish works. In nineteenth-century writing, forests are often seen as places of retreat and meditation, but only as long as the contrast with the surrounding cultivated land is sufficiently clear. When the forests are too large – as they are in the Nordic countries, for instance – they give rise to fear and superstition instead. These experiences of the mind have their counterparts in similarly contradictory ideas of the forest as shelter and as a territory where common rules are eliminated. In Shakespeare's comedies

– works that Lawless was very well acquainted with – the forest is 'the upside-down world of the Renaissance court: a place where the conventions of gender and rank are *temporarily* reversed in the interest of discovering truth, love, freedom, and above all, justice'.[45] Depending on your place in the social hierarchy, this can be either positive or negative. The cultural stereotype of Robin Hood and his equivalents in other parts of Europe is immensely powerful. Romantic stories like the cycle about Robin and his merry men figure the forest as a place of refuge and fertilises a myth of idyllic co-existence, where the insubordinate wood-people can be tolerated since they are, after all, spatially removed from the seats of power. Forests are profoundly contradictory. The deep wood is a feminine space that shelters the body, at the same time as it awakens unconscious and irrational feelings. It is also a masculine space, as the site for the hunt and guerrilla warfare. Since the meaning of the forest can fluctuate from one extreme to another, it is a very unstable symbol.

In *Maelcho,* the vast Munster forests appear as places of resistance that actively fight the English intruders, whether by working on their unconscious or ensuring that they get lost. The trees and briars obstruct the progression of the soldiers and make them easy prey for the rebels: 'They were swept apart; they were tripped up by tree roots; they were entangled amongst boughs and undergrowth, and once fallen their fate was sealed' (280). The army is perhaps the most rigorously organised environment in any society, and for the soldiers the wood becomes a frighteningly incomprehensible landscape, utterly disorganised and disorienting for the outsider:

> a good deal worse than trackless, for it was full of minute paths, intimately known to those who made use of them, but invisible to ordinary observation; paths which branched and rebranched in a complicated network, and the entrances and exits of which were sedulously concealed by those who used them. (262)

As a supernatural landscape, the forest destroys the courage of the soldiers and 'creeping along at a foot's pace through a country known to be swarming with rebels, and believed to be swarming with other things, worse even than rebels, was a trial of the nerves such as very few of them were equal to' (268). Like the great Scandinavian or German forests, the Irish woodland is a place for unnatural beings, and the soldiers shout to one another that 'the wood was full of devils; that they could see their horns, and the streams of red fire that filled their mouths and nostrils' (279). The contrast between this illogical, natural world and the Elizabethan society is immense, and the clash between the two systems becomes particularly obvious in the forest, both in *Maelcho* and *With Essex in Ireland.* Since the forest is inherently contradictory, it gives rise to diametrically opposite reactions. The invaders, naturally enough, learn to hate the woods for the very same reasons that the Irish refugees love them:

> Then, as throughout all Irish history, the forests were the close friend of the attacked, the eternal foe and torment of the attackers, and as a consequence grew to be more and more the object of detestation, which finds expression in half the State documents of the day, and has much more of the animosity which men show towards something personal and sentient, something that is capable of hating them back in return, than towards a mere aggregation of trees and bushes. (378–9)

The forests are animate, aware and sensitive, as opposed to the English army, which is represented as a machine, vulnerable only in an environment where machine-like efficiency is made impossible.

In the sections concentrating on Hugh Gaynard the forests are consequently yet another sign of Ireland's inscrutability. The sections focused on the other main character, the bard Maelcho, make more complex statements about Ireland as a contradictory space. Maelcho represents both the Irish people and the wood in the novel and, when he is first introduced into the narrative, he is described as a tree:

> He was a giant, the only giant left. It was not like a man, but like a tree he looked when he walked, yes, like a forest tree, and it was out of the forests he came in the first instance, even out of the great, dark, wind-haunted hundred-thousand-mile-long forests of Munster. (74)

The character Maelcho has his roots in the ancient bardic tradition, with connections to the druids and their reverence for trees. He has 'far-seeing eyes, like those of some big forest beast', (246) and like the clairvoyant druids and the creatures of the forest he is able to see things that are invisible to ordinary people. The later tradition of the freedom of the greenwood also contributes to the picture when Maelcho is described as an Irish Robin Hood. He is the 'big man in the green cloak' (101) and, like 'Robin Hood of earlier times in England, like Rob Roy of later ones in Scotland – nay, in some respects more redoubtable than either one or the other – he had grown to be a legend in his own lifetime' (113). Yet, when Hugh Gaynard meets this legendary figure, he performs the task of nursemaid to Lord Fitzmaurice's children (118). Like the forest itself, the forest man is ambiguously gendered.

The Maelcho sections of the narrative mainly show the forest as shelter and nurturing mother, and Lawless stresses the symbiotic relationship between the people and their place of habitation. Before the assault of the English army and its woodcutters, she suggests, there was an ecological balance between people and woodland:

> Throughout all this part of Ireland the forest had indeed modified the inhabitants very much more than the inhabitants had the forest. Their ways, their thoughts, their habit of locomotion, their very bodies, had become adapted to their environment. Strip them of their leafy sheath, and they would hardly have known how to exist. (262)

The symbiotic relationship between forest and forest people is at the centre also of one of Lawless's most anthologised poems, 'Dirge of the Munster Forest. 1581'[46] where the forest invites all its creatures to attend the funeral of those who died in the Desmond rising. Only the wolf is asked to stay away, lest he should

> lay bare my dead for gloating foes to see
> Lay bare my dead, who died, and died for me.[47]

The fate of the forest is 'yoked and linked' to the fate of the people,[48] and the underlying idea is that one cannot survive without the other. This description of mutual dependence is very close to the patronising view of the Irish as children of nature, but in other works Lawless stresses the (mainly) English exploitation of the country, and her criticism is clearly directed at the very civilisation that condemns Irish people as barbarians. In an article about County Kerry she complains about the treelessness of the area, saying that we know from Macaulay and Froude 'how the ore was imported, and how the smelting furnaces were set up, and the fires fed, until the last stick of oak and arbutus was consumed'.[49] When greedy capitalism entered the sylvan world, the trees were doomed, and 'the chief destruction of the woods', she says, occurred after the defeat of the Tyrone rebellion[50] – soon after the incidents in *Maelcho* and *With Essex in Ireland.* The place-names in the region are the only memories left of the great forests.

Lawless was clearly aware of the ecological effects of deforestation and notes that 'the destruction of a forest, it must be remembered, by no means entails the loss merely of the trees: it also entails the death or dispersal of a whole world of beings, which, having thriven under their shelter, shares their fate'.[51] Left behind is a landscape that has lost its identity: 'these slopes and highland glens, admirably adapted for forest, are to all intents and purposes useless for anything else'.[52] Against this background, her description of the forest-dwellers becomes evidence of a respectful integration with nature, to be contrasted with the destructive activities of a progressive/aggressive civilisation. In this, as in her other landscape descriptions, Lawless anticipates today's eco-feminist thought, especially since the destruction of the forests is carried out by a culture figured as predominantly masculine in her writing.

As a site that provides shelter and excludes only the invader, the forest is benign, but Lawless includes also the more frightening aspects of an incomprehensible landscape. The notion that the woods allow equality and multiplicity that accompanies the Robin Hood myth is paralleled by the understanding that heterogeneity may lead to weakness. Imagined as a forest, Ireland emerges as a fractured clan society, where personal loyalties are stronger than the abstract idea of a nation, and, ultimately, the forest cannot protect the Irish people, because the various factions in the wood fight each other. The resisting landscape becomes the suffering, killed landscape, just as the rebels become the defeated, and the main reason for this is that a heterogeneous environment is helpless against a concerted attack.

The death-blow to the Desmond rebellion, as Lawless presents it in *Maelcho,* is when its natural leader, Sir James Fitzmaurice, is killed. Riding through the forest of south Limerick, Fitzmaurice and his companions encounter the sons of Sir William Burke and Sir James is shot by them. 'In its inconsequence', Lawless comments, 'in its tragic absurdity, it might have stood as a sort of embodiment of all the disasters, and all the elaborate and ingenious blunderings that have made Irish risings, and Irish doings, a bye-word for centuries' (188). The country is divided against itself, and the war becomes 'a purely tribal one, waged in the old fashion, and for the old objects' (375). Without its leader, Ireland is helpless before the uniform machine of the English army, just as the heterogeneous forest is helpless before the woodcutters.

Basing his argument on T. W. Freeman's study *Ireland: Its Physical, Historical, Social and Economic Geography* (1950), William Linn maintains that Lawless's description of the deforestation of Munster as a result of English warfare and exploitation is actually wrong.[53] The view she puts forward in the novel was in accord with popular belief, however. As in the 'Dirge of the Munster Forest', Maelcho's fate matches the fate of the wood. Tied to a large beech tree, he awaits his execution, and 'the very forest – itself, it must be remembered, just then a culprit under sentence of death – seemed to be consciously partaking' in creating the hushed atmosphere of his last moments (416). The tree above him is also 'doomed, and would probably be cut down first thing in the morning' (415–16). After killing Maelcho, the army march off to cut down the rest of the forest. A revealing parallel to the tree metaphors in *Maelcho* is that Hugh O'Neill, the Earl of Tyrone, whose rebellion Essex was to extinguish, was described as a tree in the State Papers: 'that tree which hath been the treasonable stock from which so many poisoned plants and grafts have been derived'.[54] Lawless obviously attaches to a long tradition of describing Irish rebels as trees.

The symbolic use of the forest reflects the cultural systems the main characters belong too, so that, when Hugh Gaynard is in focus, the woods primarily underscore the strangeness of Ireland, whereas the forest functions as resistance, as shelter and finally as defeated nation in the sections about Maelcho. Anticipating the end of the novel, Lawless comments:

> They were close now to the confines of the great forest – *the* forest emphatically of South Ireland, which from this point stretched away ahead of them for more than forty miles, untouched as yet by hatchet, intact in all its virgin savagery; the forest which was adored with such passion by its inhabitants, which was detested with equal passion, and at least equal reason by their assailants; the forest which was destined within a short space of time to be cleared off so completely, that, as we gaze around us to-day at the bald nakedness which has replaced it, we are inclined to ask ourselves seriously whether as a matter of fact it can ever really have existed at all. (175)

Above all, the inscrutable forest emphasises the fundamental unavailability of the past. The forest as national symbol cannot be retrieved. Because Ireland was never really unified, nostalgia is a futile exercise and the desire to build a new national identity on the past suppresses the complexity of the truth. Seen in relation to the common celebrations of the western counties as the original Irish homeland, the forest symbolism in *Maelcho* and *With Essex in Ireland* can be read as clearly anti-revivalist.

Despite careful measures to ensure psychological realism, *Maelcho* is an uneven novel, with two equally important main characters whose brief time together is only an incident in the plot, not a pivotal event. When the focus changes to Maelcho, the novel paints a poignant picture of Irish suffering, and in these sections Hugh Gaynard is mainly absent. Lady Gregory reacted against the grimness of the tale and did not admire the novel, to a great extent because she found the characterisation weak and the presentation too impassioned:

> I finished reading *Maelcho* last night. No, it is not a fine book. She gets smothered in the horrible history of the time. The young adventurer of the story, Hugh Gaynard, drops out. Maelcho is but a poor invention, unnatural, none of the imaginative readiness of the Seanachie he is supposed to be. The whole later part of the book is of horrors, of the terrible cruelty of the English soldiers, their extermination of the people – and of the trees – the forests. Yet it is not written in a gust of anger, or wrath, although the bare unemotional putting down of the list of the horrors make them seem the more horrible.[55]

Apparently *Maelcho* is the joining of two originally separate works. In a letter to Lecky, Lawless writes:

> It is of course a very incoherent as well as a very 'bluggy' [*sic*] narrative, but its faults are a good deal due to the way it came into existence. I had the plan of <u>two</u> books ready laid out, but as I did not see a chance of getting both finished I just tied them up together, & there it is![56]

In the introductory dedication to M[aria] C[atherine] Bishop, Lawless explains that although *Maelcho* began 'as an adventure book pure and simple, this story has grown grimmer somehow, and more lugubrious, as it went on'. Given the prominence of the forest metaphor, it is perhaps logical that the writing process is described as a result of organic growth. The suggestion that the story began to live a life of its own releases Lawless from responsibility for the result, since the subject matter itself has forced her to write something she had not originally intended.

On the whole, the novel was favourably reviewed, but more, perhaps, because of the insights it gave into Irish history than its qualities as a novel. The *Atheneum* reviewer comments:

> Although the story is admittedly an historical romance, we have no
> hesitation in saying that more may be learnt as to the relations between
> England and Ireland, and more information gained as to the mode of life
> and aspect of the country three hundred years ago, than in any regular
> history with which we are acquainted.[57]

The *Times* reviewer gives a similar opinion, addressing the novel's value
as fact rather than as fiction:

> Miss Lawless's striking and delightful book 'Maelcho' is an illustration of
> a new type of historical novel, as far removed from antiquarium [*sic*]
> tedium on the one hand, as from the pure Dumas-like adventure of Mr.
> Stevenson and Mr. Stanley Weyman on the other. [. . .] Still the book is
> history as Mr. Weyman's charming tales are not history.[58]

The *Spectator* review begins with a mixture of disapproval and praise,
where the separate parts of the novel are quite severely criticised, but the
whole is admired. The reviewer suggests that the meandering nature of the
text may at some level be a manifestation of Irishness:

> In fact, take the book how you will, *Maelcho* is a paradox of literary genius.
> It is not a history, and yet has more of the stuff of history in it, more of true
> national character and fate, than any historical monograph we know. It is
> not a novel, and yet fascinates us more than any novel. It is not even a study
> of any one character, but a kind of mosaic of many such studies woven
> together by a sort of accidental 'connective tissue', which gives the book the
> air of those scraps of moss in which flowers are sometimes kept moist and
> fresh. There is a kind of Celtic arbitrariness about the story. You never
> know where it will break off, and something quite different will begin, and
> yet you feel perfectly confident, and, as it proves, justly confident, that
> however tessellated the story may be, there will be in it a wholeness of effect
> strangely Irish as well in the violence and crudeness of its contrasts, as in
> the subdued melancholy of the impression it produces.[59]

Whether the unevenness of the novel is seen as a result of organic
growth, Irishness or an attempt to produce a new kind of historical fiction,
Maelcho is clearly different from other novels at the time. Its failure to
produce a coherent picture of the past is probably an important reason why
it has been forgotten. Like *With Essex in Ireland*, *Maelcho* can serve no
partisan purposes, English no more than Irish. The characters represent
two cultural systems, and the plot relies on the circumstance that these

systems do not and cannot co-exist. There is no sense of compromise and no hope for reconciliation. The novel becomes a dialogue between opposite world-views where a synthesis is never achieved, not even with hindsight.

*

Lawless's own comments about *Maelcho* mostly concern the bleak impression of Ireland's past that it conveys. In a letter to W. E. Gladstone she indicates that she would like to turn to happier subjects for a while:

> I own that I feel myself the gloom of much of it to be too great, though it is not easy to see how such a story, laid at such a time, could have been painted in much brighter colours. If I ever again write of Irish history I must try to discover some period that will not need quite so much undiluted lamp black![60]

It may be that her third historical novel is the result of this wish to deal with the Irish past in a more light-hearted manner. *A Colonel of the Empire: From the Private Papers of Mangan O'Driscoll, Late of the Imperial Service of Austria, and a Knight of the Military Order of Maria Theresa* (1895) is certainly Lawless's slightest work, differing in tone, topic and characterisation from her previous novels. A clear sign of its minor importance is that it seems the novel was never published in Ireland or England, only in a single American edition. The only thing that strongly connects *A Colonel of the Empire* and Lawless's other works is the insistence that Ireland and Irishness are beyond categorisation.

The story is set in eighteenth-century Tipperary and narrated by Colonel O'Driscoll, newly returned to Ireland after his years in the Austrian army. O'Driscoll is a Catholic and a fond, talkative old man who advocates tolerance and understanding. At the time, Tipperary was a centre for the Whiteboys, an agrarian protest movement named after the white shirts the protesters donned over their everyday clothes. The Whiteboy Acts of 1766, 1776 and 1787 meant that several of the acts committed by the protesters were regarded as capital offences. Early in the novel Lawless refers to the harsh punishment of Whiteboy activists as well as to their activities:

> ever since Scaly Shamus had been taken, and on the road to be hanged, there had been an extraordinary quietness, and next door to no goings on

at all hereabouts – not a beast killed, nor a sod turned, nor a girl carried off, nor a thing – but now with him out again, not hung, nor like to be hung, 'twould for a certainty all begin again, and worse doings maybe than before, he gaining such credit in the country as a jail-breaker and a defier of the Government.[61]

The plot of the novel revolves around the bogus kidnapping of Alice Carew by fake Whiteboys, a plan meant to make her English suitor Captain Spencer acceptable to her father by rescuing her. The background to the story is that O'Driscoll wishes to provide a true account of the events to protect those involved, and particularly his nephew Wooden-Sword, because 'one ought always to make provision for the worst, especially in a case where the Law and the Government both come in' (2). O'Driscoll's fears for his friends are based on his knowledge of the danger of being a Catholic who can be in any way suspected of stepping out of line. Though circumstances differ, a similar realisation of the problems facing the Irish Catholics in the eighteenth century comes through very clearly in the description of the first Baron Cloncurry in the autobiography of Lawless's grandfather.[62]

Alice is the daughter of the wealthy Sir Thomas Carew, who has replaced O'Driscoll's family as the owner of Mangan Castle. Yet, O'Driscoll does not nurse any resentment but believes in leaving the past behind:

> People who are for ever recurring to the wrongs they have suffered in the past never in my experience do any good in the present, but are a nuisance to themselves and to everyone else, for what can be more tiresome than to have to listen to what's over and done with and never can be set right in this world, nor any other either. (59–60)

The parallel between the Mangans and the Aylmer family, who were the original owners of Lawless's home, Lyons Castle, is unmistakable, though it seems the Aylmers may have taken a less philosophical view of the matter.[63] William Linn sees the similar history of the castles and a few other parallels between the fictional Sir Thomas Carew and Lawless's brother Valentine as an indication that *A Colonel of the Empire* is in some part a satire of Lawless's own family.[64] The outlook she describes through O'Driscoll is present in most of her writing, however. As a returning exile – that is, someone who has been exposed to other than Irish cultures and influences – O'Driscoll is a hybrid of the same kind as the Anglo-Irish at the end of the nineteenth century. His love for his country is never in doubt, but he is less inclined to be single-minded in his opinions:

> to a man like myself, coming back with fresh eyes to the country, a stranger, and yet at home, living in the midst of the people and neither richer nor of more importance than they, though treated – Heaven bless them for it – as if able to make them all kings and queens. To such a man – meaning myself – it does seem little short of madness, the foolish talk he has to listen to, and the foolish topsy-turvey ideas that get taken up by everybody – English or Irish alike – that have anything to say to the governing of the country. (75)

Like the members of the Ascendancy, O'Driscoll is both a stranger and a native. He is fully aware of the unfairness of the situation in Ireland, but considers that neither the English nor the purist Irish position can provide all the answers. The novel ends with a symbolic union of the two countries through the marriage of the Irish Alice Carew and the English Captain Spencer.

The references to eighteenth-century agrarian outrages mean that the novel was potentially of topical interest in the Land War times of the nineteenth century. Yet, the theme of agrarian protest is mainly a backdrop to a rather trivial romantic comedy. The insistence on tolerance and the acceptance of a less than pure idea of Irishness expressed through Colonel O'Driscoll certainly makes the work a comment on Lawless's present and links it with her other novels. Even so, her attempts at comedy are rather unsuccessful and do not really suit her themes. It appears as if she had some problems publishing the novel. In a letter to W. E. H. Lecky she writes:

> I have had a good deal of worry about Mssrs Appleton, & was thinking of appealing to you for your advice, but did not like to write, feeling you were so busy. I sent them the proofs of a little story that came out in the 'Illustrated London News', as they said it was very important that the copyright should be saved, & it was the only way it could be done, & now they tell me they are not inclined to publish it themselves & that I shall have to pay for the printing, which may run to a considerable sum. I pointed out that I ought to have been warned of the possibility of this <u>before</u> the proofs were sent, & have offered to surrender the whole rights to them to dispose of as they like without my receiving <u>anything</u>. This surely ought to suffice, but I am afraid they will insist on claiming their 'pound of flesh'.[65]

A Colonel of the Empire is the only one of Lawless's works that was only published in the United States, by D. Appleton & Company, and it does not seem to have met with much success. There are no reviews of the novel in the Lawless papers in Marsh's Library in Dublin, and the library does not even hold a copy of the book.

*

Like most of Lawless's novels, *A Colonel of the Empire* builds on the idea that the strangeness of Ireland precludes definite positioning. The disintegration of categories caused by exposure to Ireland is even more apparent in Lawless's last novel, *The Race of Castlebar: Being a Narrative Addressed by Mr. John Bunbury to His Brother Mr. Theodore Bunbury* (1913), written in collaboration with Shan Bullock (1865–1935). Bullock was born in County Fermanagh, but after a few years of working on his father's farm he joined the civil service in London, where he spent the rest of his life. His first work of fiction was *The Awkward Squad, and Other Stories* (1893) and he went on to write a number of novels about rural life in Fermanagh. *The Race of Castlebar* appeared after Lawless's death, and comments about the novel often focus on Bullock's contributions. Among other things, Bullock's involvement was seen as a guarantee of objectivity. The *Irish Times* comments: 'As Miss Lawless was a staunch Unionist, while Mr. Bullock has Nationalist leanings, there should be a fine impartiality about the result of their joint labours.'[66] It seems clear, however, that the work was already planned and well under way before Bullock was involved. The preface states that Bullock took over 'from the time Bunbury reaches Castlebar down to when he leaves Killala and rejoins Lavinia'.[67] This would indicate that Lawless wrote chapters 1–14 and 26–31, treating the narrator's personal experiences, and Bullock wrote the chapters where the protagonist Bunbury is embroiled in public events, the half of the book based on Bishop Stock's description of conditions in Castlebar and Killala during the United Irishmen uprising and the French invasion of 1798.[68] Even so, Lawless seems to have been involved throughout. An article in the *Irish Book Lover* relates how Bullock sometimes 'received as many as three letters a day concerning their book, suggesting fresh incidents and corrections'.[69]

The French troops arrived at Killala Bay on 22 August 1798. They were led by General Jean Joseph Amable Humbert and numbered 1,019.

Humbert managed to raise some 3,000 local volunteers and established a provisional government under John Moore, son of a local Catholic landowner. Instead of securing his position and waiting for reinforcements, however, Humbert marched against the government army quartered in Castlebar on 27 August – the race or races of Castlebar. The loyalists were defeated, but their forces in Ireland outnumbered the French by twenty to one, and the government troops quickly regrouped. Humbert's army was surrounded at Ballinamuck, County Longford, on 8 September and forced to surrender. Harsh measures were taken against the Irish among the troops, and up to 2,000 peasant rebels may have been summarily killed. The central part of *The Race of Castlebar,* written by Bullock, deals with these events.

Since the first-person narrator is a man, Lawless's sections of the narrative are cross-gendered, while Bullock speaks, if not as himself, so at least in the voice of his own sex. As a result the novel becomes a particularly revealing example of early twentieth-century conceptions of gender. In Lawless's sections of the book, the narrator Bunbury is a lovelorn, rather insecure young Englishman who only reluctantly agrees to go to Ireland to make sure that his sister, who is married to an Irishman, is safe during the uprising and the threat of invasion. Like Essex's secretary Harvey, Bunbury is characterised through his use of language and shown to be firmly entrenched in the ideology of his time and class. One of his first encounters with the unclear divisions in Irish society is when he finds himself defending a Catholic gentleman from an uncouth Orangeman, thus opposing his supposed ally and siding with the enemy because of common class origins.[70] Before he reaches his final destination on Ireland's west coast he manages to get utterly lost in a bog (63–6), and his repeated experiences of geographical and cultural disorientation emphasise the uncertain state of affairs in Ireland, the curious alliances formed in the war and the difficulty of knowing who you are in a country where common tools of definition such as class and nationality do not entirely work.

When Shan Bullock takes over the story, Bunbury's status as a gentleman is stressed and he appears as both prudent and powerful. This change is explained as an effect of the war, which 'created a new self, a self which contemplated with no little surprise that more featherheaded and irresponsible being which it had superseded' (250). Symptomatically, the section begins with a battle , and women are conspicuously absent from Bullock's part of the novel, except for as passive victims crying in the background. The love plot in focus in Lawless's parts of the story is certainly trite and uninteresting. It adds nothing to the themes and is not very successfully described. As the *Times Literary Supplement* reviewer expresses it, Lawless was 'lost in a bog' when it came to romantic writing.[71] The decision to jettison Bunbury's love affair and concentrate on war history was therefore seen as a happy choice, at least by the *Bookman* reviewer, who ascribes the merit of the novel to Bullock's interventions and maintains that Lawless's 'share of the tale will not do full credit' to her memory.[72] There is certainly drama enough in the odd situation of English Protestants being protected from Irish rebels by French officers, and Bullock continues to problematise the categories of friend and enemy.

When Bunbury escapes from Killala, Lawless is again in charge, and women are reintroduced into the story. In overly symbolic manner Bunbury is reunited with his beloved in the centre of a labyrinth, where the tragic events of the uprising are juxtaposed with the happiness of the lovers whose 1798 is 'their *annus mirabilis;* the year in which for the first time they had definitely discovered one another' (315). History is never single and will always be infused with the particular bias of the chronicler. For Bunbury and Lavinia, 1798 is the year of love, not the year of rebellion.

The strangeness of Ireland is underscored throughout the narrative, through Bunbury's repeated failures to understand and make sense of his experiences. The Irish-French Colonel O'Byrne epitomises the blurred distinction between categories. As a French soldier he belongs to the enemy, but he is also the supplanted owner of Bunbury's sister's estate, Castle Byrne, an Irishman outmanoeuvred 'by the laws of England' (113). In this, he is a counterpart to Colonel O'Driscoll in *A Colonel of the Empire,* though O'Driscoll is described as more tolerant of the fact that he has lost his family estate. Totally unable to understand how his sister can defend the rights of a man who has at least the moral and ethical power to drive her from her home and, moreover, provide food and lodgings for his mother, Bunbury can only ascribe her attitude to the influence of Ireland, since, in 'former days', she certainly 'would not have done so' (84):

> To have one's hereditary enemy sitting at one's own dinner-table, and asking every few days who one was! Forgive my laughter. The whole affair is really beyond my comprehension. Remember, please, that I have only been a few weeks in Ireland. (85)

Nevertheless, Bunbury's final task is to save Colonel O'Byrne from English retributions, which makes him the enemy of his own English government. His experiences in Ireland thus lead to a conflict between personal and public loyalty, and ultimately it is the personal choices that count. Thus, *The Race of Castlebar* is an almost exemplary narrative of cultural encounter, where engagement with the otherness of Ireland oversets all familiar distinctions between groups.[73]

Lawless wrote a few shorter stories on Irish historical topics. As the titles indicate, 'Irish Chronicles: Gerald the Great'[74] and 'Fragments of Irish Chronicles: Gerald the Great (Concluded)'[75] concern the exploits of Sir Geroit Mor, 8th Earl of Kildare, and 'How Art Kavanagh of Wexford Fought Richard the King'[76] tells the story of Art McMurrough Kavanagh, who became King of Leinster after fighting King Richard II at the end of the fourteenth century. These stories are mainly straightforward hero-tales, and despite their dramatic themes they do not engage as the novels do. Lawless's aim seems to have been to produce exciting stories of the past, but the result is curiously wooden. One of the most successful aspects of the novels is Lawless's creation of believable narrative voices. In these stories she uses third-person narration, however, and the immediacy of *With Essex in Ireland, A Colonel of the Empire* or *The Race of Castlebar* is lost.

Where the historical novels are concerned, there is an obvious tension between a belief in plurality and the view that only a central power could have saved Ireland. As Lawless shows in the opening chapters of her history *Ireland,* the country has been invaded and settled by wave after wave of benevolent or hostile immigrants and its population is as indefinable as the land she describes. Her elusive landscapes depict this circumstance as at once Ireland's strength and its weakness. Through the forest and machine metaphors in *Maelcho* she problematises two opposite concepts of nation. The forest represents her belief that Ireland is too fractured – and always has been – to rule itself, but at the same time nationhood as represented by the machine-like English army is described as uniformity and institutionalised violence, a system where the individual is insignificant. A similar idea lies behind the depiction of Essex's disastrous choices in *With Essex in Ireland,* the description of Bunbury's decision to save his country's enemy, O'Byrne, from hanging in *The Race of Castlebar,* and even O'Driscoll's willingness to accept that his family's home is now in the hands of a Protestant upstart. Although it is normally

England, and not Ireland, that represents homogeneity in the novels, these images of nation clearly address the fears of the Anglo-Irish at the end of the nineteenth century by pitting a negative picture of nationhood against a more positive picture of a society that embraces diversity. While Lawless recognises that internal differences make the Irish weak, this heterogeneous society is, in the end, infinitely preferable to the rigid homogeneity enforced by England in the past, or the Irish nationalists in the future.

Chapter 6

Ballad, lyric and talk: poetry

Considering her impressive body of prose, it is remarkable that Lawless has been remembered mainly for her three slim volumes of poetry, and within those collections only for a few poems interpreted as expressions of romantic nationalism. The fact that her contemporaries regarded fiction as a lesser art form obviously affected her literary reputation. Due to its realist aspirations, the novel was seen as an unsuitable vehicle for the 'Celtic spirit' and was rather summarily dismissed because it did not conform to the philosophy of the Irish literary revival. Ernest Boyd's 1916 verdict that fiction and narrative prose constituted 'the weak point of the revival'[1] and Lloyd R. Morris's declaration a year later that the novel was 'the one literary form in the manipulation of which Irish writers have been conspicuously deficient'[2] bolstered the already prevalent opinion that fiction need not be taken seriously.

The continuing high regard for poetry and drama in Irish culture makes it seem that the disparagement of fiction was universal. There were, however, also critics who argued that only the Gaelic-Irish were really able to value poetry and that the Anglo-Irish community was unable to appreciate poetic works. Introducing a review of Emily Lawless's first book of poetry, *With the Wild Geese* (1902), the *Leader* commentator, Chanel (Arthur Clery), argues:

> There is probably no feature more distinctive of Anglo-Irish society than its utter distaste for poetry. In this point it has gone far beyond its English model. Whilst the more intellectual Englishman still appreciates poetry, the Anglo-Irishman has taken the lower middle-class Englishman [. . .] for his model in this regard. He is so far the antithesis of his Gaelic ancestors that verse awakes in him a feeling of utter aversion and almost of dread.[3]

With sublime disregard for the achievements of Yeats and others as well as deficient prophetical skills, the *Leader* reviewer concludes that 'Anglo-

149

Irish poetry is not a product to be developed'.[4] Poetry is seen as the province of Irish speakers, and it would be hard indeed for Lawless to find an audience outside her closest friends:

> The Gael will avoid them, because he will very properly say that they cannot be called Irish literature in any true and full sense. Englishmen will fight shy of an Irish subject. Anglo-Irishmen are sometimes ready to praise such writings, or even verbally encourage the author, but they consider it an extraordinary display of patriotic condescension if they even consent to glance through a free copy of the work.[5]

Despite such gloomy predictions, *With the Wild Geese* found plenty of readers in both England and Ireland. In complete contradiction to Chanel's view that the poems would be insufficiently Irish, the *Bookman* critic considers the collection 'Irish to the core'.[6] In a letter to Lawless, Horace Plunkett offers a similar opinion: 'I think you altogether underrate the strength, the charm, and the deeply human interest of those poems. At any time they might become enormously popular in Ireland.'[7] The verses that corresponded to popular sentiment in the early twentieth century were indeed widely appreciated. Effective rhetorical strategies make the historical ballads, in particular, attractive and easy to remember, to a great extent because the rhetoric serves to conceal their complexity. It is doubtful whether the poems would have had the same popular appeal if Lawless's questioning attitude to Ireland and the past had been fully appreciated.

The collection was first privately printed as *Atlantic Rhymes and Rhythms* (1898) and was republished only on the instigation of Stopford Augustus Brooke, with slight changes to most of the poems. A letter to Lady Gregory suggests that Lawless never intended to give the work wider distribution:

> Oddly enough I do not possess a copy of the *Wild Geese*. I only have it in the rough old form that I called "Atlantic Rhythma". I never somehow liked the get up of it in published form and had never meant to publish it at all, only to print it privately, as I have a very strong feeling that poetry should be either of the Best, or else nonexistent. Mr. Stopford Brooke kindly took a fancy to it in its old form and begged me to let him have it published and I consented. Now a good deal of it has come out in various collections, including a big profusely illustrated volume of 'Empire Poetry', where the poor old 'rebel' rhymes find themselves in very odd company.[8]

The letter corroborates Ernest Boyd's view that 'as a poet, Emily Lawless did not wish to make any great claim to public attention'.[9] It is ironic that the works she wanted attention for have been more or less forgotten, while a handful of poems that were never meant for the larger public are the only works of hers that have remained in print through most of the twentieth century. 'She is fortunate now in being only remembered by her best, those three fine poems', Lady Gregory writes in her journal.[10]

The dedicatory poem in *With the Wild Geese* is 'To the Atlantic', the 'King of our Hearts' through all the seasons, and the original title *Atlantic Rhymes and Rhythms* foregrounds the nature poems included.[11] The later title, on the other hand, shifts the emphasis to the historical ballads about the 'Wild Geese' and the Desmond rebellion of the sixteenth century. The Flight of the Wild Geese took place after the Treaty of Limerick in 1691, when Patrick Sarsfield and eleven thousand of his soldiers left for France. They were formed into four regiments by James II and became known as 'the Irish Brigade' of France. The name the Wild Geese is also applied to those Irishmen who, for more than a century after the Treaty, left Ireland to join armies abroad. Mangan O'Driscoll, the main character in Lawless's novel *A Colonel of the Empire* (1895), served in the Austrian army and could be described as one of these later Wild Geese. Two of the regiments of the Irish Brigade took part in the rescue of Cremona 1702, during the War of the Spanish Succession (1701–14). Apart from celebrating the valour and stamina of the Irish soldiers in foreign service, Lawless's poem 'Cremona' contains the refrain 'Erin's the renown' (17–22), indicating that, wherever the Irish fought, they fought for Ireland.

The most anthologised poem in the collection is 'After Aughrim', where Mother Ireland speaks about the soldiers dead and exiled after the battle of Aughrim on 12 July 1691, when Irish and French troops were defeated by William III's army. This was the poem Lady Gregory rated highest.[12] The speaker is Mother Ireland, outlining the many ways in which she has abused her children:

> She said, 'They gave me of their best,
> They lived, they gave their lives for me;
> I tossed them to the howling waste,
> And flung them to the foaming sea.'
>
> She said, 'I never gave them aught,
> Not mine the power, if mine the will;

> I let them starve, I let them bleed, –
> They bled and starved, and loved me still.' (3)

Instead of explaining how Ireland inspired the heroic deeds of the Wild Geese, the poem makes tragically clear that the exiles might actually be better off elsewhere. As Gregory A. Schirmer says, Lawless 'counters the idealized view of Mother Ireland as the nurturer of heroism with one in which she is essentially indifferent to, and unworthy of, her exiled leaders'.[13] In a similar manner, 'An Exile's Mother' describes the hardship and poverty in Ireland – 'famine in the land', 'trouble, black and bitter', 'weariness and shame' – and contrasts it with the woman speaker's only consolation: 'my Jamie's safe and well away in France' (23–5). The weather is bleak, the landscape barren and opportunities for betterment scarce in the Ireland Lawless depicts.

Nevertheless, the exile's love and longing for home comes through very strongly in the poems. The Wild Geese section of the collection is introduced by a quotation from Jeremiah 22:10–12: 'Weep not for the dead, neither bemoan him, but weep for him that goeth away, for he shall return no more, nor shall he be seen again in his own country.' In 'Clare Coast', a party of soldiers have briefly returned to Ireland to gather recruits or collect money. Their brave demeanour and outward cheerfulness hide the pain that they feel inside:

> Mirth and song on our lips
> Hearts like lead in our breasts (6)

It is made clear that it is impossible for the group to remain in Ireland and that any opportunities for the future lie elsewhere:

> Death and the grave behind
> Death and a traitor's bier;
> Honour and fame before,
> Why do we linger here? (7)

Ireland is portrayed as cold and sad, a 'sick lone landscape' full of 'struggle and woe' (12), and the only reason for the exiled soldiers' love is that it is the land of their youth. But life as a mercenary soldier is portrayed as an empty honour. The recurring line, 'my Jamie's safe and well away in France' (23–5) in 'An Exile's Mother' becomes profoundly ironic when seen in conjunction with the weary disillusion of the soldiers in 'Clare Coast':

> War-battered dogs are we,
> Fighters in every clime,
> Fillers of trench and grave,
> Mockers, bemocked by time.
> War-dogs, hungry and grey,
> Gnawing a naked bone,
> Fighters in every clime,
> Every cause but our own. (8–9)

In William Linn's opinion, the popularity of Lawless's historical ballads depended to a great extent on their 'rousing, martial rhythm and celebration of the valiant, heroic deed'.[14] The only Wild Geese poem that corresponds to this description is 'Cremona', described as a 'high-hearted story of achievement' in the *Bookman* review.[15] Otherwise, war is rarely depicted as glorious, and the soldiers are seen as tired, homesick cannon-fodder rather than gallant heroes

The value of elevated ideals is questioned in 'The Choice', where the noble motive for leaving home and loved ones is shown not to be worth the sacrifice. The poem charts the anguish of a man faced with either renouncing his faith to be able to stay in Ireland or going into exile:

> Shall I pay the needed toll, just the purchase of a soul,
> Heart and lips, faith and promises to sever?
> Six centuries of strain, six centuries of pain,
> Six centuries cry, 'Never.'
>
> Then let who will abide, for me the Fates decide,
> One road, and only one, for me they show.
> There is room enough out there, room to pray, and room to dare,
> Room out yonder – and I go! (15)

But the second part of the poem suggests that the speaker's idealism and steadfastness are not enough to sustain him in exile. Speaking to his country or his lover, he says:

> Heart of my heart, I faint, I pine to see you,
> Christ! how I hate this alien sea and shore!
> Gaily this night I'd sell my soul to see you,
> Heart of my heart – whom I shall see no more. (16)

In the end, even the price of his soul turns out to be worth paying if it could only guarantee his return home. The only exiles who are able to come home in Lawless's Wild Geese poems are dead, however. The final poem in the section is entitled 'Fontenoy. 1745'. The Battle of Fontenoy, in the Austrian Netherlands, was fought on 11 May 1745 during the War of the Austrian Succession. An army of English, Hanoverian, Dutch and Austrian units was marching to relieve Tournay, which was besieged by the French. The armies met at Fontenoy. The Irish force in the French army helped to break the Allied lines and force a retreat but suffered heavy casualties as a result. It has been estimated that 150,000 Irishmen died in the service of France alone, between 1691 and 1745.[16] Lawless's poem is divided into two parts, before and after the battle. Before the battle, the troops from Clare dream of their lost homes and of the opportunity to fight against their ancient enemy, England:

> The old foe stirs out there, God bless his soul for that!
> The old foe musters strongly, he's coming on at last,
> And Clare's Brigade may claim its own wherever blows fall fast.
> Send us, ye western breezes our full, our rightful share,
> For Faith, and Fame, and Honour, and the ruined hearths of Clare. (28–9)

After the fight, the souls of the dead men are finally able to end their exile and go home to Ireland:

> *'Jesus save you, gentry! why are ye so white,*
> *sitting all so straight and still in this misty light?'*
> 'Nothing ails us, brother; joyous souls are we
> sailing home together, on the morning sea.'

> 'Cousins, friends, and kinsfolk, children of the land,
> Here we come together, a merry rousing band;
> Sailing home together from the last great fight,
> Home to Clare from Fontenoy, in the morning light.' (30–1)

The stirring picture of valiant Irish soldiers eager to engage their ancient enemy and the moving image of the dead souls floating home at dawn ensured that the poem was one of those included in the school curriculum.[17] As Ernest Boyd says, 'Fontenoy. 1745' 'attained to the rank of a popular classic'.[18] Several poems about the battle highlight the valour and chivalry of the Irish soldiers, such as Bartholomew Dowling's 'Battle of Fontenoy' and Thomas Davis's 'Fontenoy'.[19] Lawless's poem rather emphasises the futility of heroism and can be seen as a response to the militaristic tone in these earlier pieces. The happiness of the home-coming dead is apparent, as is the deep sadness felt during the time of banishment described in the other Wild Geese poems. What is more difficult to discern is why the exiles should harbour such deep feelings for their country in the first place. The picture of Ireland that emerges in these poems is bleak in the extreme, and a poem such as 'After Aughrim' certainly problematises the connection between the mother-country and her people. The Wild Geese poems are melancholy evocations of loss, love and homesickness, but there are no celebrations of Ireland that manage to explain these feelings.

Apart from the Wild Geese poems, the most well-known piece in the collection is the 'Dirge of the Munster Forest. 1581'. The poem beautifully connects the dying forest with the conquered nation. According to Lady Gregory, Lawless wrote the poem after she had read the records of Charles Blount Mountjoy's campaign to subdue the insurrection in Ireland in the final stages of the Nine Years War.[20] A description of Mountjoy's scorched earth tactics is included in Lawless's history *Ireland* (1887):

> Mountjoy established military stations at different points in the north, and proceeded to demolish everything that lay between them. With a deliberation which left little to be desired he made his soldiers destroy every living speck of green that was to be seen, burn every roof, and slaughter every beast which could not be conveniently driven into camp. [. . .] The ground was burnt to the very sod; all harvest utterly cleared away; starvation in its most grisly forms again began to stalk the land; the people perished by tens of thousands, and the tales told by eye-witnesses of what they themselves had seen at this time are too sickening to be allowed needlessly to blacken these pages.[21]

The English army cut down the forests to ensure that the Irish rebels had nowhere to hide[22] and, in the poem, the dying forest asks all the wood creatures, save the wolf, to attend the funeral of the Irish dead:

> Bring out the hemlock! bring the funeral yew!
> The faithful ivy that doth all enfold;
> Heap high the rocks, the patient brown earth strew,
> And cover them against the numbing cold.
> Marshal my retinue of bird and beast,

Wren, titmouse, robin, birds of every hue;
Let none keep back, no, not the very least,
Nor fox, nor deer, nor tiny nibbling crew,
Only bid one of all my forest clan
Keep far from us on this funeral day.
On the grey wolf I lay my sovereign ban,
The great grey wolf who scrapes the earth away;
Lest, with hooked claw and furious hunger, he
Lay bare my dead for gloating foes to see –
Lay bare my dead, who died, and died for me.

For I must shortly die as they have died,
And lo! My doom stands yoked and linked with theirs;
The axe is sharpened to cut down my pride:
I pass, I die, and leave no natural heirs. (35–6)

The *Leader* reviewer regards the dirges that make up the second section of *With the Wild Geese* as frigid and conventional,[23] and at least 'The Dirge of the Munster Forest' seems to owe a great deal to convention or example. William Linn has noticed the striking similarities between the poem and the funeral song for Marcello sung by Vittoria Corombona's mother, Cornelia, in John Webster's *The White Devil* (1612):[24]

Call for the robin-redbreast, and the wren,
Since o'er shady groves they hover,
And with leaves and flow'rs do cover
The friendless bodies of unburied men.
Call unto his funeral dole
The ant, the field-mouse and the mole,
To rear him hillocks, that shall keep him warm,
And (when gay tombs are robb'd) sustain no harm, –
But keep the wolf far thence, that's foe to men,
For with his nails he'll dig them up agen.[25]

The images are clearly the same in both texts. It is possible, of course, that the resemblance is a matter of intertextual linking, in which case the fact that the song in Webster's play is sung over the corpse of a murdered man could install the idea that Mountjoy's war methods were no better than wholesale murder. Lawless was familiar with sixteenth- and seventeenth-century English literature, and could very well have read Webster. On the other hand, the editorial comment to Webster's play makes clear that there was a superstitious belief that when the wolf uncovered a corpse this was a sign of murder, and Lawless might have built her poem around this superstition, without conscious or unconscious reference to Webster's work.[26]

Six of the poems in *With the Wild Geese* are set in the Aran Islands. One of these, 'Above the Cliff: A Monologue', looks forward to the thought-poems in Lawless's second collection, *The Point of View* (1909), and deals with the question of God's existence and whether life is a dream. At the least the *Leader* commentator, Chanel, considered the theme unsuitable for a woman – 'strange problem for a lady!' [27] In 'Looking Eastward' the speaker looks from the island of Aranmore across to the Irish mainland.[28] The land has been forsaken by God:

> Only *thou,* only *thou,* hast stood from the dawn to the gloaming
> Holding out empty hands, pleading in vain to thy God. (51)

In Chanel's opinion, such lines make the poem next to blasphemous and the reviewer considers it 'a sad feature, indeed, of Miss Lawless's work that she seems to find little consolation in any spiritual hope'.[29] There are large exclamation marks next to these lines in the copy of the review in Marsh's Library, Dublin, presumably put there by Lawless herself or someone close to her. But Chanel's comment is partly correct: there is no sense of either spiritual or earthly faith in the future in the poem. Ireland is depicted as land without hope and there is a slight implication that, somehow, both the land and the people are responsible for this hopelessness:

> What, say what hast thou done, land not wanting in beauty?
> What, say what hast thou done, race not wanting in spirit?
> What antenatal guilt, hid in the womb of creation,
> Robbed thee of honour and pelf, robbed thee of peace and plenty? (51–2)

The poem includes the suggestion that a saint could plead for the islands and bring about the end of strife and the return of joy, but, in the end, this does not seem possible:

> Was there ever so stalwart a saint, ever so dauntless a pleader;
> Strong, persistent, resolved, vowed in the end to prevail?
> Nay, I know not, I see not; nought see I but the vapours
> Rolling eternally in; heavy, tenacious, unkind;

> Thicker and thicker still, hiding the land in their clutches,
> Wrapping it carefully round, as a corpse is wrapped in its cere-cloth;
> Leaving me, feebly lamenting, here in the mist and the darkness,
> Staring with purblind eyes; puzzled, unquiet, despondent. (55)

The concluding 'A Retort' is the only poem in the collection that contains a clear attack on English oppression:

> *You* swept them vacant! Your decree
> Bid all her budding commerce cease;
> *You* drove her from your subject sea,
> To starve in peace! (93)

Nevertheless, such pessimistic views of Ireland's past or future are balanced by the more hopeful note of, for instance, 'To a Tuft of White Bog-Cotton, Growing in the Tyrol' (75–80) and in the final lines of 'A Retort':

> I see her in those coming days,
> Still young, still gay; her unbound hair
> Crowned with a crown of starlike rays,
> Serenely fair.
>
> I see an envied haunt of peace,
> Calm and untouched; remote from roar,
> Where wearied men may from their burdens cease
> On a still shore. (94–5)

These poems hold out a promise of peace for Ireland and convey a sense of optimism that is wholly absent in 'Looking Eastward'.

Horace Plunkett wrote to Lawless that 'the "Wild Geese" appeal especially to me in my struggles with Irish sentiment. I am always grateful for any help to understand the historical basis of a moral force which seems to have so little justification in the logic of current events.'[30] It is difficult to ascertain exactly what he might have had in mind. Except for in 'A Retort', and, even there, primarily by inference, since England is not mentioned, Lawless does not explicitly blame English colonial policies for conditions in Ireland, but the unspoken accusation hovers behind her depictions of the peasants' miserable existence and the soldiers' hatred for England. The reviewer for the *Times Literary Supplement* even considers that every line 'conveys an accusation against England'.[31] Mrs Humphry Ward clearly interpreted the collection as an expression of nationalist sentiment: 'her best poems – "The Dirge of the Munster Forest," or "After Aughrim" – give a voice to Irish suffering and Irish patriotism which it would be hard to parallel in the Nationalist or rebel literature of recent years'.[32] Hugh Alexander Law, likewise, attempted to find a place for Lawless within the nationalist canon, despite his awareness of her political opinions:

> That one who was a life-long Unionist in politics, and had many English and few Gaelic sympathies, should yet have written *Clare Coast*, *The Choice*, *Cremona*, *An Exile's Mother*, *The Dirge of the Munster Forest*, and (best of all) *The Dirge for All Ireland* is one more reminder that 'poetry and patriotism are each other's guardian angels and therefore inseparable', that to-day as aforetime our poets have 'endless diversities of character, though but one spirit', and that now as always, 'there is room for all'.[33]

Commenting on the selection of Lawless's poems republished in 1965, Liam Hourican continues the project of including Lawless in the canon of nationalist literature:

> The patriotic songs, those poignant, half-realised evocations, are indispensable for the insight they give on the problem of self-definition which so afflicted Ireland throughout the nineteenth century. They are precisely the kind of thing Yeats had in mind when he spoke of 'a community bound together by imaginative possessions'.[34]

The poems nourish the cultural memory of oppression in many ways, but, even so, their questioning attitude to the past, to heroism and to Ireland as inspiring force means that they cannot be fully accommodated within a nationalist paradigm. As Gregory A. Schirmer says, Lawless not only 'affirms the value of the past but also interrogates it, rewriting the essentially monolithic tradition of popular nationalist poetry and forcing a reconsideration of the assumptions about Irish identity that lay behind it'.[35] The politics of the collection remains unclear.

*

In spite of the ambiguous messages conveyed in the poems, *With the Wild Geese* has most often been considered as a celebration of the Irish west and the Irish past. In contrast to most other critics, however, Padraic Fallon does not 'care for Emily's patriotic songs' and finds her later work much more valuable.[36] Lawless's second volume of verse, *The Point of View: Some Talks and Disputations* (1909), was sold for 'the benefit of some of the fishing people of Galway Bay'.[37] The collection contains poetry of thought rather than of place, and most of the poems have a conversational quality and specific addressees. The tone is unemotional. The opening 'Prelude' deals with the problem of communication, and several of the poems, such as 'The Friendly God', 'Shall All Then Perish' and 'Kinship', debate questions of science versus faith, God's existence, evolution, old age, death and the meaning of life. As Elizabeth Grubgeld says, this Victorian kind of poetry, reminiscent of Hopkins, Tennyson and the Pre-Raphaelites, was not appreciated by 'the post-war critical establishment', which further contributed to Lawless's disappearance from the canon of Irish literature.[38]

The poems do not seem to have been very widely appreciated in Ireland. Lady Gregory writes that 'in this little privately printed volume I cannot find anything to care for', and considers the verses 'talks' more than poems.[39] One of these talks she believes to be aimed at Yeats. From what Lady Gregory relates in her journal, Lawless and Yeats had an argument about writing for money versus writing for the sake of art, where Lawless maintained that the responsibility to family and dependants was more important than the hope to produce a masterpiece.[40] 'To Some of Us Who Put Art Above Work' repeats this claim:

> Bards, who lay bare your little gifts of rhyme
> Upon the altar of grim smiling Time,
> Who to the immortal Few would fain belong,
> And rack the very heavens for one song!
> What are your vaunted doings light or grave
> Laid beside those of one who, songless, gave
> Life's dearest peace to help, to draw, to save? (19)

'To a Rhyming Contemporary' even disputes the value of writing at all:

> Toss your visions to the wind,
> Poet! Leave no word behind,
> Better so,
> Why fond reveries rehearse,
> Meditations tell in verse? (15)

Yet, 'The End of an Argument' strikes a more conciliatory note and accepts that difference of opinion is part of the human condition and only

God, or some 'vague shadowy third' (45), can ever provide the final answer:

> So now. Be sure that neither thou nor I,
> Nor all this world's wild disputants are right;
> Whether in calm-eyed confidence, in despair,
> They stand and crouch – to all alike comes night. (45)

Published only four years before Lawless's death, many of the poems are concerned with existential problems. In 'Kinship: An Evolutionary Problem' Lawless sees all humankind as the sum of everything that has gone before, including the primeval slime that held the beginning of life. The poem looks forward to the present-day eco-feminist idea that man does not master nature, prominent also in *A Garden Diary* (1901). God does not value human beings higher than any other part of the creation:

> Only of this be sure –
> That He who ruleth hath no preference,
> No narrow choice, no blind exclusiveness;
> We and our kin, to the last drop of blood,
> The first dull dawn of hovering consciousness,
> Shall share and share. Aye, and not only we,
> But all the crowned denizens of Space,
> World after world, till the long muster-roll
> Be closed and sealed. (50–1)

At least in 'Kinship', Lawless's creed seems to be pantheistic. We are all 'myriad parts of one vast whole', where nothing is more valuable than anything else and God is the 'Wholeness' where everything can find its own 'larger Self' (*The Point of View*, 51). Most of Lawless's nature writing is informed by the idea that experiences of the natural world may lead to spiritual renewal:

> Assuredly man is by nature a devotional creature, however little of the dogmatic may mingle with his devotions. He may avert his ear from the church-going Bell, he may refuse to label himself with the label of any particular denomination, but it is only to be overtaken with awe in the heart of a forest, and to fall on his knees, as it were, in some green secluded spot of wilderness. The sense of something benignant close at hand, of some pitying eye surveying one, is so vivid at certain moments of one's life that it actually needs a rough conscious effort if one would shake it off.

Even the sense of the vastness of that arena upon which our poor little drama is played out, even this habitual impression becomes less grimly crushing at such moments than usual. What if it *is* colossal, one says to oneself, and what if, as compared to it, ourselves and our troubles *are* infinitesimal? what if they count no more in the scheme of things than do the afflictions of a broken-legged mouse, or of a crushed beetle? Very well; be it so. The mouse and the beetle have, after all, each their allotted place in that scheme. Nay for aught we know to the contrary, each may be susceptible of the same profound, if intangible, consolation.[41]

There is no difference in value between mice, insects or human beings. What distinguishes different creatures from each other is their varying purposes in the overall scheme.

The poems in *The Point of View* are closer to prose than verse, but do not really succeed as either. The metre is often uneven and unsure and, instead of using meaningful images to contain the central idea, Lawless is apt to be wordy. The thought may be interesting, but it disappears in verbosity and awkward expressions. Nevertheless, a poem like 'Kinship' is closely related to the vision of the interspace that runs through her writing in that it expresses a refusal to erect boundaries, not only between people, but between all natural phenomena.

*

The posthumous *The Inalienable Heritage and Other Poems* (1914) can be described as a combination of the previous collections, mixing pseudo-Elizabethan poetry of ideas with Irish ballad-poetry such as 'The Third Trumpet' and lyrical nature descriptions like 'From the Burren'. Many of the poems are formally weak, as Edith Sichel points out in her preface to the collection, and the eloquence Sichel admires frequently comes across as tedious wordiness today.[42] Lawless was influenced by Elizabethan poetry, but her attempts to recreate the style of the period are concentrated on language, not form or themes, and the result is an archaic tone that often seems unwarranted. Liam Hourican sees the uneven style of Lawless's poetry as a result of the uncertain aesthetic ideals of the time:

She began to write in a period of stylistic irresolution, the Romantic movement having declined into Pre-Raphaelite lethargy. Her style is timid and picturesque, appropriate enough for poetic reverie or the conjurings of the Celtic twilight, but too frail to embody with complete success the sturdy themes she sets herself.[43]

The reviewer for the *Times Literary Supplement* suggests that Lawless 'was writing verse when she ought to have been writing prose, or when her sense had not cleared itself enough to find a verse to suit it', and the pieces in *The Inalienable Heritage* are more examples of poetic diction than poetry.[44] On the whole, the collection fails to engage.

The title poem is a celebration of the early Irish missionaries who travelled throughout the known world to preach Christianity, and 'The Third Trumpet' describes a young girl who risks her life to fetch a priest to her dying mother. Such narrative poems are among the most successful pieces in the collection, partly because they succeed as stories, partly because the ballad format is suited to the poetic language Lawless employs. A few autobiographical poems, such as 'Resurgence' and 'Night Sounds', are concerned with Lawless's failing health, and contain intimate descriptions of her struggles with pain and insomnia. Most of the poems, however, deal with the west of Ireland and are variations of the themes found in most of Lawless's nature writing. 'From the Burren', for instance, shows an understanding of landscape as a source of spiritual wisdom:

> No mindless tract of earth or strand thou seem'st,
> Such as dull maps and solemn charts attest.
> Here 'mid your solitudes, as 'mid the crowds,
> Alike for me thou shinest, realm apart;
> Open to all we pine for, pray for, hope;
> Sanctified Home-land of th' unchanging heart.[45]

As in the article 'North Clare – Leaves from a Diary', Lawless envisions the Burren as an interspace that cannot be pinned down on a map, a landscape that speaks to the heart but cannot be grasped intellectually. In Ernest Boyd's view, Lawless 'never fails to voice the intimate relation of the human spirit to its natural surroundings', and landscape in Lawless's poetry acquires meaning through the emotions it inspires, not primarily because of its outward aspect.[46] In another poem about the area, 'To that Rare and Deep-Red Burnet-Moth Only to be Met with in the Burren', she describes the region as 'gaunt and grim as the halls of Death' (37), recalling the description introducing the novel *Hurrish,* where the hills are seen as skeletons embodied in the land.[47] The red moth becomes a symbol of hope and love in the bleak landscape, pointing to the possibility of beauty even in the harshest of environments.

The idea of Ireland as a country that always inspires love, even though external reasons for this seem to be absent, is prominent in almost all Lawless's Irish poetry, in *The Inalienable Heritage* as well as in the other collections. 'The Shadow on the Shore' imagines Ireland's power over her people as supernatural:

> Oh, woman-country, weak, yet strangely strong,
> What witchery doth to thy cold skies belong,
> What spells are thine, all other lands apart,
> Which cling so closely, madly to the heart?
> Is it such wandering ghosts as hover here,
> Or thine own tireless dreams that keep thee young and dear? (46)

Though the poem expresses intense love for Ireland, the references to 'cold skies' and 'wandering ghosts' strengthen the idea that this love is paradoxical. In 'Spain,' Ireland's bleakness is contrasted with the beauty of the Spanish landscape, but, even though Ireland fails to measure up, the speaker still prefers it:

> In the land I have left the skies are cold,
> The earth is green, the rocks are bare,
> Yet the devil may hold all your blue and your gold
> Were I only back there! (68)

'Spain: A Drinking Song' repeats the idea of profound love for an unlovable land:

> A queen is she, though a queen forlorn,
> A queen of tears from her birth.
> Ragged and hungry, woeful and worn,
> Yet the fairest Fair on the earth. (69)

'A Famine Cry' questions the idealised image of Ireland even more clearly:

> Oh skeleton with the hungry jaw,
> Corpse-snatcher, armed with tooth and claw,
> Not satiate yet? Thy lustful maw?
>
> Eiré, to *you* our love we gave,
> Our mother-mistress, now our grave,
> Be pitiful for once, and save!

In these poems, as in 'After Aughrim' in *With the Wild Geese,* Ireland is figured as a woman, but without the characteristics usually connected with femininity, except, sometimes, for weakness. The 'woman-country' is barren, uninviting, unable to protect her people and beautiful only against the odds. Whereas national feeling is present throughout, nationalism understood as trust and belief in Ireland's future is not and, in this, the poems express a critique of popular nationalism at the time. Most of Lawless's Irish poems problematise rather than eulogise the connection between country and people.

Although the collections *With the Wild Geese, The Point of View* and *The Inalienable Heritage* could not be defined as feminist poetry, it could be argued that they to some extent encompass a feminist attitude to both the world and the woman poet. The image of Ireland as a woman who is neither nurturing nor kind to her children contains a challenge to both conventional perceptions of women and romanticised representations of Ireland. Lawless's forms – historical ballads and philosophical poetry of thought rather than pretty lyrics – suggest that she wrote herself into a masculine instead of a feminine tradition, as does the fact that her main influences were the Elizabethan poets. The themes of war, natural science, evolution and the world of ideas are also more readily connected with male writers, and the *Leader* reviewer Chanel's contention that the exploration of life as a dream in the poem 'Above the Cliff: A Monologue' was a strange issue for a woman to tackle indicates that some of Lawless's subjects were indeed regarded as unfeminine. Lawless's poetry emanates from the double legacy of romantic nationalism and intellectual scepticism. This doubleness in her poetry has frequently been ignored. The attempts to integrate her work in the nationalist canon and thus create a place for Lawless in the male-dominated field of Irish literature have paradoxically feminised her poetry by emphasising its romantic and sentimental aspects and downplaying its complexity.

Chapter 7

Writing the interspace

The tendency among critics, now and historically, to overemphasise political themes and writers' political allegiances has led to a vision of literary culture in nineteenth-century Ireland as a system of polarities where writers occupy either-or positions. Works that transcend political boundaries – nationalist, unionist, feminist or other – have frequently been ignored. Reading paradigms that privilege clear and unambiguous standpoints has served to deny or at least conceal the possibility of a third alternative and have rarely managed to accommodate texts that fluctuate between opposite positions.

There may be problems reclaiming writers who do not fit neatly into a camp, but it is eminently necessary if criticism is not to establish new sets of exclusions and silencings. Retrieving the works of nineteenth-century Irish women writers requires the critic too scrutinise his or her own activities more closely and be open enough to acknowledge ambivalent and seemingly reactionary ideas in the texts. An open attitude is necessary not only because what may look reactionary now may well have been radical in the past, but also because ideologies like nationalism and feminism have many faces, and their nineteenth-century appearances may be very different from their twenty-first-century manifestations. Without knowledge about Emily Lawless and other women writers, the picture of Irish history and culture would be skewed and incomplete. Readers and writers alike would lose important links with the tradition, and would have to start afresh again and again and again.

Taken as a whole, and frequently also in individual instances, the works of Emily Lawless are deeply contradictory. They cannot even be described as advocating a third position or a hybrid alternative, but shift between opposites in a dialogue that never settles into a coherent resolution. They blur the boundaries between genres, with poetry that resembles prose, descriptions of naturalist pursuits included in fictional texts and scientific observations presented in semi-fictional form or in a highly personal manner. Her early novels introduce feminist ideas into the patriarchal genre of the popular romance. The Irish novel *Grania* is a strong plea for women's right to autonomy, yet Lawless publicly dissociated herself from the struggle for women's suffrage. She writes herself into the male-dominated disciplines of natural science, geography, historiography and biography-writing, but does not assume the voice of authority that governs these fields. In *Hurrish* she offers caricatures of Irish people, though in other works she rejects the notion of national types and throughout her writing she questions the idea of an essential definition of Irishness. The conflict between place-defined and group-defined identity recurs throughout her work. Her historical novels present poignant pictures of Irish suffering at the same time as they make clear that English oppression was a logical effect of the ideological views of the age. On the one hand, she expresses the belief that a strong leader might have saved Ireland, on the other, she returns to the pantheistic vision that all life is connected and every living thing has equal value. The binary oppositions underwriting rigid gender definitions and national loyalties are interrogated but not resolved or reversed.

Lawless was aware that it was an impossible task to try to communicate an unbroken picture of reality: 'We are but poor, bedimmed mirrors all of us, and what we reflect is rarely the real thing, more often only some blurred and distorted image projected by our own sad selves'.[1] The doubleness that characterises her writing expresses her negotiations between ultimately incompatible positions. As a woman and an intellectual, she struggled with finding a place for herself as a writer at a time when women were expected to deal with only domestic themes. Lawless engaged with issues like science, history and war, areas that were clearly in the masculine domain, and when she uses the male narrative voice or a personal style that seems to diminish her claim to authority, this might be seen as a way of minimising the challenge of a woman entering fields regarded as unfeminine. She was writing for predominantly English readers, yet trying to establish a distinguishably Irish voice, and her attempts to negotiate the expectations of both English and Irish readers are frequently manifested as dialogic writing. Her position as an Anglo-Irish writer with nationalist sympathies but unionist politics lies behind the tension between an intense love for the country but a lack of trust in the emerging nation that permeates her work. Above all, her dialogic writing embodies her reluctance to accept a single identity, whether in gender or national terms.

There is room for opposites in an environment understood as an interspace, because this space is inherently contradictory and constantly shifting. If, as Simon Schama maintains, landscapes are mental representation of what we experience on the inside,[2] Lawless's vision of the interspace reveals a great deal about how she looked upon her own position. Apart from being spatially incoherent, the interspace is clearly ambiguously gendered, and this insistence on indistinctness is deeply bound up with Lawless's need to envision an Irish and a female identity that allows difference. The interspace signifies openness, allowance and accommodation, profoundly meaningful concepts in relation to Lawless's situation as a professional woman writer and an Anglo-Irish aristocrat insecure about her future in the country she loves. By representing Ireland as an interspace, Lawless is able to acknowledge the complexities, contradictions and ambiguities that characterised both her world and her own place in it. At a time when divisions between Us and Them were too often seen as absolute, this is a powerful challenge.

Bibliography

Primary sources

Lawless, Emily, 'An Addition to Mr. Birchall's List of 'The Lepidoptera of Ireland', *Entomologist's Monthly Magazine* vol. 3, Jan. 1867, p. 187

——, *Atlantic Rhymes and Rhythms*. Printed by S. S. [Lady Sarah Spencer] for herself and four others, 1898

——, 'A Bardic Chronicle', *Nineteenth Century* vol. 30, 1891, pp. 643–57

——, 'A Biscayan Stroll', *The Gentleman's Magazine* vol. 28, 1882, pp. 26–39

——, *The Book of Gilly: Four Months Out of a Life*, London: Smith & Elder, 1906

——, 'Borroughdale of Borroughdale I-II', *Macmillan's Magazine* vol. 51, 1884, pp. 38–56. Rpt. in *Littell's Living Age* 163, 20 Dec. 1884, pp. 738–46 and in *Plain Frances Mowbray and Other Tales,* London: John Murray, 1889

——, 'Borroughdale of Borroughdale III–IV', *Macmillan's Magazine* vol. 51, Dec. 1884, pp. 134–49. Rpt. in *Littell's Living Age* vol. 164, 3 Jan. 1885, pp. 13–23; vol. 164, 10 Jan. 1885, pp. 75–84, and in *Plain Frances Mowbray and Other Tales,* London: John Murray, 1889

——, 'The Builder of the Round Towers: A Chronicle of the Eighth Century', *Nineteenth Century,* vol. 37, 1895, pp. 421–34. Rpt. in *Littell's Living Age* vol. 205, 13 Apr. 1895, pp. 104–13

——, *A Chelsea Householder,* 3 vols., London: Sampson Low, 1882

——, *A Chelsea Householder,* 1882; New York: Henry Holt, 1883

——, 'Collaboration – a Note', in Emily Lawless and Shan Bullock, *The Race of Castlebar: Being a Narrative Addressed by Mr. John Bunbury to His Brother Mr. Theodore Bunbury,* London: John Murray, 1913, n. p.

——, *A Colonel of the Empire: From the Private Papers of Mangan O'Driscoll, Late of the Imperial Service of Austria, and a Knight of the Military Order of Maria Theresa,* New York: Appleton, 1895

——, 'Compensation', *Outlook* vol. 16.402, Oct. 1905, p. 516. Rpt. in *Littell's Living Age* vol. 247, 10 Dec. 1905, p. 770

——, 'Connaught Homes', *Monthly Review* vol. 31.11.1, April 1903, pp. 143 ff. Rpt. in *Littell's Living Age* vol. 237, 1903, pp. 556–72

——, 'A Dredging Ground', *Nineteenth Century* vol. 10, 1881, pp. 131–41

——, 'Earnest Tommy', *Vanity Fair,* 7 Dec. 1905, n. p.

——, 'Florentine Gardens in March', *Nineteenth Century* vol. 45, 1899, pp. 327–35. Rpt. in *Littell's Living Age* vol. 220, 18 Mar. 1899, pp. 689–95

——, 'Fragments of Irish Chronicles: Gerald the Great (Concluded)', *Nineteenth Century* vol. 29, 1891, pp. 429–44

——, *A Garden Diary: September, 1899–September, 1900,* London: Methuen, 1901

——, *Grania: The Story of an Island,* 2 vols., London: Smith & Elder, 1892

——, *Grania: The Story of an Island,* 2 vols., 1892; New York: Garland, 1979

——, 'How Art Kavanaugh Fought Richard the King: A Fourteenth Century Chronicle', *Nineteenth Century* vol. 28, 1890, pp. 355–68. Rpt. as 'How Art Kavanaugh of Wexford Fought Richard the King' in *Traits and Confidences,* London: Methuen, 1897

——, *Hurrish: A Study,* 2 vols., Edinburgh: Blackwood & Sons, 1886

——, *Hurrish: A Study,* 1886; Leipzig: Bernard Tauchnitz, 1888

——, *Hurrish: A Study,* 2 vols., 1886; New York: Garland, 1979

——, *Hurrish: A Study,* 1886; Belfast: Appletree, 1992

——, 'Iar-Connaught: A Sketch', *Cornhill Magazine* vol. 45, Mar. 1882, pp. 319–33

——, *The Inalienable Heritage and Other Poems,* privately printed, London: R. Clay, 1914

——, 'In the Kingdom of Kerry', *The Gentleman's Magazine* vol. 28, 1882, pp. 540–53

——, 'In the Night', *Littell's Living Age* vol. 282, 19 Sep. 1914, p. 706

——, *Ireland: With Some Additions by Mrs. Arthur Bronson,* London: Fisher Unwin, 1887, 1898

——, *Ireland: With Some Additions by Mrs. Arthur Bronson,* New York: G. P. Putnam's, 1887

——, *Ireland: With Some Additions by Mrs. Arthur Bronson,* rev. ed. with two new chapters, London: Fisher Unwin, 1912

——, *Ireland: With Some Additions by Mrs. Arthur Bronson,* 3rd rev. ed., London: Fisher Unwin, 1923

——, 'Irish Captures in 1870 and 1871', *Entomologist* vol. 6, 1882, pp. 74–78 and 97–100

——, 'Irish Chronicles: Gerald the Great', *Nineteenth Century* vol. 28, 1890, pp. 733–49

——, 'Irish Memories–West and East', in Margaret Waterfield (ed.), *Flower Grouping in English, Scotch and Irish Gardens,* London: J. M. Dent, 1907, pp. 3–26

——, 'Lament of Ireland for Her Children', *Littell's Living Age* vol. 234, 1902, p. 448

——, *Maelcho: A Sixteenth Century Narrative,* London: Smith & Elder, 1894

——, *Maelcho: A Sixteenth Century Narrative,* 1894; London: Methuen, 1895

——, *Maelcho: A Sixteenth Century Narrative,* 1894; New York: Garland, 1979

——, *Major Lawrence, F. L. S.,* 3 vols., London: John Murray, 1887

——, *Major Lawrence, F. L. S.,* New York: Henry Holt, 1887

——, 'Major Lawrence, F. L. S', *Murray's Magazine* vol. 1, 1887, pp. 81–835. Rpt. in *Littell's Living Age* vol. 173, 23 Apr. 1887, pp. 203–20; vol. 173, 30 Apr. 1887, pp. 269–84; vol. 173, 14 May 1887, pp. 397–408; vol. 173,

21 May 1887, pp. 462–73; vol. 173, 4 Jun. 1887, pp. 589–600; vol. 174, 2. Jul. 1887, pp. 47–55; vol. 174, 9 Jul. 1887, pp. 76–81; vol. 174, 6 Aug. 1887, pp. 336–45; vol. 174, 13 Aug. 1887, pp. 414–19; vol. 174, 27 Aug. 1887, pp. 532–9; vol. 174, 3 Sep. 1887, pp. 587–93; vol. 175, 22 Oct. 1887, pp. 153–62; vol. 175, 29 Oct. 1887, pp. 224–30; vol. 175, 12 Nov. 1887, pp. 334–43; vol. 175, 19 Nov. 1887, pp. 412–18; vol. 175, 3 Dec. 1887, pp. 528–43. Republished as *Major Lawrence, F. L. S.,* London: Jhn Murray, 1887

——, *Maria Edgeworth,* London: Macmillan, 1904

——, *A Millionaire's Cousin: A Story,* London: Macmillan, 1885

——, 'A Millionaire's Cousin: A Story I–III', *Macmillan's Magazine* vol. 51, Jan. 1885, pp. 215–30. Rpt. in *Littell's Living Age* vol. 164, 7 Feb. 1885, pp. 329–42. Republished as *A Millionaire's Cousin: A Story,* London: Macmillan, 1885

——, 'A Millionaire's Cousin: A Story IV–VI', *Macmillan's Magazine* vol. 51, Feb. 1885, pp. 295–309; 375–91. Rpt. in *Littell's Living Age* vol. 164, 7 Mar. 1885, pp. 621–32. Republished as *A Millionaire's Cousin: A Story,* London: Macmillan, 1885

——, 'A Millionaire's Cousin: A Story VII–IX', *Macmillan's Magazine* vol. 51, Mar. 1885, pp. 375–91. Rpt. in *Littell's Living Age* vol. 164, 28 Mar. 1885, pp. 784–97. Republished as *A Millionaire's Cousin: A Story,* London: Macmillan, 1885

——, 'Mrs. O'Donnell's Report', *English Illustrated Magazine* (?) vol. 10, 717 ff. Rpt. in *Traits and Confidences,* London: Methuen, 1897

——, 'A Munster Skirmish (Circa 1581)', *Irish Review* vol. 1, 1911, pp. 217–18

——, 'Namesakes', *Temple Bar* vol. 69, Dec. 1883, pp. 495–507. Rpt. in *Plain Frances Mowbray and Other Tales,* London: John Murray, 1889

——, 'North Clare – Leaves from a Diary', *Nineteenth Century* vol. 46, 1899, pp. 603–12

——, 'A Note on the Ethics of Literary Forgery', *Nineteenth Century* vol. 41, 1897, pp. 84–95. Rpt. in *Littell's Living Age* vol. 212, 1897, 613 ff.

——, 'Notes in the Morbihan', *National Review,* vol. 4, 1884–85, pp. 492–503

——, 'Of the Personal Element in History', *Nineteenth Century* vol. 50, 1901, pp. 790–8. Rpt. in *Eclectic Magazine* vol. 138, 183 ff., and in *Littell's Living Age* vol. 231, 1901, 835 ff.

——, 'Old Lord Kilconnell', *Murray's Magazine* vol. 8, n. d., 229 ff. Rpt. in *Littell's Living Age* vol. 186, 6 Sep. 1890, pp. 614–22, and in *Traits and Confidences,* London: Methuen, 1897

——, 'Overstrand–Evening', *Littell's Living Age* vol. 282, 5 Sep. 1914, p. 578

——, *Plain Frances Mowbray and Other Tales,* London: John Murray, 1889

——, *Plain Frances Mowbray and Other Tales,* 1889; New York: Garland, 1979

——, 'Plain Frances Mowbray: Part I', *Blackwood's Magazine* vol. 137, Feb. 1885, pp. 245–68. Rpt. in *Plain Frances Mowbray and Other Tales,* London: John Murray, 1889

——, 'Plain Frances Mowbray: Part II', *Blackwood's Magazine* vol. 137, Mar. 1885, pp. 326–53. Rpt. in *Plain Frances Mowbray and Other Tales,* London: John Murray, 1889

——, *The Poems of Emily Lawless,* ed. Padraic Fallon, Dublin: Dolmen Press, 1965

——, *The Point of View: Some Talks and Disputations,* privately printed, London: Richard Clay & Sons, 1909

——, 'Quin Lough', *Murray's Magazine* vol. 4, n. d., 509 ff. Rpt. in *Littell's Living Age* 179, 10 Nov. 1888, pp. 331–45, and in *Plain Frances Mowbray and Other Tales,* London: John Murray, 1889

——, 'A Reminiscence', *Monthly Review* vol. 14, 1903, p. 112

——, 'A Renegade: I–II', *Macmillan's Magazine* vol. 49, Mar. 1884, pp. 350–62. Rpt. as 'A Ligurian Episode' in *Plain Frances Mowbray and Other Tales,* London: John Murray, 1889

——, 'A Renegade: III–V', *Macmillan's Magazine* vol. 49, Apr. 1884, pp. 444–59. Rpt. as 'A Ligurian Episode' in *Plain Frances Mowbray and Other Tales,* London: John Murray, 1889

——, 'Reply', *Living Age* vol. 248, 1906, p. 322

——, 'Some Mothing Memories', *Monthly Review* vol. 7.3, 147 ff. Rpt. in *Eclectic Magazine* vol. 139, 688 ff., and *Littell's Living Age* vol. 234, 1902, pp. 414–19

——, *Traits and Confidences,* London: Methuen, 1897

——, *Traits and Confidences,* 1897; New York: Garland, 1979

——, 'Two Leaves from a Note-Book', *Alexandra College Magazine,* Jun. 1895, pp. 242–50

——, 'An Upland Bog', *Belgravia* vol. 45, 1881, pp. 417–30

——, 'Verse: A Reply', *Outlook* 16.411, Dec. 1905, p. 863. Rpt. in *Littell's Living Age* vol. 248, 10 Feb. 1906, p. 322

——, 'Vision of England', *Eclectic Magazine* vol. 139, n. d., p. 476. Rpt. in *Littell's Living Age* vol. 234, 1902, p. 640

——, 'Vision of Law', *Eclectic Magazine* vol. 139, n. d., p. 476

——, 'W. E. H. Lecky: A Reminiscence', *Monthly Review,* vol. 14.41, Feb. 1904, pp. 112–26

——, 'Wide is the Shannon', *Outlook* vol. 17.423, Mar. 1906, p. 340. Rpt. in *Littell's Living Age* vol. 249, 26 May 1906, p. 250

——, *With Essex in Ireland, Being Extracts from a Diary Kept in Ireland during the Year 1599 by Mr. Henry Harvey, Edited by Hon. Emily Lawless,* London: Smith & Elder, 1890

——, *With Essex in Ireland,* 1890; New York: Garland, 1979

——, *With the Wild Geese,* London: Isbister, 1902

Lawless, Emily and Shan Bullock, *The Race of Castlebar: Being a Narrative Addressed by Mr. John Bunbury to His Brother Mr. Theodore Bunbury* London: John Murray, 1913

Letters

Cloncurry, Elizabeth, Letter to W. E. H. Lecky, Lecky correspondence, Trinity College Dublin, MS 1827–36/455

Cooper, Venetia, Letter to Mr Graves, 17 Jul. 1914, National Library Dublin, MS 13829

Lawless, Emily, Letters, University of Illinois, Bentley papers

——, Letter to Mrs Boyle, Oxford, Bodleian Library, MS. Autogr. b. 9, p. 471

——, Letter to Rhoda Broughton, 9 Oct. n. y., Delves Broughton Collection, DDB 16 /M/L/2/, Chester, Cheshire Record Office

——, Letters to Lord Castletown, 2 Aug. n. y., 10 Aug. n. y., Lord Castletown Papers, National Library, Dublin, MS 35304 (4)

——, Letter to A. V. Dicey, 24 July, n. y., University of Glasgow Library, MS. Gen 508 (47)

——, Letters to W. E. Gladstone, Gladstone Papers, British Library, Add. MSS. 44518/202; 44519/149

——, Letters to Edmund Gosse 2 Apr. 1894, 3 Jul. 1908, Gosse correspondence, Brotherton Collection, Brotherton Library, Leeds

——, Letter to Sir M. E. Grant Duff, Skibbereen, County Cork, Royal Commission on Historical Manuscripts, Castlehaven House, Vol. VI (3), 42

——, Letters to Lady Gregory, New York Public Library, Berg Collection

——, Letters to W. E. H. Lecky, Lecky correspondence, Trinity College, Dublin, MS 1827–36/531, 550, 639, 2472–2482

——, Letters to Sir Alfred Lyall, British Library [London, India Office Library and Records] MSS Eur. F. 132/53, 72, 74, 78–79 & 109

——, Letters to Macmillan's, Macmillan Archive, British Library, London, Add. Mss. 54966/128–86

——, Letter to Lord Monteagle, 31 Aug. 1907, Monteagle papers, National Library, Dublin, MS 11141 (3)

——, Letter to Clement K. Shorter, 11 Apr. 1895, L 96, University College Dublin Library

——, Letter to Seumas O'Sullivan, Dublin, Trinity College Library, MSS4630–4649/183

——, Letter to Mrs Humphry Ward, Oxford, Pusey House Library, Mrs Humphry Ward papers, Section 3a

Martin, Violet (Martin Ross), Letter to Hildegarde (Somerville) Coghill, 22 May 1895, Coghill archive

Oliphant, Margaret, Letters to Emily Lawless, MS 23194–206–7, 215–18, 223–24, 233–38, 248–53, National Library of Scotland

——, Letter to Emily Lawless, Jul. 1890, Lawless Papers, Marsh's Library, Dublin

Plunkett, Horace, Letter to Emily Lawless, 26 Jul. 1902, Lawless Papers, Marsh's Library, Dublin

——, Letter to Emily Lawless, 30 Jul. 1902, Lawless Papers, Marsh's Library, Dublin

——, Letter to Emily Lawless, 3 Oct. 1902, Lawless Papers, Marsh's Library, Dublin

Secondary sources

'Accident to Lord Cloncurry', *The Times,* 7 Nov. 1916, p. 10, col. b

Annan, Noel Gilroy, *Leslie Stephen: His Thought and Character in Relation to his Time,* London: MacGibbon, 1951

'An Appeal Against Women's Suffrage', *Nineteenth Century* vol. 148.25, Jun. 1889, pp. 781–8

'The Author of "Hurrish" ', review of *The Race of Castlebar,* by Emily Lawless and Shan Bullock, *Times Literary Supplement,* 1913, p. 589

Aylmer, Sir Fenton John, *The Aylmers of Ireland,* London: Mitchell Hughes and Clark, 1931.

Bakhtin, M. M., *The Dialogic Imagination: Four Essays,* ed. Michael Holquist, trans. Caryl Emerson and Michael Holquist, 1981; Austin: University of Texas Press, 1985

Belanger, Jacqueline, 'The Desire of the West: The Aran Islands and Irish Identity in *Grania*', in Leon Litvack and Glenn Hooper (eds.), *Ireland in the Nineteenth Century: Regional Identity,* Dublin: Four Courts, 2000, pp. 95–107

Bell, Mrs G. H. (ed.), *The Hamwood Papers of the Ladies of Llangollen and Caroline Hamilton,* London: Macmillan, 1930

Bell, Susan Groag, and Marilyn Yalom (eds.), *Revealing Lives: Autobiography, Biography, and Gender,* Albany: State University of New York Press, 1990

Belsey, Catherine, *Desire: Love Stories in Western Culture,* Oxford: Blackwell, 1994

Bender, Barbara, 'Introduction: Landscape–Meaning and Action', in Barbara Bender (ed.), *Landscape, Politics and Perspectives,* Oxford: Berg, 1993, pp. 1–17

Best, Sue, 'Sexualizing Space', in Elizabeth Grosz and Elspeth Probyn (eds.), *Sexy Bodies: The Strange Carnalities of Feminism,* London: Routledge, 1995, pp. 181–94

Birke, Lynda, *Feminism, Animals and Science: The Naming of the Shrew,* Buckingham: Open University Press, 1994

'Book Reviews', review of *The Story of Ireland,* by Emily Lawless, *Overland Monthly and Out West Magazine* vol. 12.67, Jul. 1887, pp. 109–11 [110]

'Book Reviews', review of *Grania: The Story of an Island,* by Emily Lawless, *Overland Monthly and Out West Magazine* vol. 26.155, Nov. 1895, pp. 568–72 [572]

'Book Reviews and Notices', review of *The Story of Ireland,* by Emily Lawless, *North American Review,* vol. 146, Mar. 1888, p. 357

'Books of the Month', review of *A Millionaire's Cousin,* by Emily Lawless, *Atlantic Monthly,* vol. 56.336, Oct. 1885, p. 574–76 [576]

'Books of the Month', review of *The Story of Ireland,* by Emily Lawless, *Atlantic Monthly* vol. 61.364, Feb. 1888, p. 286–8 [287]

Bourdieu, Pierre, *Distinction: A Social Critique of the Judgement of Taste,* trans. Richard Nice, 1984; London: Routledge, 1994

Boyd, Ernest, *Ireland's Literary Renaissance,* 1916, rev. ed. 1922; Dublin: Allen Figgis, 1968

Breathnach, Eibhlín, 'Charting New Waters: Women's Experience in Higher Education, 1879–1908', in Mary Cullen (ed.), *Girls Don't Do Honours: Irish Women in Education in the 19th and 20th Centuries,* Dublin: Women's Education Bureau, 1987, pp. 55–78

Brewer, Betty Webb, ' "She Was a Part of It": Emily Lawless (1845–1913)', *Éire-Ireland: A Journal of Irish Studies* vol. 18.4, 1983, pp. 119–31

Brooke, Stopford, Preface, Emily Lawless, *With the Wild Geese* (London: Isbister, 1902), pp. vii–xxiv

Brown, John Russell, Editorial note to John Webster, *The White Devil,* V. iv. 103–4, in John Russell Brown (ed.), John Webster, *The White Devil,* London: Methuen, 1960, p. 165

Bull, Philip, *Land, Politics and Nationalism: A Study of the Irish Land Question,* Dublin: Gill & Macmillan, 1996

Burke, Martin J., 'The Politics and Poetics of Nationalist Historiography: Mathew Carey and the *Vindiciae Hibernicae*', in Joep Leerssen, A. H. van der Weel and Bart Westerweel (eds.), *Forging in the Smithy: National Identity and Representation in Anglo-Irish Literary History,* Amsterdam: Rodopi, 1995, pp. 183–94

Bush, Julia, 'British Women's Anti-Suffragism and the Forward Policy, 1908–14', *Women's History Review* vol. 11.3, 2002, pp. 431–54

Butler, Marilyn, *Maria Edgeworth: A Literary Biography,* Oxford: Clarendon Press, 1972

Cahalan, James M., 'Forging a Tradition: Emily Lawless and the Irish Literary Canon', *Colby Quarterly* vol. 27.1, 1991, pp. 27–39

——, *Double Visions: Women and Men in Modern and Contemporary Irish Fiction,* Syracuse, NY: Syracuse University Press, 1999

Cameron, Deborah, *Verbal Hygiene,* London: Routledge, 1995

Carson, James, 'Narrative Cross-Dressing and the Critique of Authorship in the Novels of Richardson', in Elizabeth C. Goldsmith (ed.), *Writing the Female Voice: Essays on Epistolary Literature,* London: Pinter, 1989, pp. 95–113

Casteleyn, Mary, *A History of Literacy and Libraries in Ireland: The Long Traced Pedigree,* Aldershot: Gower, 1984

Chanel [Arthur Clery], 'The Bread of Exile', review of *With the Wild Geese,* by Emily Lawless, *Leader,* 30 Aug. 1902, n. p. Clipping in the Lawless Papers, Marsh's Library, Dublin

'A Chelsea Householder', review of *A Chelsea Householder,* by Emily Lawless, *Spectator,* 4 Nov. 1882, pp. 1416–17

Cloncurry, Valentine, 'To the Editor of the *Times',* 29 Oct. 1880, p. 6 col. a [On Irish landlords]

——, 'To the Editor of the *Times*', *The Times*, 2 Jan. 1886, p. 6 col. c [On the Irish Land question]

——, 'To the Editor of the *Times*', *The Times*, 20 Sep. 1880, p. 11 col. e [Comment on M. Sharman Crawford's letter]

Coates, Jennifer, *Women, Men and Language: A Sociolinguistic Account of Sex Differences in Language*, 1986; London: Longman, 1991

Coghill, Mrs Harry [Annie L.] (ed.), *The Autobiography and Letters of Mrs. M. O. W. Oliphant. Arranged and Edited by Mrs. Harry Coghill*, Edinburgh: W. Blackwood & Sons, 1899

'Comment on New Books', review of *Grania: The Story of an Island*, by Emily Lawless, *Atlantic Monthly* vol. 69, 416, Jun. 1892, pp. 846–51 [848]

Connolly, S. J., 'Culture, Identity and Tradition: Changing Definitions of Irishness', in Brian Graham (ed.), *In Search of Ireland: A Cultural Geography*, London: Routledge, 1997, pp. 43–63

Coogan, Tim Pat, *The IRA*, 1971; London: HarperCollins, 2000

Corkery, Daniel, *The Hidden Ireland*, 1924; Dublin: Gill & Macmillan, n. d.

Costello-Sullivan, Kathleen, 'Novel Traditions: Realism and Modernity in *Hurrish* and *The Real Charlotte*', in Jacqueline Belanger (ed.), *The Irish Novel in the Nineteenth Century*, Dublin: Four Courts Press, 2005, pp. 150–66

Crawford, M. Sharman, 'To the Right Hon. Lord Cloncurry, & c.', *The Times*, 18 Oct. 1836, p. 3 col. e

'Current Fiction: *Maelcho*', review of *Maelcho*, by Emily Lawless, *Globe*, 16 Nov. 1894, n. p. Clipping in the Lawless Papers, Marsh's Library, Dublin

'Current Literature', review of *Plain Frances Mowbray and Other Tales*, by Emily Lawless, *Spectator*, 15 Jun. 1889, pp. 835–6

'Daniel O'Connell's Correspondence', *Living Age*, vol. 180, 19 Jan 1889, p. 131–48. Reprinted from the *Quarterly Review*

Deane, Seamus, 'Irish National Character 1790–1900', in Tom Dunne (ed.), *The Writer as Witness: Literature as Historical Evidence*, Cork: Cork University Press, 1987, pp. 90–113

——, *Strange Country: Modernity and Nationhood in Irish Writing since 1790*, Oxford: Clarendon Press, 1997

'Death of Lord Cloncurry', *The Times*, 31 Oct. 1853, p. 9 col. a

Delaney, Frank, *The Celts*, London: Hodder and Stoughton, 1986

Digby, Margaret, *Horace Plunkett: An Anglo-American Irishman*, Oxford: Basil Blackwell, 1949

Egan, Maurice F., 'A Chat About New Books', review of *Hurrish: A Study*, by Emily Lawless, *Catholic World* vol. 43.254, May 1886, pp. 270–83 [274]

Elizabeth, Countess of Fingall, *Seventy Years Young: Memories of Elizabeth, Countess of Fingall. Told to Pamela Hinkson*, 1937; Dublin: Lilliput, 1995, p. 175

'Elizabethan Ireland', review of *With Essex in Ireland*,' by Emily Lawless, *Speaker*, 27 Sept. 1890, pp. 358–60

'English Authors in Office', *Living Age,* vol. 35, 13 Nov. 1852, p. 304

'Estate of Lord Cloncurry', *The Times,* 29 Oct. 1929, p. 22, col. d [Frederick, Fifth and last Baron]

Fallon, Padraic, Introduction, *The Poems of Emily Lawless,* ed. Padraic Fallon, Dublin: Dolmen, 1965, pp. 7–9

'Father Mathew', *Living Age* vol. 3, 21 Dec. 1844, pp. 467–8

Fenton, Seamus, 'The Honourable Emily Lawless: An Inspirational Poetess and Novelist. Lecture delivered November 1944 to the Women's Social and Progressive League, Dublin', National Library Dublin, pamphlet 2034

'Fiction', review of *The Book of Gilly: Four Months Out of a Life,* by Emily Lawless, *Times Literary Supplement,* 14 Dec. 1906, p. 417

Finke, Laurie A., *Feminist Theory, Women's Writing,* Ithaca: Cornell University Press, 1992

Floto, Inga, *Historie: nyere og nyeste tid,* København: Gyldendal, 1985

Fludernik, Monika, *Towards a 'Natural' Narratology,* London: Routledge, 1996

'Forthcoming Works,' *Irish Book Lover* vol. 3, Jul. 1912, p. 216

'Forthcoming Works', *Irish Book Love,* vol. 5, Aug. 1913, pp. 16–18

Foster, John Wilson, *Colonial Consequences: Essays in Irish Literature and Culture,* Dublin: Lilliput, 1991

Foster, Roy, *The Irish Story: Telling Tales and Making it up in Ireland,* 2001; London: Penguin, 2002

Foucault, Michel, *Power/Knowledge: Selected Interviews and Other Writings 1972–1977,* ed. Colin Gordon, trans. Colin Gordon, Leo Marshall, John Mepham, Kate Soper, Brighton: Harvester, 1980

——, *The Order of Things: An Archaeology of the Human Sciences,* trans. unknown, London: Tavistock, 1970

——, 'Space, Knowledge, and Power', in Paul Rabinow (ed.), *The Foucault Reader,* New York: Pantheon, pp. 239–56

Francis, S. M., 'Maria Edgeworth', review of *Maria Edgeworth,* by Emily Lawless, *Atlantic Monthly* vol. 96, 1905, pp. 423–4

Freedman, Diane P. 'Discourse as Power: Renouncing Denial', in Carol J. Singley and Susan Elizabeth Sweeney (eds.), *Anxious Power: Reading, Writing, and Ambivalence in Narrative by Women,* Albany: State University of New York Press, 1993, pp. 363–78

Friedman, Susan Stanford, *Mappings: Feminism and the Cultural Geographies of Encounter,* Princeton NJ: Princeton University Press, 1998

Garnett, Richard, 'Maria Edgeworth', review of *Maria Edgeworth,* by Emily Lawless, *Bookman* vol. 26, Aug. 1904, pp. 168–70

Gilligan, Carol, *In a Different Voice: Psychological Theory and Women's Development,* 1982; Cambridge MA: Harvard University Press, 1993

Gooch, G. P., *History and Historians in the Nineteenth Century,* 1913; Boston: Beacon Press, 1959

Gladstone, W. E., 'Notes and Queries on the Irish Demands', in *Special Aspects of the Irish Question: A Series of Reflections in and since 1886. Collected from various sources and reprinted*, London: J. Murray, 1892

Graham, Brian, 'Ireland and Irishness: Place, Culture and Identity', in Brian Graham (ed.), *In Search of Ireland: A Cultural Geography*, London: Routledge, 1997, pp. 1–15

'Grania', review of *Grania: The Story of an Island*, by Emily Lawless, *Bookman*, 2 Apr. 1892, p. 27

Grant Duff, Mountstuart Elphinstone, *Notes from a Diary: 1892–1895, I*, London: 1904

'A Great Irish Novelist', review of *Grania: The Story of an Island*, by Emily Lawless, *United Ireland*, Apr. 1892, n. p. Clipping in the Lawless Papers, Marsh's Library, Dublin

Greene, David H., and Edward M. Stephens, *J. M. Synge, 1871–1909*, 1959; New York: Collier, 1961

Griswold, William MacCrillis, *A Descriptive list of British Novels*, Cambridge, Mass., 1891

Grubgeld, Elizabeth, 'Emily Lawless's *Grania: The Story of an Island* (1892)', *Éire-Ireland: A Journal of Irish Studies* vol. 22.3, 1987, pp. 115–29

——, 'The Poems of Emily Lawless and the Life of the West', *Turn-of-the-Century Women* vol. 3.2, 1986, pp. 35–41

[Gwynn, Stephen], 'Novels of Irish Life', *Macmillan's Magazine*, vol. 75, 1897, pp. 182–91. Rpt. in Littell's *Living Age* vol. 212, 6 Feb. 1897, pp. 389–97

Hadfield, Andrew, and John McVeagh (eds.), *Strangers to that Land: British Perceptions of Ireland from the Reformation to the Famine*, Gerrards Cross: Colin Smythe, 1994

'Happiness', review of *Grania: The Story of an Island*, by Emily Lawless, *Spectator* vol. 69, 6 Aug. 1892, pp. 186–7

Heilmann, Ann, *New Woman Fiction: Women Writing First-Wave Feminism*, Basingstoke: Macmillan, 2000

Hewlett, Henry G., 'Forged Literature', *Living Age* vol. 188, 28 Mar. 1891, pp. 771–83. First published in the *Nineteenth Century*

'Hon. Emily Lawless: Irish Authoress', *Daily Telegraph*, 24 Oct. 1913, n. p. Clipping in the Lawless Papers, Marsh's Library, Dublin

'The Hon. Emily Lawless', *Irish Times*, n. d., n. p. Clipping in the Lawless Papers, Marsh's Library, Dublin

Hourican, Liam, review of *The Poems of Emily Lawless*, ed. Padraic Fallon, *Dublin Magazine*, Summer 1965, pp. 78–9

Hutcheon, Linda, *A Poetics of Postmodernism: History, Theory, Fiction*, 1988; New York: Routledge, 1992

'Hurrish', review of *Hurrish: A Study*, by Emily Lawless, *St. James's Gazette*, 5 Feb. 1886, n. p. Clipping in the Lawless Papers, Marsh's Library, Dublin

Hutton, Richard Holt, '*Maelcho*', review of *Maelcho*, by Emily Lawless, *Spectator* vol. 73, 27 Oct. 1894, pp. 559–61

'Inquests', *The Times,* 11 Nov. 1891, p. 7, col. d

'Ireland', *The Times,* 7 Apr. 1869, p. 10

'Ireland', *The Times,* 14 Jul. 1882, p. 10, col. b

'Ireland', *The Times,* 30 Jul. 1883, p. 6, col. d

'Ireland', *The Times,* 1 Feb. 1884, p. 7, col. a [Lord Cloncurry and his tenants]

'Ireland', *The Times,* 2 Jul. 1888, p. 9, col. e [Lord Cloncurry and his tenants]

'Ireland', *The Times,* 17 Dec. 1907, p. 5, col. f [Cattle-driving on Cloncurry lands]

'The Ireland of Today', *Living Age,* vol. 199, 30 Dec. 1893, pp. 771–85. First published in the *Fortnightly Review*

'An Irish Book of the Week: Hon. Emily Lawless' "Maelcho" ', review of *Maelcho,* by Emily Lawless, *Evening Telegraph,* 8 Dec. 1894, n. p. Clipping in the Lawless Papers, Marsh's Library, Dublin

'The Irish Did Not Understand Her', *Daily Sketch,* 25 Oct. 1913, n. p. Clipping in the Lawless Papers, Marsh's Library, Dublin

'Irish Literary Society', *Irish Book Lover,* vol. 7, Feb./Mar. 1916, pp. 129–30

'An Irish Novel', review of *Hurrish: A Study,* by Emily Lawless, *John Bull,* 20 Feb. 1886, n. p. Clipping in the Lawless Papers, Marsh's Library, Dublin

'Irish Spies and Informers', *Living Age,* vol. 195, 8 Oct. 1892, pp. 88–108. Reprinted from the *Edinburgh Review*

Jay, Elizabeth, (ed.), *The Autobiography of Margaret Oliphant,* Missisauga, Canada: Broadview, 2002

——, *Mrs Oliphant: 'A Fiction to Herself': A Literary Life,* Oxford: Clarendon Press, 1995

Jeffares, Norman, 'Place, Space and Personality and the Irish Writer', in Andrew Carpenter (ed.), *Place, Personality and the Irish Writer,* Gerrards Cross: Colin Smythe, 1977, pp. 11–40

Jones, Ann Rosalind, and Peter Stallybrass, 'Dismantling Irena: The Sexualising of Ireland in Early Modern England', in Andrew Parker, Mary Russo, Doris Sommer and Patricia Yaeger (eds.), *Nationalisms and Sexualities,* New York: Routledge, 1992, pp. 157–71

Joyce, P. W., *A Smaller Social History of Ancient Ireland,* Dublin: M. H. Gill & Son, 1906

Kaplan, Carla, *The Erotics of Talk: Women's Writing and Feminist Paradigms,* New York: Oxford University Press, 1996

Kay, Charles de, 'Woman in Ireland of Old', *Catholic World* vol. 43.225, Jun. 1886, pp. 372–83 [381–2]

Kearney, Richard, Introduction, in Richard Kearney (ed.), *The Irish Mind: Exploring Intellectual Traditions,* Dublin: Wolfhound, 1985, pp. 7–14

Kelleher, Margaret, 'Writing Irish Women's Literary History', *Irish Studies Review* vol. 9.1, 2001, pp. 5–14

——, '*The Field Day Anthology* and Irish Women's Literary Studies', *The Irish Review* vol. 30, 2003, pp. 82–94

Kiberd, Declan, *Inventing Ireland: The Literature of the Modern Nation,* 1995; London: Vintage, 1996

Kickham, Lisbet, *Protestant Women Novelists and Irish Society 1879–1922,* Lund Studies in English 106, Lund: Dept. of English, Lund University, 2004

Kilfeather, Siobhán, 'Sex and Sensation in the Nineteenth-Century Novel', in Margaret Kelleher and James H. Murphy, (eds.), *Gender Perspectives in Nineteenth-Century Ireland: Public and Private Spheres,* Dublin: Irish Academic Press, 1997, pp. 83–92

Kingsley, William L., 'Current Literature', review of *The Story of Ireland,* by Emily Lawless, *New Englander and Yale Review* vol. 48.215, 1888, pp. 131–7

Kristeva, Julia, *Desire in Language: A Semiotic Approach to Literature and Art,* ed. Leon S. Roudiez, trans. Thomas Gora, Alice Jardine and Leon S. Roudiez, Oxford: Basil Blackwell, 1980

Krontiris, Tina, *Oppositional Voices: Women as Writers and Translators of Literature in the English Renaissance,* London: Routledge, 1992

Lacey, Robert, *Robert, Earl of Essex: An Elizabethan Icarus,* 1971; London: Phoenix, 2001

'Lady Morgan', *Living Age* vol. 66, 11 Aug. 1860, pp. 374–6

Laird, Heather, *Subversive Law in Ireland 1879–1920,* Dublin: Four Courts Press, 2005, pp. 43–59

Laird, Helen, 'A bohareen of Irish botany. With a poem entitled Dirge of the Munster Forest, 1581, by Miss Lawless', *Limerick Field Club Journal* vol 2, 1901–4, pp 196–210

Lanser, Susan Sniader, *Fictions of Authority: Women Writers and Narrative Voice,* Ithaca NY: Cornell University Press, 1992

'The Last Poems of Emily Lawless', *Times Literary Supplement,* 25 Jun. 1914, p. 309

Law, Hugh Alexander, *Anglo-Irish Literature,* Dublin: Talbot, 1926

Lawless, Valentine Browne, Baron Cloncurry, *Letter from the Right Honorable Lord Cloncurry, to the Most Noble the Marquis of Downshire, on the Conduct of the Kildare-Street Education Society, and the Employment of the Poor,* Dublin: Thomas Reilly, 1826

——, *Personal Recollections of the Life and Times, with Extracts from the Correspondence, of Valentine, Lord Cloncurry,* Dublin, 1849

——, *Thoughts on the Projected Union between Great Britain and Ireland,* Dublin: J. Moore, 1797

Le Juen, Yves, 'The Abbé MacGeoghegan Dies', *Eighteenth-Century Ireland* vol. 13, 1998, 135 ff.

[Lecky, Elizabeth], *A Memoir of the Right Hon. William Edward Hartpole Lecky M. P., O. M., LL. D., D. C. L., LITT. D., Member of the French Institute and of the British Academy, by His Wife,* London: Longmans, Green, and Co., 1909

Lecky, W. E. H. 'Noticeable Books', review of *With Essex in Ireland,* by Emily Lawless, *Nineteenth Century* vol. 28, Aug. 1890, pp. 236–8

Leerssen, Joep, *Remembrance and Imagination: Patterns in the Historical and Literary Representation of Ireland in the Nineteenth Century*, Cork: Cork University Press, 1996

'The Library', review of *Maelcho*, by Emily Lawless, *Province*, 9 Feb. 1895, n. p. Clipping in the Lawless Papers, Marsh's Library, Dublin

Linn, William, 'The Life and Works of the Hon. Emily Lawless, First Novelist of the Irish Literary Revival', dissertation, New York University, 1971

'List of One Hundred Books Towards the Formation of a Village Library', *Irish Homestead*, 20 Jan. 1900, n. p.

'Lord Cloncurry and His Tenantry, *The Times*, 26 Aug. 1845, p. 6 col. f

'Lord Cloncurry on Coercion', *The Times*, 10 Mar. 1846, p. 7 col. f

'Lord Cloncurry', *The Times*, 10 Sep. 1849, p. 2 col. d

'Lord Cloncurry', *The Times*, 19 Jul. 1929, p. 16 col. c [Death of Lord Cloncurry, Frederick, Fifth and last Baron]

Lyall, Sir Alfred, *The Life of the Marquis of Dufferin and Ava*, 1905; London: Thomas Nelson & Sons, n. d.

Lysaght, Edward E., *Sir Horace Plunkett and His Place in the Irish Nation*, Dublin: Maunsel, 1916

Macaulay, G. C., 'A Local Historian', *Macmillan's Magazine* vol. 63, 1890–1, pp. 464–73

McBride, Lawrence W., 'Imagining the Nation in Irish Historical Fiction, c. 1870–c. 1925', in Stewart J. Brown and David W. Miller (eds.), *Piety and Power in Ireland 1760–1950: Essays in Honour of Emmet Larkin*, Notre Dame, IN: University of Notre Dame Press, 2000, pp. 81–107

MacLennan, Gordon W., 'Digression in Oral Tradition: The Case of Anna Nic Grianna', in Cyril J. Byrne, Margaret Harry and Pádraig Ó Siadhail (eds.), *Celtic Languages and Celtic Peoples: Proceedings of the Second North American Congress of Celtic Studies*, Halifax Nova Scotia: D'Arcy McGee Chair of Irish Studies, n. d.

'Maelcho: A Sixteenth Century Narrative', review of *Maelcho: A Sixteenth Century Narrative*, by Emily Lawless, *Atheneum*, vol. 104, 10 Nov. 1894, p. 638

'Maelcho', review of *Maelcho*, by Emily Lawless, *Sun*, 7 Nov. 1894, n. p. Clipping in the Lawless Papers, Marsh's Library, Dublin

'Maelcho', review of *Maelcho: A Sixteenth Century Narrative*, by Emily Lawless, *The Times*, 30 Nov. 1894, p. 14, col. c

'Maelcho', review of *Maelcho: A Sixteenth Century Narrative*, by Emily Lawless, *Spectator* vol. 73, 27 Oct. 1894, pp. 559–61

Mag Fhearaigh, Críostóir, and Tim Stampton, *Ogham: An Irish Alphabet*, 1993; Indreabhán: Cló Iar-Chonnachta, 1997

'Major Lawrence', review of *Major Lawrence* by Emily Lawless, *Pall Mall Gazette*, 23 Jan. 1888, n. p. Clipping in the Lawless Papers, Marsh's Library, Dublin

'Maria Edgeworth', review of *Maria Edgeworth*, by Emily Lawless, *Oxford Magazine*, 14 Jun. 1905, n. p. Clipping in the Lawless Papers, Marsh's Library, Dublin

'Maria Edgeworth', review of *Maria Edgeworth,* by Emily Lawless, *Times Literary Supplement,* 22 Jul. 1904, p. 228

Matthews-Kane, Bridget, 'Emily Lawless's *Grania:* Making for the Open', *Colby Quarterly* vol. 33.3, 1997, pp. 223–35

Meaney, Gerardine, 'Decadence, Degeneration and Revolting Aesthetics: The Fiction of Emily Lawless and Katherine Cecil Thurston', *Colby Quarterly* vol. 36.2, 2000, pp. 157–75

'Memoirs of Richard Whately', *Living Age* vol. 83, 12 Nov. 1864, pp. 321–432

Miller, J. Hillis. 'Trollope's Thackeray', *Nineteenth-Century Fiction* vol. 37.3, 1982, pp. 350–7

Mills, Lia, 'Forging History: Emily Lawless's *With Essex in Ireland*', *Colby Quarterly* vol. 36.2, 2000, pp. 132–44

'Miss Lawless's "Grania"', review of *Grania: The Story of an Island,* by Emily Lawless, *Spectator* vol. 68, 26. Mar. 1892, pp. 431–3

'Miss Lawless's New Tale', review of *Maelcho,* by Emily Lawless, *Daily Chronicle,* 6 Nov. 1894, n. p. Clipping in the Lawless Papers, Marsh's Library, Dublin

'Miss Lawless's Poems', review of *With the Wild Geese,* by Emily Lawless, *Times Literary Supplement,* 11 Apr. 1902, p. 98

Mitchel, John, *The History of Ireland from the Treaty of Limerick to the Present Time,* 2 vols., Dublin: James Duffy, 1869

Morris, Lloyd R., *The Celtic Dawn: A Survey of the Renascence in Ireland, 1889–1916,* 1917; New York: Cooper Square, 1970

'Mrs. Oliphant's Autobiography', review of *The Autobiography of Margaret Oliphant,* by Margaret Oliphant, *Living Age* vol. 223, 7 Oct. 1899, pp. 1–10

Murphy, Cliona, *The Women's Suffrage Movement and Irish Society in the Early Twentieth Century,* Philadelphia: Temple University Press, 1989

——, 'Women's History, Feminist History, or Gender History', *The Irish Women's History Reader,* ed. Alan Hayes and Diane Urquhart, London: Routledge, 2001, pp. 21–5

Murphy, Daniel J., (ed.), *Lady Gregory's Journals, Volume Two, Books Thirty to Forty-Four, 21 February 1925–9 May 1932,* Gerrards Cross: Colin Smythe, 1987

Nagy, Joseph Falaky, *Conversing with Angels: Literary Myths of Medieval Ireland,* Dublin: Four Courts, 1997

Nash, Catherine, 'Embodied Irishness: Gender, Sexuality and Irish Identities', in Brian Graham (ed.), *In Search of Ireland: A Cultural Geography,* 1997; London: Routledge, 1998, pp. 108–27

——, 'Remapping the Body/Land: New Cartographies of Identity, Gender, and Landscape in Ireland', in Alison Blunt and Gillian Rose (eds.), *Writing Women and Space: Colonial and Postcolonial Geographies,* New York: Guilford, 1994, pp. 227–50

'New Novels', review of *Grania: The Story of an Island,* by Emily Lawless, *Jonquille, or The Swiss Smuggler,* by T. Combe, *Eline Vere,* by Louis

Couperus, *San Salvador,* by Mary Agnes Tincker, *Nation* vol. 54, 26 May 1892, pp. 401–2

No title, *Commercial* [?], New York, 9 Nov. 1892, n. p. Clipping in the Lawless Papers, Marsh's Library, Dublin

No title, *Irish Times,* 7 Jul. 1905, n. p. Clipping in the Lawless Papers, Marsh's Library, Dublin

No title, *Irish Times,* 4 Nov. 1913, n. p. Clipping in the Lawless Papers, Marsh's Library, Dublin

No title, *Literary World,* 7 Jun. 1895, n. p. Clipping in the Lawless Papers, Marsh's Library, Dublin

No title, *Piccadilly Magazine,* 17 Oct. 1889, n. p. Clipping in the Lawless Papers, Marsh's Library, Dublin

No title, *Southern Weekly Review,* 5 Nov. 1892, n. p. Clipping in the Lawless Papers, Marsh's Library, Dublin

No title, *The Times,* 15 Sep. 1789 p. 3, col. a [Dignity of Baron granted to Nicholas Lawless]

No title, *The Times,* 18 Sep. 1789 p. 4 [Vacancies in the House of Commons]

No title, *The Times,* 4 Sep. 1799, p. 4, col. a [Succession of Valentine Browne Lawless, Second Baron Cloncurry]

No title, *The Times,* 24 Feb. 1807, p. 4, col. a [Trial between Lord Cloncurry and Sir John Piers]

No title, *The Times,* 29 Feb. 1832, p. 1, col. f [Parliament]

No title, *The Times,* 1 Jun. 1838, p. 3, col. d [Parliament]

No title, *The Times,* 18 Jun. 1841, p. 11, col. b [Death of Lady Emily Cloncurry]

No title, *The Times,* 31 May 1842, p. 3, col. d [Parliament]

No title, *The Times,* 10 Mar. 1846, p. 7, col. f

No title, *The Times,* 11 Mar. 1867, p. 10, col. d [Letter from Lord Cloncurry to Lord Howth]

No title, *The Times,* 3 Aug. 1867, p. 5, col. f [Parliament]

No title, *The Times,* 25 Oct. 1867, p. 1, col. a [Marriage of Edward Lawless]

No title, *The Times,* 5 Apr. 1869, p. 5, col. e [Death of Lord Cloncurry, Edward, Third Baron]

No title, *The Times,* 6 Apr. 1869, p. 9, col. f [Inquest on Lord Cloncurry's death, Edward, Third Baron]

No title, *The Times,* 7 Apr. 1869, p. 5, col. b [Death of Lord Cloncurry, Edward, Third Baron]

No title, *The Times,* 22 Feb. 1882, p. 10, col. c [Lord Cloncurry and his tenants]

No title, *The Times,* 9 Jun. 1882, p. 5, col. e [Letter from Archbishop Croke on the evicted tenants of Lord Cloncurry]

No title, *The Times,* 14 Aug. 1896, p. 4, col. b [Parliament]

No title, *The Times,* 10 Jun. 1907, p. 7, col. d [Cattle-driving on Cloncurry lands]

No title, *The Times,* 8 Nov. 1916, p. 11, col. b [Health of Lord Cloncurry, Valentine, Fourth Baron]

No title, *The Times,* 13 Feb. 1928, p 15, col. e [Death of Lord Cloncurry, Valentine, Fourth Baron]

No title, *The Times,* 27 June 1928, p. 10, col. e [Will of Lord Cloncurry, Valentine, Fourth Baron]

'Novels', review of *With Essex in Ireland,* by Emily Lawless, *Saturday Review,* 4 Oct 1890, n. p. Clipping in the Lawless Papers, Marsh's Library, Dublin

'Novels of the Week', review of *Grania: The Story of an Island,* by Emily Lawless, *Dr. Willoughby Smith,* by Mrs. A. M. Marks, *A Masquerader,* by Algernon Gissing, *An East-End Mystery,* by Adeline Sergeant, *That Stick,* by Charlotte M. Yonge, *Athenæum* vol. 99, 16 Apr. 1892, pp. 496–7

'Novels', review of *Maelcho,* by Emily Lawless, *Daily News,* 23 Nov. 1894, n. p. Clipping in the Lawless Papers, Marsh's Library, Dublin

'Novels', review of *Major Lawrence,* by Emily Lawless, *Saturday Review,* 28 Jan. 1888, n. p. Clipping in the Lawless Papers, Marsh's Library, Dublin

O'Connell, Daniel, 'To Lord Cloncurry', *The Times,* 19 Jan. 1831, p. 3 col. b

Ó Corráin, Donnchadh, 'Legend as Critic', in Tom Dunne (ed.), *The Writer as Witness: Literature as Historical Evidence,* Cork: Cork University Press 1987, pp. 23–38

O'Donoghue, D. J., 'Emily Lawless: A Great Loss to Literature', *Irish Independent,* 24 Oct. 1913

O'Dowd, Mary, 'From Morgan to MacCurtain: Women Historians in Ireland from the 1790s to the 1990s', in Alan Hayes and Diane Urquhart (eds.), *The Irish Women's History Reader,* London: Routledge, 2001, pp. 7–14

O'Grady, Standish, *Early Bardic Literature, Ireland,* 1879; New York: Lemma, 1970

O'Neill, Marie, 'Emily Lawless', *Dublin Historical Record* vol. 48.2, Autumn 1995, pp. 125–41

O'Toole, Fintan, 'Booking Now for 2100', *Irish Times,* 4 Nov. 2000, n. p.

Ó Tuama, Seán, 'Stability and Ambivalence: Aspects of the Sense of Place and Religion in Irish Literature', in Joseph Lee (ed.), *Ireland Towards a Sense of Place,* Cork: Cork University Press, 1985, pp. 21–33

Ó Tuama, Seán, and Thomas Kinsella, *An Duanaire 1600–1900: Poems of the Dispossessed,* 1981; Portlaoise: Dolmen, 1994

Obituary of Elizabeth, Dowager Lady Cloncurry, *The Times,* 10 May 1895, p. 10, col. f

Obituary of Emily Lawless, *Daily Graphic,* 24 Oct. 1913, n. p. Clipping in the Lawless Papers, Marsh's Library, Dublin

Obituary of Emily Lawless, *Irish Book Lover* vol. 5, Dec. 1913, pp. 84–5

Obituary of Emily Lawless, *Irish Independent,* 23 Oct. 1913, n. p. Clipping in the Lawless Papers, Marsh's Library, Dublin

Obituary of Emily Lawless, *Morning Post,* 24 Oct. 1913, n. p. Clipping in the Lawless Papers, Marsh's Library, Dublin

Obituary of Emily Lawless, *Westminster Gazette,* 24 Oct. 1913, n. p. Clipping in the Lawless Papers, Marsh's Library, Dublin

Obituary of Emily Lawless, *Yorkshire Post*, 24 Oct. 1913, n. p. Clipping in the Lawless Papers, Marsh's Library, Dublin

Obituary of Major Denis Lawless, *The Times*, 9 Oct. 1900, p. 4, col. a

Oliphant, Margaret, 'Hurrish', review of *Hurrish: A Study*, by Emily Lawless, *Spectator* vol. 30, Jan. 1886, pp. 147–8

——, 'A Noble Lady', *New Review* vol. 14, Mar. 1896, pp. 241–7

——, *Sheridan*, London: Macmillan and Co., 1883

——, 'The Old Saloon 4', review of *Hurrish: A Study*, by Emily Lawless, *Blackwood's Magazine* vol. 141, Apr. 1887, pp. 552–72 [568–70]

——, 'The Old Saloon 16', review of *Plain Frances Mowbray, and Other Stories*, by Emily Lawless, *Blackwood's Magazine* vol. 145, Jun. 1889, pp. 809–34 [830–3]

——, 'The Old Saloon 26', review of *Grania: The Story of an Island*, by Emily Lawless, *Blackwood's Magazine* vol. 152, Oct. 1892, pp. 574–96 [591–6]

'Our Scrap Book', *Irish Book Lover*, vol. 5.6, 1914, pp. 108–9

'Parliamentary Intelligence', *The Times*, 8 Feb. 1832, p. 1, col. d

'Parliamentary Intelligence', *The Times*, 12 Feb. 1836, p. 3, col. d

Parnell, Anna, *The Tale of a Great Sham*, ed. Dana Hearne, Dublin: Arlen House, 1986

Patten, Eve, 'With Essex in India? Emily Lawless's Colonial Consciousness', *European Journal of English Studies* vol. 3.3, 1999, pp. 285–97

Paul, Herbert, 'The Apotheosis of the Novel under Queen Victoria', *Living Age* vol. 213, 19 Jun. 1897, pp. 779–97. First published in the *Nineteenth Century*

Pethica, James (ed.), *Lady Gregory's Diaries 1892–1902. Edited and Introduced by James Pethica*, Gerrards Cross: Colin Smythe, 1996

Petre, M. D. (ed.), *George Tyrrell's Letters*, London: Fisher Unwin, 1920

Plumwood, Val, *Feminism and the Mastery of Nature*, London: Routledge, 1993

Plunkett, Horace, Ellice Pilkington and George Russell, *The United Irishwomen: Their Place, Work and Ideals*, Dublin: Maunsel & Co., 1911

'Post Bag', *Irish Book Lover* vol. 5, Apr. 1914, pp. 165–6

Protheroe, R. E., 'Irish Novelists on Irish Peasants', *Living Age* vol. 181, 20 Apr. 1889, pp. 181–8. First published in the *National Review*

Prothero, R. E., 'Grania', review of *Grania: The Story of an Island*, by Emily Lawless, *Nineteenth Century* vol. 31, Apr. 1892, pp. 693–5

'The Race of Castlebar', review of *The Race of Castlebar*, by Emily Lawless and Shan Bullock, *Bookman* vol. 45, 1914, p. 283

'The Real Historian', *Macmillan's Magazine* vol. 66, 1892, pp. 221–7

'Recent Fiction: Miss Emily Lawless's New Novel', review of *Maelcho*, by Emily Lawless, *Observer*, 4 Nov. 1894, n. p. Clipping in the Lawless Papers, Marsh's Library, Dublin

'Recent Fiction', review of *Hurrish: A Study*, by Emily Lawless, *Overland Monthly and Out West Magazine* vol. 7.42, Jun. 1886, pp. 649–56 [651]

'Recent Novels and Tales', review of *With Essex in Ireland,* by Emily Lawless, *The Times,* 21 Jul. 1890, p. 13, col. a. Clipping in the Lawless Papers, Marsh's Library, Dublin

'Recent Novels: Hurrish', review of *Hurrish: A Study,* by Emily Lawless, *Morning Post,* n. d., n. p. Clipping in the Lawless Papers, Marsh's Library, Dublin

'Reformers', *The Times,* 30 Oct. 1819, p. 2, col. e

Reid, Mark, 'Our Young Historians', *Macmillan's Magazine* vol. 68, 1892–3, pp. 91–8

Reilly, Eileen, 'Rebel, Muse, and Spouse: The Female in '98 Fiction', *Éire-Ireland: A Journal of Irish Studies* vol. 34.2, 1999, pp. 135–54

Review of 'The Builder of the Round Towers', by Emily Lawless, *Builder,* 9 Mar. 1895, n. p. Clipping in the Lawless Papers, Marsh's Library, Dublin

Review of *A Chelsea Householder,* by Emily Lawless, *Athenæum* vol. 2870, 28 Oct. 1882, n. p. Clipping in the Lawless Papers, Marsh's Library, Dublin

Review of *A Chelsea Householder,* by Emily Lawless, *Daily News,* 30 Nov. 1882, n. p. Clipping in the Lawless Papers, Marsh's Library, Dublin

Review of *A Chelsea Householder,* by Emily Lawless, *Dublin Evening Mail,* 22 Nov. 1882, n. p. Clipping in the Lawless Papers, Marsh's Library, Dublin

Review of *A Chelsea Householder,* by Emily Lawless, *Dublin Evening Mail,* 22 Nov. 1882. n. p. Clipping in the Lawless Papers, Marsh's Library, Dublin

Review of *A Chelsea Householder,* by Emily Lawless, *Morning Post,* 26 Dec. 1882, n. p. Clipping in the Lawless Papers, Marsh's Library, Dublin

Review of *A Chelsea Householder,* by Emily Lawless, *Queen,* 18 Nov. 1882, n. p. Clipping in the Lawless Papers, Marsh's Library, Dublin

Review of *A Chelsea Householder,* by Emily Lawless, *Standard,* 8 Jan. 1883, n. p. Clipping in the Lawless Papers, Marsh's Library, Dublin;

Review of *A Garden Diary,* by Emily Lawless, *The Times,* 31 Aug. 1901, p. 3 col. b

Review of *Grania: The Story of an Island,* by Emily Lawless, *Athenæum* vol. 99, 16 Apr. 1892, p. 496

Review of *Grania: The Story of an Island,* by Emily Lawless, *Manchester Guardian,* 29 Mar. 1892, n. p. Clipping in the Lawless Papers, Marsh's Library, Dublin

Review of *Grania: The Story of an Island,* by Emily Lawless, *Massachusetts,* 4 May 1892, n. p. Clipping in the Lawless Papers, Marsh's Library, Dublin

Review of *Grania: The Story of an Island,* by Emily Lawless, *North British Daily Mail,* 25 Mar. 1892, n. p. Clipping in the Lawless Papers, Marsh's Library, Dublin

Review of *Grania: The Story of an Island,* by Emily Lawless, *Spectator* vol. 68, 26 Mar. 1892, pp. 431–3

Review of *Grania: The Story of an Island,* by Emily Lawless, *Spectator* vol. 69, 6 Aug. 1892, pp. 186–7

Review of *Grania: The Story of an Island,* by Emily Lawless, *Standard,* 25 Jun. 1892, n. p. Clipping in the Lawless Papers, Marsh's Library, Dublin

Review of *Grania: The Story of an Island,* by Emily Lawless, *The Times,* 8 Apr. 1892, n. p. Clipping in the Lawless Papers, Marsh's Library, Dublin

Review of *Grania: The Story of an Island,* by Emily Lawless, *Tribune,* 23 Jul. 1892, n. p. Clipping in the Lawless Papers, Marsh's Library, Dublin

Review of *Grania: The Story of an Island,* by Emily Lawless, *Truth,* 14 May 1892, n. p. Clipping in the Lawless Papers, Marsh's Library, Dublin

Review of *Grania: The Story of an Island,* by Emily Lawless, *World,* 3 Mar. 1892 [?], n. p. Clipping in the Lawless Papers, Marsh's Library, Dublin

Review of *Hurrish: A Study,* by Emily Lawless, *Morning Post,* n. d., n. p. Clipping in the Lawless Papers, Marsh's Library, Dublin

Review of *Hurrish: A Study,* by Emily Lawless, *St. James's Gazette,* 5 Feb. 1886, n. p. Clipping in the Lawless Papers, Marsh's Library, Dublin

Review of *Hurrish: A Study,* by Emily Lawless, *Tablet,* 11 Sep. 1886, n. p. Clipping in the Lawless Papers, Marsh's Library, Dublin

Review of *Hurrish: A Study,* by Emily Lawless, *Times Literary Supplement,* 1 Apr. 1994, p. 23

Review of *Hurrish: A Study,* by Emily Lawless, *Whitehall Review,* 11 Feb. 1886, n. p. Clipping in the Lawless Papers, Marsh's Library, Dublin

Review of *The Inalienable Heritage and Other Poems,* by Emily Lawless, *Irish Homestead,* 25 Jul. 1914, n. p. Clipping in the Lawless Papers, Marsh's Library, Dublin

Review of *Ireland,* by Emily Lawless, *Stonecutter,* 28 Feb., n. d., n. p. Clipping in the Lawless Papers, Marsh's Library, Dublin

Review of *Maelcho,* by Emily Lawless, *Irish Daily Independent,* 5 Nov. 1894, n. p. Clipping in the Lawless Papers, Marsh's Library, Dublin

Review of *Maelcho,* by Emily Lawless, *Manchester Guardian,* 6 Nov. 1894, n. p. Clipping in the Lawless Papers, Marsh's Library, Dublin

Review of *Major Lawrence,* by Emily Lawless, *Academy,* 14 Jan. 1888, n. p. Clipping in the Lawless Papers, Marsh's Library, Dublin

Review of *Major Lawrence,* by Emily Lawless, *Court Journal,* 26 Jan. 1889 [?], p. 103. Clipping in the Lawless Papers, Marsh's Library, Dublin

Review of *Maria Edgeworth,* by Emily Lawless, *Dial* vol. 37, Jul. 1–Dec. 16 1904, p. 170

Review of *Maria Edgeworth,* by Emily Lawless, *International Quarterly* vol. 10, Dec. 1904, pp. 190–5

Review of *Maria Edgeworth,* by Emily Lawless, *Oxford Magazine,* 14 Jun. 1905, n. p. Clipping in the Lawless Papers, Marsh's Library, Dublin

Review of *Plain Frances Mowbray and Other Tales,* by Emily Lawless, *Saturday Review,* 27 Jul. 1889, n. p. Clipping in the Lawless Papers, Marsh's Library, Dublin

Review of *The Race of Castlebar,* by Emily Lawless and Shan Bullock, *Irish Book Lover* vol. 5.6, Jan. 1914, p. 103

Review of *The Story of Ireland,* by Emily Lawless, *Detroit Tribune,* 1 Jan. 1888 [?], n. p. Clipping in the Lawless Papers, Marsh's Library, Dublin

Review of *Traits and Confidences,* by Emily Lawless, *Outlook* vol. 1, 1898, p. 405

Review of *Traits and Confidences,* by Emily Lawless, *Spectator* vol. 80, 28 May 1898, pp. 760–1

Review of *With Essex in Ireland,* by Emily Lawless, *Athenæum* vol. 95, 14 Jun. 1890, pp. 765–6

Review of *With Essex in Ireland,* by Emily Lawless, *Boston England,* 12 Jul. 1890, n. p. Clipping in the Lawless Papers, Marsh's Library, Dublin

Review of *With Essex in Ireland,* by Emily Lawless, *Church Times,* 31 Oct. 1902, n. p. Clipping in the Lawless Papers, Marsh's Library, Dublin

Review of *With Essex in Ireland,* by Emily Lawless, *Critic* vol. 17, 1 Nov. 1890, p. 217

Review of *With Essex in Ireland,* by Emily Lawless, *Manchester Examiner,* 6 Jun. 1890, n. p. Clipping in the Lawless Papers, Marsh's Library, Dublin

Review of *With Essex in Ireland,* by Emily Lawless, *Outlook,* 25 Oct. 1902, n. p. Clipping in the Lawless Papers, Marsh's Library, Dublin

Review of *With Essex in Ireland,* by Emily Lawless, *Pall Mall Gazette,* 8 Jul. 1890, n. p. Clipping in the Lawless Papers, Marsh's Library, Dublin

Review of *With Essex in Ireland,* by Emily Lawless, *Queen,* 13 Dec. 1890, n. p. Clipping in the Lawless Papers, Marsh's Library, Dublin

Review of *With the Wild Geese,* by Emily Lawless, *Bookman,* 22 May 1902, p. 70

Robinson, Lennox (ed.), *Lady Gregory's Journals 1916–1930,* London: Putnam, 1946

Rose, Gillian, *Feminism and Geography: The Limits of Geographical Knowledge,* Cambridge: Polity Press, 1993

Roy, James Charles, 'Landscape and the Celtic Soul', *Éire-Ireland: A Journal of Irish Studies* vol. 31.3–4, 1996, pp. 228–54

Saintsbury, George, 'Some Great Biographies', *Macmillan's Magazine,* vol. 66.392, 1892, pp. 97–107

Schama, Simon, *Landscape and Memory,* 1995; New York: Vintage, 1996

Schirmer, Gregory A., *Out of What Began: A History of Irish Poetry in English,* Ithaca: Cornell University Press, 1998

Shildrick, Margrit, *Leaky Bodies and Boundaries: Feminism, Postmodernism and (Bio)ethics,* London: Routledge, 1997

Sichel, Edith, Preface, *The Inalienable Heritage and Other Poems,* by Emily Lawless, privately printed, London: R. Clay, 1914, pp. v–viii

——, 'Emily Lawless', *Nineteenth Century and After* vol. 76, Jul. 1914, pp. 80–100

Simms, Katharine, 'Bardic Poetry as a Historical Source', in Tom Dunne (ed.), *The Writer as Witness: Literature as Historical Evidence,* Cork: Cork University Press, 1987, pp. 58–75

Singley, Carol J., 'Female Language, Body, and Self', in Carol J. Singley and Susan Elizabeth Sweeney (eds.), *Anxious Power: Reading, Writing, and Ambivalence in Narrative by Women,* Albany: State University of New York Press, 1993, pp. 3–15

Singley, Carol J. and Susan Elizabeth Sweeney, Preface, in Carol J. Singley and Susan Elizabeth Sweeney (eds.), *Anxious Power: Reading, Writing, and Ambivalence in Narrative by Women*, Albany: State University of New York Press, 1993, pp. ix–x

'Sixteenth-Century Narrative', review of *Maelcho*, by Emily Lawless, *Pall Mall Gazette* vol. 19, Nov. 1894, n. p. Clipping in the Lawless Papers, Marsh's Library, Dublin

Smyth, William J., 'A Plurality of Irelands: Regions, Societies and Mentalities', in Brian Graham (ed.), *In Search of Ireland: A Cultural Geography* (1997; London: Routledge, 1998), pp. 19–42

'Some New Novels', review of *Maelcho*, by Emily Lawless, *Standard*, 10 Dec. 1894, n. p. Clipping in the Lawless Papers, Marsh's Library, Dublin

Southern Weekly Review, 15 Nov. 1892, n. p. Clipping in the Lawless Papers, Marsh's Library, Dublin

Spender, Dale, *Mothers of the Novel: 100 Good Women Writers before Jane Austen*, London: Pandora, 1986

Stephen, Sir Leslie, *George Eliot*, London: Macmillan, 1902

Stevenson, Jane, 'The Politics of Historiography: or, Novels with Footnotes', in Joep Leerssen, A. H. van der Weel and Bart Westerweel (eds.), *Forging in the Smithy: National Identity and Representation in Anglo-Irish Literary History*, Amsterdam: Rodopi, 1995, pp. 195–206

[Stock, Joseph], *A Narrative of what Passed at Killala, in the County of Mayo, and the Parts Adjacent, during the French Invasion in the Summer of 1798. By an Eye-Witness*, Dublin: R. E. Mercier & John Jones, 1800

'The Story of the Nations: Ireland', review of *Ireland*, by Emily Lawless, *Spectator*, 14 Jan. 1888, pp. 60–1

Strachey, Lytton, *Elizabeth and Essex: A Tragic History*, London: Chatto & Windus, 1928

'Talk about New Books', review of *Grania: The Story of an Island*, by Emily Lawless, *Catholic World* vol. 55, Apr. 1892, pp. 129–45 [130–1]

'Talks and Disputations in Verse', review of *The Point of View*, by Emily Lawless, *Times Literary Supplement*, n. d. 1909, p. 136

Tannen, Deborah, *Gender and Discourse*, Oxford: Oxford University Press, 1994

Thompson, Nicola Diane, *Reviewing Sex: Gender and the Reception of Victorian Novels*, Basingstoke: Macmillan, 1996

Tillyard, Stella, *Citizen Lord: Edward Fitzgerald, 1763–1798*, 1997; London: Vintage, 1998

Todd, Janet, *Rebel Daughters: Ireland in Conflict 1798*, 2003; London: Penguin, 2004

Tuchman, Gaye with Nina E. Fortin, *Edging Women Out: Victorian Novelists, Publishers, and Social Change*, London: Routledge, 1989

Tynan, Katharine, *The Years of the Shadow*, London: Constable, 1919

Wall, Richard, 'Politics and Language in Anglo-Irish Literature', in Joep Leerssen, A. H. van der Weel and Bart Westerweel (eds.), *Forging in the Smithy:*

   National Identity and Representation in Anglo-Irish Literary History,
   Amsterdam: Rodopi, 1995, pp. 119–31

Ward, Mary A. [Mrs. Humphry Ward], Review of *Grania: The Story of an Island,*
   by Emily Lawless, *New Review* 6, pp. 399–407

——, *A Writer's Recollections,* London: Collins, 1918

——, *Delia Blanchflower,* 1915; London: Ward, Lock & Co., 1917

Warren, Karen J. (ed.), *Ecofeminism: Women, Culture, Nature,* Bloomington:
   Indiana University Press, 1997

Watson, Cresap S., 'The Date of Emily Lawless' "Grania"', *Notes and Queries* vol.
   CXCIX, Mar. 1954, p. 129

Webster, John, *The White Devil,* ed. John Russell Brown, London: Methuen,
   1960

Weekes, Ann Owens, *Unveiling Treasures: The Attic Guide to The Published Works
   of Irish Women Literary Writers,* Dublin: Attic, 1993

'Well-Known Irish Writer Dead', *Pall Mall Gazette,* 23 Oct. 1913, n. p. Clipping
   in the Lawless Papers, Marsh's Library, Dublin

White, Hayden, *Tropics of Discourse: Essays in Cultural Criticism,* 1978; Baltimore:
   Johns Hopkins University Press, 1990

Williams, Merryn, 'Feminist or Antifeminist? Oliphant and the Woman
   Question', in D. J. Trela (ed.), *Margaret Oliphant: Critical Essays on a Gentle
   Subversive,* Selinsgrove: Susquehanna University Press, 1995, pp. 165–80.

'Wills and Bequests', *The Times,* 7 Aug. 1869, p. 6, col. b

'With Essex in Ireland', review of *With Essex in Ireland,* by Emily Lawless, *Boston
   Literary World,* Oct. 1890, n. p. Clipping in the Lawless Papers, Marsh's
   Library, Dublin

'With Essex in Ireland', review of *With Essex in Ireland,* by Emily Lawless, *Irish
   Society,* 12 Jul. 1890, n. p. Clipping in the Lawless Papers, Marsh's Library,
   Dublin

'With Essex in Ireland', review of *With Essex in Ireland,* by Emily Lawless,
   Nonconformist and Independent, 10 Jul. 1890, n. p. Clipping in the Lawless
   Papers, Marsh's Library, Dublin

'With Essex in Ireland', review of *With Essex in Ireland,* by Emily Lawless,
   Spectator vol. 64, 7 Jun. 1890, pp. 799–800

Yeats, W. B. 'Irish National Literature, II: Contemporary Prose Writers – Mr.
   O'Grady, Miss Lawless, Miss Barlow, Miss Hopper, and the Folklorists'
   Bookman, Aug. 1895. Rpt. in John P. Frayne (ed.), *Uncollected Prose by W.
   B. Yeats 1: First Reviews and Articles 1886–1896,* London: Macmillan,
   1970, pp. 366–73.

——, 'Irish National Literature, IV: A List of the Best Irish Books', in John P.
   Frayne (ed.), *Uncollected Prose by W. B. Yeats 1: First Reviews and Articles
   1886–1896,* London: Macmillan, 1970, pp. 382–7

——, Letter to the Editor of the *Dublin Daily Express,* 27 Feb. 1895, in Allan
   Wade (ed.), *The Letters of W. B. Yeats,* London: Rupert Hart-Davis, 1954,
   pp. 246–51

Young, Arlene, *Culture, Class and Gender in the Victorian Novel: Gentlemen, Gents and Working Women,* Houndmills: Macmillan, 1999

Internet sources

http://humphrysfamilytree.com/Butler/lawless.html. Access date 10 Mar. 2006

http://www.chapters.eiretek.org/books/Cloncurry/cloncurry5.htm. Access date 8 Mar. 2006

http://www.thepeerage.com/p92.htm#i920. Access date 10 Mar. 2006

Lynch, Ronan, Letter to the Editor, *Tuam Herald,* 21 Mar. 2003, http://www.unison.ie/tuam_herald/stories.php3?ca=53&si=939103&issue_id=8918. Access date 6 Sep. 2004

Seoighe, Mainchin, 'Poems of the Wild Geese', *Limerick Leader,* 29 May 1999, online edition, http://www.limerick-leader.ie/issues/19990529/seoighe.html. Access date 8 Feb. 2005

Notes

Notes to 'Behind the book'

1. Emily Lawless, *A Garden Diary: September, 1899 – September, 1900* (London: Methuen, 1901), p. 123.

2. Lawless, *A Garden Diary,* p. 123.

3. Emily Lawless, 'An Addition to Mr. Birchall's List of "The Lepidoptera of Ireland"', *Entomologist's Monthly Magazine,* vol. 3, Jan. 1867, p. 187.

4. Emily Lawless, 'North Clare – Leaves from a Diary', *Nineteenth Century,* vol. 46, 1899, p. 606. The identity of Lawless's correspondent is unclear. Lawless refers to him as her 'Commander-in-Chief' in the field of entomology, and the context seems to indicate that this should be the Mr Birchall of the note's title. The natural scientist Augustus Birchall died several years before the note was published, however.

5. [Stephen Gwynn], 'Novels of Irish Life', *Macmillan's Magazine,* vol. 75, 1897, p. 182.

6. The historian W. E. H. Lecky ends his review of Lawless's *With Essex in Ireland* by saying: 'It has often been lamented that no writer has arisen in Ireland who could do for Irish history what Scott did for the history of his own country. If Miss Lawless can produce only a few more books like *Essex in Ireland* this misfortune and reproach will be effectually removed.' W. E. H. Lecky, 'Noticeable Books', review of *With Essex in Ireland* by Emily Lawless, *Nineteenth Century,* vol. 28, 1890, p. 238.

7. [Stephen Gwynn], 'Novels of Irish Life', p. 182.

8. [Stephen Gwynn], 'Novels of Irish Life', p. 187, 190.

9. 'List of One Hundred Books Towards the Formation of a Village Library', *Irish Homestead,* 20 Jan. 1900, n. p.

10. 'The Hon. Emily Lawless', *Irish Times,* n. d., n. p. Clipping in the Lawless Papers, Marsh's Library, Dublin.

11. Fintan O'Toole, 'Booking Now for 2100', *Irish Times*, 4 Nov. 2000, n. p.

12. *Southern Weekly Review*, 15 Nov. 1892, n. p. Clipping in the Lawless Papers, Marsh's Library, Dublin.

13. Apart from Yeats, both J. M. Synge and Lady Gregory expressed critical opinions of Lawless's work.

14. W. B. Yeats, 'Irish National Literature, IV: A List of the Best Irish Books', in John P. Frayne (ed.), *Uncollected Prose by W. B. Yeats 1: First Reviews and Articles 1886–1896* (London: Macmillan, 1970), p. 386.

15. W. B. Yeats, Letter to the Editor of the *Dublin Daily Express* 27 Feb. 1895, in Allan Wade (ed.), *The Letters of W. B. Yeats* (London: Rupert Hart-Davis, 1954), p. 248.

16. W. B. Yeats, 'Irish National Literature, II: Contemporary Prose Writers – Mr O'Grady, Miss Lawless, Miss Barlow, Miss Hopper, and the Folklorists', in John P. Frayne (ed.), *Uncollected Prose by W. B. Yeats 1: First Reviews and Articles 1886–1896* (London: Macmillan, 1970), p. 369.

17. *Ibid.*, p. 370.

18. Lloyd R. Morris, *The Celtic Dawn: A Survey of the Renascence in Ireland, 1889–1916* (1917; New York: Cooper Square, 1970), p. 186.

19. 'The Irish Did Not Understand Her', *Daily Sketch*, 25 Oct. 1913, n. p. Clipping in the Lawless Papers, Marsh's Library, Dublin.

20. Obituary of Emily Lawless, *Irish Book Lover*, vol. 5, 1913, p. 84.

21. 'A Great Irish Novelist', review of *Grania: The Story of an Island* by Emily Lawless, *United Ireland*, Apr. 1892, n. p. Clipping in the Lawless Papers, Marsh's Library, Dublin.

22. 'A Great Irish Novelist', n. p.

23. 'Irish Literary Society', *Irish Book Lover*, vol. 7, 1916, p. 129.

24. Seamus Fenton, 'The Honorable Emily Lawless', pamphlet in the National Library, Dublin, p 2034, pp. 8–9.

25. *Ibid.*, p. 8.

26. Tim Pat Coogan, *The IRA* (1971; London: HarperCollins, 2000), p. 247.

27. Padraic Fallon, Introduction, *The Poems of Emily Lawless*, ed. Padraic Fallon (Dublin: Dolmen, 1965), p. 8.

28. Marie O'Neill, 'Emily Lawless', *Dublin Historical Record*, vol. 48.2, Autumn 1995, pp. 125–141.

29. See, for instance, Betty Webb Brewer, '"She Was a Part of It": Emily Lawless (1845–1913)', *Éire-Ireland: A Journal of Irish Studies*, vol. 18.4, 1983, pp. 119–31; Elizabeth Grubgeld, 'Emily Lawless's *Grania: The Story of an Island* (1892)', *Éire-Ireland: A Journal of Irish Studies*, vol. 22.3, 1987, pp. 115–29; James M. Cahalan, 'Forging a Tradition: Emily Lawless and the Irish Literary Canon', *Colby Quarterly*, vol. 27.1, 1991, pp. 27–39; Bridget Matthews-Kane, 'Emily Lawless's *Grania:* Making for the Open', *Colby Quarterly*, vol. 33.3, 1997, pp. 223–35; Gerardine Meaney, 'Decadence, Degeneration and Revolting Aesthetics: The Fiction of Emily Lawless and Katherine Cecil Thurston', *Colby Quarterly*, vol. 36.2, 2000, pp. 157–75.

30. See Margaret Kelleher, 'Writing Irish Women's Literary History', *Irish Studies Review* 9.1, 2001, p. 10 and Margaret Kelleher, '*The Field Day Anthology* and Irish Women's Literary Studies', *The Irish Review*, 30, 2003, pp. 82–94. See also Cliona Murphy, 'Women's History, Feminist History, or Gender History', in Alan Hayes and Diane Urquhart (eds.), *The Irish Women's History Reader* (London: Routledge, 2001), pp. 21–5.

31. Margrit Shildrick, *Leaky Bodies and Boundaries: Feminism, Postmodernism and (Bio)ethics* (London: Routledge, 1997), p. 9.

32. *Ibid.*, p. 12.

33. Richard Kearney, Introduction, *The Irish Mind: Exploring Intellectual Traditions*, ed. Richard Kearney (Dublin: Wolfhound, 1985), p. 9.

34. Lawless, 'North Clare', p. 604.

35. Gillian Rose, *Feminism and Geography: The Limits of Geographical Knowledge* (Cambridge: Polity Press, 1993), p. 140.

36. Michel Foucault, *The Order of Things: An Archaeology of the Human Sciences*, trans. unknown (London: Tavistock, 1970), p. xvii.

37. Michel Foucault, 'Space, Knowledge, and Power', in Paul Rabinow (ed.), *The Foucault Reader* (New York: Pantheon, 1984), p. 253.

38. Linda Hutcheon, *A Poetics of Postmodernism: History, Theory, Fiction* (New York: Routledge, 1988), p. 3.

Notes to Chapter 1

1. Valentine Browne Lawless, Baron Cloncurry, *Personal Recollections of the Life and Times, with Extracts from the Correspondence, of Valentine, Lord Cloncurry* (Dublin: 1849), p. 18.

2. *Ibid.*, p. 18.

3. Sir Fenton John Aylmer, *The Aylmers of Ireland* (London: Mitchell Hughes and Clark, 1931), pp. 198–99. Lyons was owned by University College Dublin for many years and is now (2006) owned by Tony Ryan, founder of RyanAir.

4. Mrs G. H. Bell (ed.), *The Hamwood Papers of the Ladies of Llangollen and Caroline Hamilton* (London: Macmillan, 1930), pp. 205–6. Also referred to in William Linn, 'The Life and Works of the Hon. Emily Lawless, First Novelist of the Irish Literary Revival', dissertation, New York University, 1971, p. 1.

5. Aylmer, p. 198.

6. An item in *The Times* 15 Sep. 1789, p. 3, reports that the dignity of Baron has been granted to Nicholas Lawless and in *The Times*, 18 Sep. 1789, p. 4, it is noted that the creation of new peers has left vacancies in the House of Commons.

7. Valentine Browne Lawless, Baron Cloncurry, *Personal Recollections*, p. 20.

8. Valentine Lawless was still confined in the Tower of London at the time of his succession to the title. *The Times*, 4 Sep. 1799, p. 4.

9. Valentine Browne Lawless, Baron Cloncurry, *Personal Recollections*, pp. 12–13.

10. Stella Tillyard, *Citizen Lord: Edward Fitzgerald, 1763–1798* (1997; London: Vintage, 1998), pp. 210, 228–9. Tillyard gives the first name of Lady Cloncurry as Anne, while she is called Margaret, née Browne, in other sources, such as http://www.thepeerage.com/p92.htm#i920, access date 10 Mar. 2006, and http://humphrys familytree.com/Butler/lawless.html, access date 10 Mar. 2006.

11. Janet Todd, *Rebel Daughters: Ireland in Conflict 1798* (2003; London: Penguin, 2004), p. 185.

12. 'Irish Spies and Informers', *Living Age*, vol. 195, 8 Oct. 1892, p. 95. Reprinted from the *Edinburgh Review*.

13. Valentine Browne Lawless, Baron Cloncurry, *Thoughts on the Projected Union between Great Britain and Ireland* (Dublin: J. Moore, 1797).

14. Tillyard, p. 229.

15. Todd, p. 201.

16. http://www.chapters.eiretek.org/books/Cloncurry/cloncurry5.htm, access date 8 Mar. 2006.

17. *Ibid.*

18. 'Daniel O'Connell's Correspondence', *Living Age,* vol. 180, 19 Jan 1889, p. 131. Reprinted from the *Quarterly Review.*

19. Valentine Browne Lawless, Baron Cloncurry, *Personal Recollections,* pp. 164, 169–174, 323.

20. Daniel O'Connell, 'To Lord Cloncurry', *The Times,* 19 Jan. 1831, p. 3.

21. 'Ireland', *The Times,* 26 Aug. 1845, p. 6.

22. Valentine Browne Lawless, Baron Cloncurry, *Letter from the Right Honorable Lord Cloncurry, to the Most Noble the Marquis of Downshire, on the Conduct of the Kildare-Street Education Society, and the Employment of the Poor* (Dublin: Thomas Reilly, 1826); No title, *The Times,* 29 Feb. 1832, p. 1. See also 'Reformers', *The Times,* 30 Oct. 1819, p. 2; 'Parliamentary Intelligence', *The Times,* 12 Feb. 1836, p. 3; No title, *The Times,* 1 Jun. 1838, p. 3; No title, *The Times,* 31 May 1842, p. 3; 'Lord Cloncurry on Coercion', *The Times,* 10 Mar. 1846, p. 7.

23. 'Parliamentary Intelligence', *The Times,* 8 Feb. 1832, p. 1.

24. 'Death of Lord Cloncurry', *The Times,* 31 Oct. 1853, p. 9.

25. No title, *The Times,* 24 Feb. 1807, p. 4, col. a.

26. The story of Sir John Piers's seduction of Lady Cloncurry is told, for instance, in the John Betjeman poem 'Sir John Piers'.

27. Emily Lawless, *A Garden Diary: September, 1899–September, 1900* (London: Methuen, 1901), pp. 68–9.

28. *Ibid.*

29. Marie O'Neill, 'Emily Lawless', *Dublin Historical Record,* vol. 48.2, Autumn 1995, p. 128.

30. Margaret Oliphant, 'A Noble Lady', *New Review,* vol. 14, 1896, p. 244.

31. Ronan Lynch, Letter to the Editor, *Tuam Herald,* 21 Mar. 2003 (http://www.unison.ie/tuam_herald/stories.php3?ca=53&si=93910 3&issue_id=8918, access date 6 Sep. 2004).

32. 'Ireland', *The Times,* 7 Apr. 1869, p. 10.

33. 'Inquests', *The Times,* 11 Nov. 1891, p. 7.

34. Daniel J. Murphy (ed.), *Lady Gregory's Journals, Volume Two, Books Thirty to Forty-Four, 21 February 1925–9 May 1932* (Gerrards Cross: Colin Smythe, 1987), p. 153.

35. Emily Lawless, Letter to W. E. H. Lecky, 13 May [1895?], Lecky correspondence, Trinity College, Dublin, MS 1827–36/2474.

36. Elizabeth, Countess of Fingall, *Seventy Years Young: Memories of Elizabeth, Countess of Fingall. Told to Pamela Hinkson* (1937; Dublin: Lilliput, 1995), p. 175.

37. *Ibid.*

38. Murphy (ed.), *Lady Gregory's Journals, Volume Two,* p. 153.

39. Emily Lawless, Letter to Mr Macmillan, 28 Jun. 1904, Macmillan Archive, British Library, Add. Mss. 54966, pp. 176–7.

40. Lennox Robinson (ed.), *Lady Gregory's Journals 1916–1930* (London: Putnam, 1946), p. 217.

41. Emily Lawless, Letter to Rhoda Broughton, 9 Oct. n. y., Delves Broughton Collection, DDB 16/M/L/2/, Chester, Cheshire Record Office.

42. Emily Lawless, Letter to Edmund Gosse, 3 Jul. 1908, Gosse correspondence, Brotherton Collection, Brotherton Library, Leeds.

43. Emily Lawless, Letter to W. E. H. Lecky, 5 Nov. [1895?], Lecky correspondence, Trinity College, Dublin, MS 1827–36/2477.

44. Emily Lawless, Letter to Mr Macmillan, 14 Mar. [1904], Macmillan Archive, British Library, Add. Mss. 54966, pp. 172–3.

45. Edith Sichel, 'Emily Lawless', *Nineteenth Century and After,* vol. 76, Jul. 1914, p. 87.

46. Edward E. Lysaght, *Sir Horace Plunkett and His Place in the Irish Nation* (Dublin: Maunsel, 1916), pp. 24–5.

47. Margaret Digby, *Horace Plunkett: An Anglo-American Irishman* (Oxford: Basil Blackwell, 1949), p. 98.

48. Horace Plunkett, Letter to Emily Lawless, 3 Oct. 1902, Lawless Papers, Marsh's Library, Dublin.

49. Horace Plunkett, Letter to Emily Lawless, 30 Jul. 1902, Lawless Papers, Marsh's Library, Dublin.

50. Emily Lawless, Letter to Lord Monteagle, 31 Aug. 1907, Monteagle papers, National Library, Dublin, MS 11141 (3).

51. Digby, p. 88.

52. Emily Lawless, Letter to Lord Castletown, 10 Aug. n. y., Lord Castletown Papers, National Library of Ireland, Dublin, MS 35304 (4).

53. Lecky correspondence, Trinity College, Dublin, MS 1827–36/455, 531, 550, 639, 2472–2482; [Elizabeth Lecky], *A Memoir of the Right Hon. William Edward Hartpole Lecky M. P., O. M., LL. D., D. C. L., LITT. D., Member of the French Institute and of the British Academy, by His Wife* (London: Longmans, Green, and Co., 1909), p. 222.

54. Apart from inscribing her history *Ireland* to Lord Dufferin and Ava, Lawless also sent him a signed copy of *Hurrish* for his 'Helen's Tower Library', a collection of books containing 'something or other by the hand of the writer'. Letter from Lord Dufferin to Emily Lawless, 13 Jul. 1887, quoted in Sir Alfred Lyall, *The Life of the Marquis of Dufferin and Ava* (1905; London: Thomas Nelson & Sons, n. d.), p. 442.

55. Digby, p. 153.

56. M. D. Petre (ed.), *George Tyrrell's Letters* (London: Fisher Unwin, 1920), pp. 271–6.

57. Emily Lawless, Letter to Edmund Gosse, 2 Apr. 1894, Gosse correspondence, Brotherton Collection, Brotherton Library, Leeds.

58. Emily Lawless, Letter to Edmund Gosse, 3 Jul. 1908.

59. *Ibid.*

60. *Ibid.*

61. Sichel, p. 99.

62. *Ibid.*

63. The friendship with Lawless and her mother was important also to Margaret Oliphant: 'A friendship of Mrs. Oliphant's later life, enchanting and enchanted, which she used to liken to the friendship of husband and wife, was that with Lady Cloncurry. Miss Emily Lawless, Lady Cloncurry's gifted daughter, the rise of whose genius was such a pleasure to Mrs. Oliphant, also shared in the joys and sorrows of these years.' 'Mrs. Oliphant's Autobiography', review of *The Autobiography of Margaret Oliphant*, by Margaret Oliphant, *Living Age*, vol. 223, 7 Oct. 1899, p. 7. See also Margaret Oliphant's

letters to Lawless, MS 23194–206–7, 215–18, 223–24, 233–38, 248–53, National Library of Scotland.

64. Sichel, p. 99.

65. Mrs Humphry Ward, *A Writer's Recollections* (London: Collins, 1918), p. 262.

66. Murphy (ed.), *Lady Gregory's Journals, Volume Two,* p. 423.

67. It should be noted that most of Lawless's friends abroad were English or Irish expatriates, however, many of them in imperial service, like the Marquis of Dufferin and Ava or Sir Alfred Lyall.

68. Elizabeth Jay (ed.), *The Autobiography of Margaret Oliphant* (Missisauga, Canada: Broadview, 2002), p. 171.

69. Quoted in William Linn, 'The Life and Works of the Hon. Emily Lawless', p. 42.

70. Quoted in Sichel, p. 87.

71. Emily Lawless, Letter to Lord Castletown, 2 Aug. n. y., National Library, Dublin, MS 35304 (4).

72. Murphy (ed.), *Lady Gregory's Journals Volume Two,* p. 424.

73. *Ibid.,* p. 152.

74. Sichel, p. 80.

75. Emily Lawless, Letter to Mr Macmillan, 10 Feb. n. y., Macmillan Archive, British Library, Add. Mss. 54966, pp. 180–1.

76. See, for instance, Emily Lawless, Letter to Mr Craik, 29 Aug. 1891, Macmillan Archive, British Library, Add. Mss. 54966, 147–8; Emily Lawless, Letter to Macmillan's, 3 Sep. 1891, Macmillan Archive, British Library, Add. Mss. 54966, 149; Emily Lawless, Letter to Macmillan's, 8 Sep. 1891, Macmillan Archive, British Library, Add. Mss. 54966, 150; Emily Lawless, Letter to Macmillan's, 23 Sep. 1891, Macmillan Archive, British Library, Add. Mss. 54966, 151–2.

77. Emily Lawless, Letter to Clement K. Shorter, 11 Apr. 1895, L 96, University College Dublin Library.

78. Emily Lawless, Letter to Macmillan's, 21 Mar. 1904, Macmillan Archive, British Library, Add. Mss. 54966 165–166.

79. Emily Lawless, Letter to Mr Macmillan, 5 Jul. n. y., Macmillan Archive, British Library, Add. Mss. 54966, 177–8.

80. Emily Lawless, Letter to Mr Macmillan, 13 Feb. n. y., Macmillan Archive, British Library, Add. Mss. 54966, 182–3.

81. 'Irish Literary Society', *Irish Book Lover,* vol. 7, 1916, p. 130.

82. Linn, p. 47.

83.   *Literary World,* n. d. 1895, n. p. Clipping in the Lawless Papers, Marsh's Library, Dublin.

84.   Sichel, p. 97. See also Linn, pp. 44–5.

85.   *The Diaries of Sir Horace Plunkett,* entry for 21 Oct. 1913. Quoted in Linn, p. 47, n. 253.

86.   Katharine Tynan, *The Years of the Shadow* (London: Constable, 1919), p. 94.

87.   In the Preface to his *Anglo-Irish Literature,* Hugh Alexander Law deplores the effects of the tendency in Irish literary criticism to judge works in terms of nationalism: 'Mr. Yeats' right to be esteemed the chief of modern Anglo-Irish poets was long unquestioned. But only the other day, chancing upon a copy of a widely-read Irish weekly paper, I read in it the startling phrase – "Mr. Yeats, an Englishman wherever he may have been born". Again, a writer in a well-known review has recently denounced those very persons whom Mr. Boyd – justly as I think – delights to honour, as un-Irish and even as anti-Irish. "Yeats and his school", so the writer informs us, "are foreigners here . . . They are worse than foreigners. They simply have no point of contact at all with Ireland save with the very basest". They are, it appears, distinguished "by their rancorous enmity to the Irish people".' Hugh Alexander Law, *Anglo-Irish Literature* (Dublin: Talbot, 1926), pp. x–xi. Such a critical climate can obviously not tolerate the political ambiguity that characterises Emily Lawless's writing.

Notes to Chapter Two

1.   Ann Heilmann, *New Woman Fiction: Women Writing First-Wave Feminism* (Basingstoke: Macmillan, 2000), p. 4.

2.   For an overview of Irish women's access to higher education in the late nineteenth and early twentieth centuries, see Eibhlín Breathnach, 'Charting New Waters: Women's Experience in Higher Education, 1879–1908', in Mary Cullen (ed.), *Girls Don't Do Honours: Irish Women in Education in the 19th and 20th Centuries* (Dublin: Women's Education Bureau, 1987), pp. 55–78.

3.   Gaye Tuchman with Nina E. Fortin, *Edging Women Out: Victorian Novelists, Publishers, and Social Change* (London: Routledge, 1989), pp. 7–8.

4.   Edith Sichel, 'Emily Lawless', *Nineteenth Century and After*, vol. 76, 1914, p. 80.

5.   Emily Lawless, *Traits and Confidences* (1897; New York: Garland, 1979), pp. 8–9.

6.   Sichel, p. 80.

7.   James M. Cahalan, *Double Visions: Women and Men in Modern and Contemporary Irish Fiction* (Syracuse, NY: Syracuse University Press, 1999), p. 30.

8.   See Cliona Murphy, *The Women's Suffrage Movement and Irish Society in the Early Twentieth Century* (Philadephia: Temple University Press, 1989).

9.   Horace Plunkett, Ellice Pilkington and George Russell, *The United Irishwomen: Their Place, Work and Ideals* (Dublin: Maunsel & Co., 1911), p. 11.

10. *Ibid.*, pp. 43–4.

11. *Ibid.*, p. 1.

12. See Merryn Williams, 'Feminist or Antifeminist? Oliphant and the Woman Question', in D. J. Trela (ed.), *Margaret Oliphant: Critical Essays on a Gentle Subversive* (Selinsgrove: Susquehanna University Press, 1995), pp. 165–80. Williams concludes that 'Margaret Oliphant is a complex figure, typecast as antifeminist, yet concerned throughout her life with the problems of women and the author of several novels that are rooted in this concern', p. 179.

13. Margaret Oliphant, 'A Noble Lady', *New Review*, vol. 14, 1896, p. 246.

14. Elizabeth Jay, *Mrs Oliphant: 'A Fiction to Herself': A Literary Life* (Oxford: Clarendon Press, 1995), p. 48.

15. Arlene Young, *Culture, Class and Gender in the Victorian Novel: Gentlemen, Gents and Working Women* (Houndmills: Macmillan, 1999), p. 131.

16. Jay, pp. 48–9.

17. Sichel, p. 98.

18. 'An Appeal Against Women's Suffrage', *Nineteenth Century*, vol. 148.25, Jun. 1889, pp. 781–8. Lawless's name appears on page 786.

19. *Ibid.*, p. 782.

20. See Julia Bush, 'British Women's Anti-Suffragism and the Forward Policy, 1908–14', *Women's History Review*, vol. 11.3, 2002, pp. 431–54, for an account of Mary A. Ward's involvement in the

organisation the Forward Policy and its attempts to support positive policies for women.

21. Mrs Humphry Ward, *Delia Blanchflower* (1915; London: Ward, Lock & Co., 1917).

22. Emily Lawless, Letter to A. V. Dicey, 24 July, n. y., University of Glasgow Library, MS. Gen 508 (47).

23. *Ibid.*

24. *Ibid.*

25. *Ibid.* The battle of Majuba or Amajuba took place 27 Feb. 1881 during the first Boer War and led to English defeat.

26. Heilmann, p. 12.

27. Although published after Lawless's first Irish novel, *Hurrish* (1886), *Major Lawrence, F.L.S.* belongs with the early novels because of its English and continental setting.

28. Emily Lawless, *A Chelsea Householder* (1882; New York: Henry Holt, 1883), p. 148. Subsequent references to this work are given parenthetically in the text.

29. Quoted in William MacCrillis Griswold, *A Descriptive List of British Novels* (Cambridge, MA, 1891).

30. *Ibid.*

31. Review of *A Chelsea Householder,* by Emily Lawless, *Dublin Evening Mail,* 22 Nov. 1882, n. p. Clipping in the Lawless Papers, Marsh's Library, Dublin.

32. Emily Lawless, Letter to Macmillan's, 6 Feb. 1883, Macmillan Archive, British Library, Add. Mss. 54966, 128–9.

33. Sichel, p. 84.

34. William Linn, 'The Life and Works of the Hon. Emily Lawless' First Novelist of the Irish Literary revival, dissertation, New York University, 1971, p. 52.

35. Review of *A Chelsea Householder,* by Emily Lawless, *Standard,* 8 Jan. 1883, n. p. Clipping in the Lawless Papers, Marsh's Library, Dublin; 'A Chelsea Householder', review of *A Chelsea Householder,* by Emily Lawless, *Spectator,* 4 Nov. 1882, pp. 1416–17.

36. *Ibid.*, p. 1417.

37. Nicola Diane Thompson, *Reviewing Sex: Gender and the Reception of Victorian Novels* (Basingstoke: Macmillan, 1996), pp. 8–24.

38. Emily Lawless, Letter to Mr Macmillan, 4 Jan. 1885, Macmillan Archive, British Library, Add. Mss. 54966, 140–1.

39. Emily Lawless, Letter to Macmillan's, 18 May 1885, Macmillan Archive, British Library, Add. Mss. 54966, 143–4.

40. 'Books of the Month', review of *A Millionaire's Cousin,* by Emily Lawless, *Atlantic Monthly,* vol. 56.336, Oct. 1885, p. 576.

41. Emily Lawless, Letter to Mr Macmillan, 21 May 1885, Macmillan Archive, British Library, Add. Mss. 54966, 145–6.

42. Emily Lawless, 'A Biscayan Stroll', *The Gentleman's Magazine,* vol. 28, 1882, p. 28.

43. Emily Lawless, *A Millionaire's Cousin: A Story* (London: Macmillan, 1885), p. 1. Subsequent references to this work are given parenthetically in the text.

44. See, for instance, Tina Krontiris, *Oppositional Voices: Women as Writers and Translators of Literature in the English Renaissance* (London: Routledge, 1992), pp. 3–23, for an overview of women's situation in the sixteenth and early seventeenth centuries.

45. Dale Spender, *Mothers of the Novel: 100 Good Women Writers before Jane Austen* (London: Pandora, 1986), p. 158.

46. Bell's immediate response that there are no convents for Protestants hints at a religious dimension to the problem that Lawless does not explore, except for very briefly in a conversation between Bell and Miss Bonson about the situation of Islamic women. Lawless, *A Millionaire's Cousin,* pp. 61–4.

47. James M. Cahalan, 'Forging a Tradition: Emily Lawless and the Irish Literary Canon', *Colby Quarterly,* vol. 27.1, 1991, p. 35.

48. Emily Lawless, *Major Lawrence, F. L. S.* (1887; New York: Henry Holt, 1887), p. 273.

49. 'Major Lawrence', review of *Major Lawrence,* by Emily Lawless, *Pall Mall Gazette,* 23 Jan. 1888, n. p. Clipping in the Lawless Papers, Marsh's Library, Dublin.

50. Linn, p. 67.

51. 'Novels', review of *Major Lawrence,* by Emily Lawless, *Saturday Review,* 28 Jan. 1888, n. p. Clipping in the Lawless Papers, Marsh's Library, Dublin.

52. 'Major Lawrence', *Pall Mall Gazette,* 23. Jan. 1888, n. p. Clipping in the Lawless Papers, Marsh's Library, Dublin.

53. Emily Lawless, Letter to Macmillan's, 18 Sep. 1883, Macmillan Archive, British Library, Add. Mss. 54966, 134.

54. Emily Lawless, *Plain Frances Mowbray and Other Tales* (London: John Murray, 1889), p. 60. Subsequent references to this work will be given parenthetically in the text.

55. Margaret Oliphant, 'The Old Salon 16', review of *Plain Frances Mowbray and Other Stories,* by Emily Lawless, *Blackwood's Magazine,* vol. 145, Jan. 1889, p. 831.

56. Linn, p. 165.

57. Oliphant, 'The Old Salon 16', p. 833.

58. *Ibid.*, p. 833.

59. See chapter 1.

60. Review of *Plain Frances Mowbray and Other Tales,* by Emily Lawless, *Saturday Review,* 27 Jul. 1889, n. p. Clipping in the Lawless Papers, Marsh's Library, Dublin.

61. Oliphant, 'The Old Salon 16', p. 830.

62. 'Current Literature', review of *Plain Frances Mowbray and Other Tales,* by Emily Lawless, *Spectator,* 15 Jun. 1889, p. 835.

63. *Ibid.*, p. 836.

Notes to Chapter Three

1. Barbara Bender, 'Introduction: Landscape–Meaning and Action', in Barbara Bender (ed.), *Landscape, Politics and Perspectives* (Oxford: Berg, 1993), pp. 1–2.

2. Catherine Nash, 'Remapping the Body/Land: New Cartographies of Identity, Gender, and Landscape in Ireland', in Alison Blunt and Gillian Rose (eds.), *Writing Women and Space: Colonial and Postcolonial Geographies* (New York: Guilford, 1994), p. 234.

3. Emily Lawless, *A Garden Diary: September, 1899–September, 1900* (London: Methuen, 1901), p. 8. Subsequent references to this work will be given parenthetically in the text.

4. Michel Foucault, *Power/Knowledge: Selected Interviews and Other Writings 1972–1977,* ed. Colin Gordon, trans. Colin Gordon, Leo Marshall, John Mepham, Kate Soper (Brighton: Harvester, 1980), p. 73.

5. John Wilson Foster, *Colonial Consequences: Essays in Irish Literature and Culture* (Dublin: Lilliput, 1991), p. 30.

6. Philip Bull, *Land, Politics and Nationalism: A Study of the Irish Land Question* (Dublin: Gill & Macmillan, 1996), p. 95. The most intensive phase of what is termed 'the Irish Land War' is the period

of Land League mobilisation (1879–1882), but the conflict lasted longer – it could be argued that it did not end until after the proclamation of the Irish Free State in 1922.

7. S. J. Connolly, 'Culture, Identity and Tradition: Changing Definitions of Irishness', in Brian Graham (ed.), *In Search of Ireland: A Cultural Geography* (London: Routledge, 1997), p. 57.

8. The nineteenth century saw the development from a rather inclusive variety of nationalism, represented by, for instance, Wolfe Tone at the end of the eighteenth century, to a more exclusive form, where from the 1820s onwards Irish nationalism was increasingly identified with Catholicism. It is this late nineteenth-century version of nationalism that is intended here.

9. There was no law forbidding women to own land, however, and there are several both real and fictional exceptions to the rule that women seldom were landowners, one of them the female protagonist of Emily Lawless's *Grania: The Story of an Island*. It could be argued, also, that the Ladies' Land League constitutes an example of women defining their Irish identity by claiming land rights, though in most cases the women in the group did not claim the land for themselves. The Ladies' Land League was headed by Charles Stewart Parnell's sister, Anna Parnell, and was in operation only until 1882, since Anna Parnell felt that the group had no power, only responsibilities. See Anna Parnell, *The Tale of a Great Sham*, ed. Dana Hearne (Dublin: Arlen House, 1986).

10. Emily Lawless, 'Notes in the Morbihan', *National Review*, vol. 4, 1884–5, p. 492.

11. *Ibid.*, p. 498.

12. Emily Lawless, 'North Clare – Leaves from a Diary,' *Nineteenth Century*, vol. 46, 1899, p. 604.

13. Emily Lawless, 'Iar-Connaught: A Sketch', *Cornhill Magazine*, vol. 45, Mar. 1882, p. 321.

14. Lawless, 'North Clare', p. 607.

15. Gillian Rose, *Feminism and Geography: The Limits of Geographical Knowledge* (Cambridge: Polity Press, 1993), p. 140.

16. James M. Cahalan, *Double Visions: Women and Men in Modern and Contemporary Irish Fiction* (Syracuse, NY: Syracuse University Press, 1999), p. 34.

17. See, for instance, Val Plumwood, *Feminism and the Mastery of Nature* (London: Routledge, 1993) and Karen J. Warren (ed.), *Ecofeminism: Women, Culture, Nature* (Bloomington: Indiana University Press, 1997).

18. See, for instance, Lynda Birke, *Feminism, Animals and Science: The Naming of the Shrew* (Buckingham: Open University Press, 1994).

19. The *Times* review of *A Garden Diary* suggests affinities with both Elizabeth von Arnim's *Elizabeth and her German Garden* (1898) and Maria Theresa Earle's *Pot-Pourri from a Surrey Garden* (1897). There are certainly similarities in the ways these writers use musings on their plants and gardens as points of departure for more wide-ranging philosophical reflections, though the proto-feminist tone is much more prominent in von Arnim's work than in Lawless's text. Review of *A Garden Diary*, by Emily Lawless, *The Times*, 31 Aug. 1901, p. 3, col. b.

20. Rose, p. 115.

21. Lawless, 'North Clare', pp. 610–11.

22. *Ibid.*, p. 612.

23. See, for instance, Emily Lawless, 'An Addition to Mr. Birchell's List of 'The Lepidoptera of Ireland"', *Entomologist's Monthly Magazine*, vol. 3, Jan. 1867, p. 187; 'A Dredging Ground', *Nineteenth Century*, vol. 10, 1881, pp. 131–41; 'Florentine Gardens in March', *Nineteenth Century*, vol. 45, 1899, pp. 327–35; 'Irish Captures in 1870 and 1871', *Entomologist*, vol. 6, 1882, pp. 74–8 and 97–100; 'Irish Memories–West and East', in Margaret Waterfield (ed.), *Flower Grouping in English, Scotch and Irish Gardens* (London: J. M. Dent, 1907), pp. 3–26; 'Some Mothing Memories', *Monthly Review*, vol. 7.3. Report in *Littell's Living Age*, vol. 234, 1902, pp. 414–19; 'Two Leaves from a Note-Book', *Alexandra College Magazine*, Jun. 1895, pp. 242–50; 'An Upland Bog', *Belgravia*, vol. 45, 1881, pp. 417–30. Lawless's interest in nature studies is apparent in most of her writing, though not only in texts directly concerned with botany, etc.

24. Emily Lawless, 'In the Kingdom of Kerry', *The Gentleman's Magazine*, vol. 28, 1882, p. 548.

25. *Ibid.*, p. 545.

26. *Ibid.*, p. 552.

27. Lawless, 'North Clare', p. 607.

28. *Ibid.*, pp. 608–9.

29. Susan Stanford Friedman, *Mappings: Feminism and the Cultural Geographies of Encounter* (Princeton, NJ: Princeton University Press, 1998), p. 19.

30. Emily Lawless, *Traits and Confidences* (1897; New York: Garland, 1979), pp. 150–8.

31. Gillian Rose strongly criticises the idea of a readable landscape, claiming that '[t]he metaphor of landscape as text works to establish an authoritative reading, and to maintain that authority whenever emotion threatens to erupt and mark the author as a feeling subject. Knowledge/texts/evidence are asserted over and against emotion' (Rose, pp. 100–1). Textualising landscape, Rose maintains, 'encourages a retreat back to a disinterested and therefore disembodied search for evidence and truth' (Rose, p. 101). The meanings of Lawless's textual landscapes are precisely emotional, however, and they are fixed only insofar as the viewer is attuned to these emotions.

32. Lawless, 'Iar-Connaught', p. 325. Andrew Hadfield comments on the destruction of Irish woodland in the introduction to the section 'Land and Landscape' in Andrew Hadfield and John McVeagh (eds.), *Strangers to that Land: British Perceptions of Ireland from the Reformation to the Famine* (Gerrards Cross: Colin Smythe, 1994), p. 63: 'The importance of woodland in Ireland should not be underestimated. Woods were valued as raw material, particularly for the Pipe-staving industry [. . .], and timber was so over-used that a severe shortage occurred in the early 1600s. However, woods also served to hide Irish "rebels" and were removed for this reason. Ulster, once a vast forest, is still virtually treeless today after the destruction performed to establish the plantation and the re-establishment of woodland is by no means a dead political issue.'

33. Emily Lawless, *Hurrish: A Study* (1886; Belfast: Appletree, 1992), p. 3. Subsequent references to this work will be given parenthetically in the text.

34. Lisbet Kickham, *Protestant Women Novelists and Irish Society 1879–1922,* Lund Studies in English, 106 (Lund: Lund University, 2004), p. 38.

35. Charles de Kay, 'Woman in Ireland of Old', *Catholic World,* vol. 43.225, Jun. 1886, p. 382.

36. Ernest Boyd, *Ireland's Literary Renaissance* (1916, rev. ed. 1922; Dublin: Allen Figgis, 1968), p. 374.

37. Margaret Oliphant, Letter to Emily Lawless, Jul. 1890. Lawless Papers, Marsh's Library, Dublin.

38. 'Hurrish', review of *Hurrish: A Study*, by Emily Lawless, *St James's Gazette*, 5 Feb. 1886, n. p. Clipping in the Lawless Papers, Marsh's Library, Dublin.

39. 'Recent Novels: Hurrish', review of *Hurrish:* A Study, by Emily Lawless, *Morning Post*, n. d., n. p. Clipping in the Lawless Papers, Marsh's Library, Dublin.

40. 'Recent Fiction', review of *Hurrish: A Study*, by Emily Lawless, *Overland Monthly and Out West Magazine*, vol. 7.42, Jun. 1886, p. 651.

41. 'A Great Irish Novelist', review of *Grania: The Story of an Island*, by Emily Lawless, *United Ireland*, Apr. 1892, n. p. Clipping in the Lawless Papers, Marsh's Library, Dublin.

42. Maurice F. Egan, 'A Chat About New Books', review of *Hurrish: A Study*, by Emily Lawless, *Catholic World*, vol. 43.254, May 1886, p. 274.

43. *Nation*, 20 Feb. 1886, quoted in William Linn, 'The Life and Works of the Hon. Emily Lawless, First Novelist of the Irish Literary Revival,' dissertation, New York University, 1971, pp. 74–5.

44. Daniel J. Murphy (ed.), *Lady Gregory's Journals, Volume Two, Books Thirty to Forty-Four, 21 February 1925–9 May 1932* (Gerrards Cross: Colin Smythe, 1987), pp. 418–19.

45. Betty Webb Brewer, '"She was a Part of it": Emily Lawless (1845–1913)', *Éire-Ireland: A Journal of Irish Studies*, vol. 18:4, 1983, p. 123.

46. Boyd, p. 376.

47. For a discussion of *Hurrish* and law, see Heather Laird, *Subversive Law in Ireland 1879–1920* (Dublin: Four Courts Press, 2005), pp. 43–59.

48. W. E. Gladstone, 'Notes and Queries on the Irish Demands', *Special Aspects of the Irish Question: A Series of Reflections in and since 1886. Collected from various sources and reprinted* (London: J. Murray, 1892), p. 151.

49. 'Ireland', *The Times*, 30 Jul. 1883, p. 6. The notice continues with some information about the other side of Irish life at the time:

'Eighty emigrants, 40 male and 40 female, left Dublin on Thursday morning from the South Dublin Union Work house. Captain Boyd, one of the guardians, took charge of them.'

50. [Stephen Gwynn], 'Novels of Irish Life', *Living Age*, vol. 212, 2744, 1897, p. 396.

51. Mountstuart Elphinstone Grant Duff, *Notes from a Diary: 1892–1895, I* (London: 1904), p. 82. Quoted in Linn, p. 32.

52. According to William Linn, 'M. C.' was Mary Cole, née Mary de Vere. Linn, p. 33, n 187, and p. 90, n 49.

53. Murphy (ed.), *Lady Gregory's Journals, Volume Two*, p. 423. Lady Gregory was displeased with Lawless's description of the language in her plays as 'a convention' and commented that it 'was all from the spoken word' (p. 424).

54. Review of *Grania: The Story of an Island*, by Emily Lawless, *Manchester Guardian*, 29 Mar. 1892, n. p. Clipping in the Lawless Papers, Marsh's Library, Dublin.

55. 'Happiness', review of *Grania: The Story of an Island*, by Emily Lawless, *Spectator*, vol. 69, 6 Aug. 1892, pp. 186–7; 'Miss Lawless's "Grania"', review of *Grania: The Story of an Island*, by Emily Lawless, *Spectator*, vol. 68, 26. Mar. 1892, pp. 431–3.

56. 'Novels of the Week', review of *Grania: The Story of an Island*, by Emily Lawless, *Dr. Willoughby Smith*, by Mrs. A. M. Marks, *A Masquerader*, by Algernon Gissing, *An East-End Mystery*, by Adeline Sergeant, *That Stick*, by Charlotte M. Yonge, *Athenæum*, vol. 99, 16 Apr. 1892, pp. 496–7.

57. 'Grania', review of *Grania: The Story of an Island*, by Emily Lawless, *Bookman*, 2 Apr. 1892, p. 27.

58. 'New Novels', review of *Grania: The Story of an Island*, by Emily Lawless, *Jonquille, or The Swiss Smuggler*, by T. Combe, *Eline Vere*, by Louis Couperus, *San Salvador*, by Mary Agnes Tincker, *Nation*, 26 May 1892, pp. 401–2.

59. 'Comment on New Books', review of *Grania: The Story of an Island*, by Emily Lawless, *Atlantic Monthly*, vol. 69, 416, 1892, p. 848.

60. R. E. Prothero, 'Grania', review of *Grania: The Story of an Island*, by Emily Lawless, *Nineteenth Century*, vol. 31, Apr. 1892, p. 695.

61. 'Book Reviews', review of *Grania: The Story of an Island*, by Emily Lawless, *Overland Monthly and Out West Magazine*, vol. 26.155, Nov. 1895, p. 572.

62. 'A Great Irish Novelist', n. p.

63. Review of *Grania: The Story of an Island,* by Emily Lawless, *North British Daily Mail,* 25 Mar. 1892, n. p. Clipping in the Lawless papers, Marsh's Library, Dublin.

64. Mrs Humphry Ward, *A Writer's Recollections* (London: Collins, 1918), p. 263.

65. Grant Duff, p. 82. Quoted in Linn, p. 32.

66. Emily Lawless, *With the Wild Geese* (London: Isbister, 1902), p. 43. The poem was first published in the privately printed *Atlantic Rhythms and Rhymes,* where it is specified that it is set on Inishmaan.

67. Emily Lawless, *Grania: The Story of an Island,* 2 vols. (1892; New York: Garland, 1979), vol. 1, p. 52. Subsequent references to this work will be given parenthetically in the text.

68. Linn, p. 82.

69. Grant Duff, p. 82. Quoted in Linn, p. 32.

70. Edith Sichel, 'Emily Lawless', *Nineteenth Century and After,* vol. 76, Jul. 1914, p. 99.

71. Lawless, *With the Wild Geese,* p. 48.

72. Quoted in David H. Greene and Edward M. Stephens, *J. M. Synge, 1871–1909* (1959; New York: Collier, 1961), pp. 95–6.

73. Violet Martin (Martin Ross), Letter to Hildegarde (Somerville) Coghill, 22 May 1895, Coghill archive. I am grateful to Gifford Lewis for providing me with an extract from this letter.

74. 'Irish Literary Society', *Irish Book Lover,* vol. 7, 1916, pp. 129–30.

75. Elizabeth Grubgeld interprets *Grania* as 'a vivid, obsessive response to the processes of erosion and geologic change as dramatically revealed on the island of Inishmaan. Like her Victorian predecessors, Lawless reads in the landscape itself the evidence of private and national upheaval.' Elizabeth Grubgeld, 'Emily Lawless's *Grania: The Story of an Island* (1892)', *Éire-Ireland: A Journal of Irish Studies,* vol. 22.3, 1987, p. 115.

76. For a comment on this passage, see Siobhán Kilfeather, 'Sex and Sensation in the Nineteenth-Century Novel', in Margaret Kelleher and James H. Murphy (eds.), *Gender Perspectives in Nineteenth-century Ireland: Public and Private Spheres* (Dublin: Irish Academic Press, 1997), p. 83.

77. See Gerardine Meaney, 'Decadence, Degeneration and Revolting Aesthetics: The Fiction of Emily Lawless and Katherine Cecil

Thurston', *Colby Quarterly*, vol. 36.2, 2000, p. 167, for a useful commentary on Murdough Blake's loquacity.

78. Jacqueline Belanger also sees Grania's only place as in-between the islands and the mainland. See Jacqueline Belanger, 'The Desire of the West: The Aran Islands and Irish Identity in *Grania*', in Leon Litvack and Glenn Hooper (eds.), *Ireland in the Nineteenth Century: Regional Identity* (Dublin: Four Courts, 2000), p. 103.

79. Bridget Matthews-Kane, 'Emily Lawless's *Grania:* Making for the Open,' *Colby Quarterly*, vol. 33.3, 1997, p. 234.

80. Cahalan, p. 33.

81. Friedman, p. 138.

82. As Jacqueline Belanger makes clear, there is obviously also a temporal aspect to Grania's development, and her experience in Galway in particular draws attention to this temporality, since Grania sees her future self in the abused peasant woman whose home she visits. Belanger, pp. 102–3.

83. Brian Graham, 'Ireland and Irishness: Place, Culture and Identity', in Brian Graham (ed.), *In Search of Ireland: A Cultural Geography* (London: Routledge, 1997), p. 7.

84. Seán Ó Tuama, 'Stability and Ambivalence: Aspects of the Sense of Place and Religion in Irish Literature', in Joseph Lee (ed.), *Ireland Towards a Sense of Place* (Cork: Cork University Press, 1985), p. 24.

85. Foster, p. 253.

86. Norman Jeffares, 'Place, Space and Personality and the Irish Writer', in Andrew Carpenter (ed.), *Place, Personality and the Irish Writer* (Gerrards Cross: Colin Smythe, 1977), p. 22.

87. Emily Lawless, 'Connaught Homes', *Monthly Review*, vol. 31.11.1, April 1903, pp. 152–3.

88. Nash, p. 235.

89. Belanger, p. 98.

90. Lawless, 'Connaught Homes', p. 144.

91. Emily Lawless, 'A Note on the Ethics of Literary Forgery', *Nineteenth Century*, vol. 41, 1897, p. 92.

92. See Belanger, pp. 95–107, for a discussion of centre and margin in relation to the Aran Islands as the setting of the novel.

93. Grania's refusal to learn English and her total identification with Inishmaan might be said to point towards an essential understanding of Irishness, but the circumstance that Lawless resists

such a definition in her other work makes it more plausible that Grania should be seen as an illustration of the problems and possibilities of being both an insider and an outsider.

94. Brewer, p. 124.

95. Lawless, 'Iar-Connaught', p. 319.

96. Rose, p. 137.

97. Emily Lawless, *The Book of Gilly: Four Months Out of a Life* (London: Smith and Elder, 1906), p. 187. Subsequent references to this work will be given parenthetically in the text.

98. See Seamus Deane, 'Irish National Character 1790–1900', in Tom Dunne (ed.), *The Writer as Witness: Literature as Historical Evidence* (Cork: Cork University Press, 1987), pp. 109–10.

99. Quoted in Hugh Alexander Law, *Anglo-Irish Literature* (Dublin: Talbot, 1926), pp. 276–7.

100. James Charles Roy, 'Landscape and the Celtic Soul', *Éire-Ireland: A Journal of Irish Studies,* vol. 31.3–4, 1996, p. 234.

101. Graham, p. 4.

102. Lawless, 'Connaught Homes', p. 153.

Notes to Chapter Four

1. See, for instance, Jennifer Coates, *Women, Men and Language: A Sociolinguistic Account of Sex Differences in Language* (1986; London: Longman, 1991), Carol Gilligan, *In a Different Voice: Psychological Theory and Women's Development* (1982; Cambridge, MA: Harvard University Press, 1993), and Deborah Tannen, *Gender and Discourse* (Oxford: Oxford University Press, 1994) for discussions of women's and men's language.

2. See Deborah Cameron, *Verbal Hygiene* (London: Routledge, 1995), pp. 166–211, for a discussion of advice literature and women's language. Advice books concerned with changing the way women speak and react to language do, of course, rely on essentialist notions of gender and are, as Cameron argues, fundamentally conservative.

3. Diane P. Freedman, 'Discourse as Power: Renouncing Denial', in Carol J. Singley and Susan Elizabeth Sweeney (eds.), *Anxious Power: Reading, Writing, and Ambivalence in Narrative by Women* (Albany: State University of New York Press, 1993), p. 364.

4. Susan Sniader Lanser, *Fictions of Authority: Women Writers and Narrative Voice* (Ithaca, NY: Cornell University Press, 1992), p. 18.

5.   Carol J. Singley, 'Female Language, Body, and Self', in Carol J. Singley and Susan Elizabeth Sweeney (eds.), *Anxious Power: Reading, Writing, and Ambivalence in Narrative by Women* (Albany: State University of New York Press, 1993), p. 7.

6.   Monika Fludernik, *Towards a 'Natural' Narratology* (London: Routledge, 1996), p. 362.

7.   See, for instance, Tina Krontiris, *Oppositional Voices: Women as Writers and Translators of Literature in the English Renaissance* (London: Routledge, 1992).

8.   Carol J Singley and Susan Elizabeth Sweeney, Preface, in Carol J. Singley and Susan Elizabeth Sweeney (eds.), *Anxious Power: Reading, Writing, and Ambivalence in Narrative by Women* (Albany: State University of New York Press, 1993), p. ix.

9.   See, for instance, Linda Hutcheon, *A Poetics of Postmodernism: History, Theory, Fiction* (1988; New York: Routledge, 1992).

10. M. M. Bakhtin, *The Dialogic Imagination: Four Essays,* ed. Michael Holquist, trans. Caryl Emerson and Michael Holquist (1981; Austin: University of Texas Press, 1985), pp. 304–5.

11. Laurie A. Finke, *Feminist Theory, Women's Writing* (Ithaca: Cornell University Press, 1992), pp. 13, 8.

12. Joseph Falaky Nagy, *Conversing with Angels: Literary Myths of Medieval Ireland* (Dublin: Four Courts, 1997), p. 21.

13. Emily Lawless, 'A Note on the Ethics of Literary Forgery', *Nineteenth Century,* vol. 41, 1897, p. 86.

14. Nagy, p. 328.

15. Hayden White, *Tropics of Discourse: Essays in Cultural Criticism* (1978; Baltimore: Johns Hopkins University Press, 1990), p. 83.

16. Roy Foster, *The Irish Story: Telling Tales and Making it up in Ireland* (2001; London: Penguin, 2002), pp. 2, 25.

17. See Foster, pp. 6–16, for a discussion of A. M. Sullivan's and Standish O'Grady's histories of Ireland.

18. See Chapter 6 for a discussion of Emily Lawless's cross-gendered historical fictions.

19. Inga Floto, *Historie: nyere og nyeste tid* (København: Gyldendal, 1985), pp. 13–50.

20. 'The Real Historian', *Macmillan's Magazine,* vol. 66, 1892, p. 221.

21. Mark Reid, 'Our Young Historians', *Macmillan's Magazine,* vol. 68, 1892–93, p. 95.

22. Reid, p. 98.

23. Emily Lawless, 'W. E. H. Lecky: A Reminiscence', *Monthly Review*, vol. 14.41, 1904, p. 116.

24. Emily Lawless, Letter to W. E. H. Lecky, 30 December 1890, Lecky correpondence Trinity College Dublin, MS 1827–36/639. Also quoted in William Linn, 'The Life and Works of the Hon. Emily Lawless, First Novelist of the Irish Literary Revival,' dissertation, New York University, 1971, p. 182. Linn sees the letter extract as evidence that Lawless considered the role of the historian to be 'to assess and portray the influence of dominant personalities upon their era'. Linn, pp. 181–2. To the extent that a story needs characters, this was certainly true.

25. Emily Lawless, 'Irish History Considered as a Pastime', in Emily Lawless, *Traits and Confidences* (London: Methuen, 1897), pp. 224–5.

26. Mary O'Dowd, 'From Morgan to MacCurtain: Women Historians in Ireland from the 1790s to the 1990s', in Alan Hayes and Diane Urquhart (eds.), *The Irish Women's History Reader* (London: Routledge, 2001), p. 10.

27. Linn, pp. 179–80.

28. Emily Lawless, *Ireland: With Some Additions by Mrs. Arthur Bronson* (1887; London: Fisher Unwin, 1898), p. x. Subsequent references to this text will be given parenthetically in the text.

29. Emily Lawless, *Ireland,* rev. ed. with two new chapters (London: Fisher Unwin, 1912), pp. 434–5. A third edition with chapters on the Free State by Michael MacDonagh appeared in 1923.

30. 'Book Reviews', review of *The Story of Ireland,* by Emily Lawless, *Overland Monthly and Out West Magazine,* vol. 12.67, Jul. 1887, p. 110.

31. Emily Lawless, Letter to W. E. H. Lecky, Aug. 24 [1887?], Lecky correpondence Trinity College Dublin, MS 1827–36/2476.

32. Linn, pp. 183–5.

33. Standish O'Grady, *Early Bardic Literature, Ireland* (1879; New York: Lemma, 1970), p. 15. For more recent discussions of the historical value of bardic literature, see Donnchadh Ó Corráin, 'Legend as Critic', in Tom Dunne (ed.), *The Writer as Witness: Literature as Historical Evidence* (Cork: Cork University Press 1987), pp. 23–38; Katharine Simms, 'Bardic Poetry as a Historical Source', in Tom

Dunne (ed.), *The Writer as Witness: Literature as Historical Evidence* (Cork: Cork University Press 1987), pp. 58–75.

34. John Mitchel, *The History of Ireland from the Treaty of Limerick to the Present Time*, 2 vols., (Dublin: James Duffy, 1869), vol. 1, pp. v–vi. Despite its clear nationalist outlook, Mitchel's work – though not A. M. Sullivan's far more popular *The Story of Ireland* – appears in Lawless's list of Authorities for her history.

35. Carla Kaplan, *The Erotics of Talk: Women's Writing and Feminist Paradigms* (New York: Oxford University Press, 1996), p. 11.

36. Review of *The Story of Ireland*, by Emily Lawless, *Detroit Tribune*, 1 Jan. 1888 [?], n. p. Clipping in the Lawless Papers, Marsh's Library, Dublin.

37. See Sir Alfred Lyall, *The Life of the Marquis of Dufferin and Ava* (1905; London: Thomas Nelson & Sons, n. d.), particularly Chapter VI 'Ireland', pp. 151–190, for an account of Lord Dufferin's views on the Irish Land question. Dufferin argued for the rights of the landlords and protested against the 'three Fs' of Free Sale, Fair Rent and Fixity of Tenure.

38. Review of *The Story of Ireland*, *Detroit Tribune*.

39. Spelling and form of 'Tuatha-da-Danaans' as the word appears in Emily Lawless's *Ireland*.

40. There are numerous variants of Abbé's name, the most common being MacGeoghegan. The spelling McGecghehan is almost certainly a misprint, since Lawless uses the form McGeoghegan in her list of Authorities (p. 422) and the spelling McGeoghan in the Index (p. 431). See Yves Le Juen, 'The Abbé MacGeoghegan Dies', *Eighteenth-Century Ireland*, vol. 13, 1998, p. 135. Abbé James MacGeoghegan published his *History of Ireland* in France between 1758 and 1762, which meant that he could include critical opinions that could not be printed in Ireland at the time. It is a Catholic, nationalist and Jacobite work, and was widely read in the nineteenth century as a classic of Irish nationalism. It is also profoundly anti-democratic, however, and propounds ideas such as the divine right of kings, hereditary nobility and patriarchal monarchy.

41. Finke, p. 17.

42. Elizabeth Cloncurry, Letter to W. E. H. Lecky, 20 Jul. 1887, Lecky correpondence Trinity College Dublin, MS 1827–36/455.

43. Lawless, 'W. E. H. Lecky', pp. 117, 119.

44. Emily Lawless, 'Of the Personal Element in History', *Nineteenth Century,* vol. 50, 1901, p. 798.

45. 'The Story of the Nations: Ireland', *Spectator,* 14 Jan. 1888, p. 61.

46. William L. Kingsley, 'Current Literature', review of *The Story of Ireland,* by Emily Lawless, *New Englander and Yale Review,* vol. 48.215, 1888, p. 131.

47. Linn, p. 183.

48. 'Books of the Month', review of *The Story of Ireland,* by Emily Lawless, *Atlantic Monthly,* vol. 61.364, 1888, p. 287.

49. Emily Lawless, *Maria Edgeworth* (London: Macmillan, 1904), p. 1. Subsequent references to this work are given parenthetically in the text.

50. Betty Webb Brewer, '"She Was a Part of It": Emily Lawless (1845–1913)', *Éire-Ireland: A Journal of Irish Studies,* vol. 18.4, 1983, p. 127.

51. Obituary of Emily Lawless, *Irish Book Lover,* vol. 5, 1913, p. 85.

52. Richard Garnett, 'Maria Edgeworth', review of *Maria Edgeworth,* by Emily Lawless, *Bookman,* vol. 26, 1904, p. 168.

53. 'Maria Edgeworth', review of *Maria Edgeworth,* by Emily Lawless, *Times Literary Supplement,* 22 Jul. 1904, p. 228.

54. S. M. Francis, 'Maria Edgeworth', review of *Maria Edgeworth,* by Emily Lawless, *Atlantic Monthly,* vol. 96, 1905, p. 423.

55. 'Maria Edgeworth', review of *Maria Edgeworth,* by Emily Lawless, *Oxford Magazine,* 14 Jun. 1905, n. p. Clipping in the Lawless Papers, Marsh's Library, Dublin.

56. Linn, p. 191.

57. *Ibid.,* p. 193.

58. George Saintsbury, 'Some Great Biographies', *Macmillan's Magazine,* vol. 66.392, 1892, p. 97.

59. *Ibid.,* p. 103.

60. J. Hillis Miller, 'Trollope's Thackeray', *Nineteenth-Century Fiction,* vol. 37.3, 1982, p. 350.

61. In a letter to Macmillan's Lawless wrote: 'I shall be very glad to undertake Maria Edgeworth's life for your "English men (!) of Letters" series, & hope I should succeed in doing so to your satisfaction.' As her biography shows, Lawless perceived Edgeworth as Irish, apart from the fact that she was of course a woman, and the exclamation mark indicates her awareness of the irony of including

a life of Maria Edgeworth in a series of English Men of Letters. Emily Lawless, Letter to Macmillan's, 8 Mar. 1903, Macmillan Archive, British Library, Add. Mss. 54966 153.

62. See Noel Gilroy Annan, *Leslie Stephen: His Thought and Character in Relation to his Time* (London: MacGibbon, 1951), pp. 49–109 and 222–79 in particular for an overview of Stephen's opinions about biography and literary criticism.

63. Sir Leslie Stephen, *George Eliot* (London: Macmillan, 1902), p. 5. It should be noted that Lawless's novel *Hurrish* is also to a great extent a study of an 'organism' in his environment.

64. Sources are of course quite often omitted from nineteenth- and early twentieth-century works, and the importance of their absence from Stephen's biography of George Eliot should not be overstated.

65. Margaret Oliphant's biography of Richard Brinsley Sheridan (1883) is quite patronising in its descriptions of the Irish character. Thus, her style offers no guidance for somebody whose intention it is to celebrate the Irishness of her subject.

66. In Julia Kristeva's definition, intertexts are all the previously experienced texts which writer and reader bring to the work when creating or reading it. These texts are not only literary, but in a broad sense of the word include social and political context, both of the time when the work was written and the time when it is read, as well as oral sources and visual images that, in combination with written material, create popular stereotypes. Intertexts draw attention to important ideas in the dominant work, or offer contrastive views, and function as textual strategies or metaphors. Julia Kristeva, *Desire in Language: A Semiotic Approach to Literature and Art,* ed. Leon S. Roudiez, trans. Thomas Gora, Alice Jardine and Leon S. Roudiez (Oxford: Basil Blackwell, 1980).

67. Lawless writes: 'Please do not think that my suggestion about Mrs Oliphant means that I wish myself to write her life! It would be an intensely hard task & I knew her almost too well I may say! For several years we were almost constantly together. Would not Mr Lang for instance, as a Scotchman, & with an interest in the occult undertake it? Or better still Sir Leslie Stephen, if he is well enough? He knew her so well, & admired her so much.' Emily Lawless, Letter to Mr Macmillan, 12 Jun. 1903, Macmillan Archive, British Library, Add. Mss. 54966 154–6.

68. Emily Lawless, Letter to Sir Alfred Lyall, 27 Oct. [1902], British Library [London, India Office Library and Records] MS Eur.F.132/109/25.

69. As William Linn sees it, breaks in the chronology show that Lawless had not mastered her material sufficiently: 'Emily Lawless also occasionally disrupts chronological order, which suggests that she does not have full control of her sources.' Linn, p. 192, n. 45.

70. Gordon W. MacLennan, 'Digression in Oral Tradition: The Case of Anna Nic Grianna', in Cyril J. Byrne, Margaret Harry and Pádraig Ó Siadhail (eds.), *Celtic Languages and Celtic Peoples: Proceedings of the Second North American Congress of Celtic Studies* (Halifax Nova Scotia: D'Arcy McGee Chair of Irish Studies, n. d.), p. 123.

71. Finke, p. 138.

72. *Ibid.*, p. 138.

73. Freedman, p. 364.

74. Cameron, *Verbal Hygiene*.

75. Stephen, p. 40.

76. *Ibid.*, p. 183.

77. S. M. Francis disagrees with Lawless's opinion about Edgeworth's feelings for Edelcrantz, as Mrs Edgeworth ought to have been a better judge of the situation since she was actually present at the time: 'In a rather summary manner she dismisses the comments of Mrs. Edgeworth on the feelings of Maria towards her Swedish suitor, M. Edelcrantz, though frankly owning that the writer was unquestionably in a position to know the actual facts,–and we may venture to add, was likely to report them accurately.' Francis, p. 424.

78. Emily Lawless, Letter to Mr Macmillan, 12 Jun. 1903, Macmillan Archive, British Library, Add. Mss. 54966 154–6.

79. Lawless, 'Of the Personal Element in History', p. 797.

80. Lawless, 'A Note on the Ethics of Literary Forgery', pp. 84–5.

81. *Ibid.*, p. 85.

82. Edith Sichel, 'Emily Lawless,' *Nineteenth Century and After,* vol. 76, 1914, p. 98. See also chapter 3.

83. Marilyn Butler, *Maria Edgeworth: A Literary Biography* (Oxford: Clarendon Press, 1972), p. 6.

84. George Tyrrell, Letter to Emily Lawless, 25 Aug. 1904, in M. D. Petre (ed.), *George Tyrrell's Letters* (London: Fisher Unwin, 1920), p. 272.

85. The *Times Literary Supplement* reviewer strongly disagrees with Lawless's negative view of Edgeworth's father: 'A stranger to Miss Edgeworth would come away from Miss Lawless's monograph with at least three wrong ideas prominently in his head, – (1) That Richard Lowell Edgeworth had an unvaryingly bad influence on his daughter's intellectual life; (2) that Miss Edgeworth's stories for children are, with the exception of "Simple Susan", negligible; and (3) that Miss Edgeworth stands beside Sir Walter Scott and Charles Lamb as the third "most eminently likeable" writer in English literature. For our own part we disagree with Miss Lawless in respect of them all.' 'Maria Edgeworth', review of *Maria Edgeworth*, by Emily Lawless, *Times Literary Supplement*, 22 Jul. 1904, p. 228.

86. James M. Cahalan, 'Forging a Tradition: Emily Lawless and the Irish Literary Canon', *Colby Quarterly*, vol. 27.1, 1991, p. 35.

Notes to Chapter Five

1. See also the discussion in chapter 2 of male narrative voice in *A Millionaire's Cousin*.

2. James Carson, 'Narrative Cross-Dressing and the Critique of Authorship in the Novels of Richardson', in Elizabeth C. Goldsmith (ed.), *Writing the Female Voice: Essays on Epistolary Literature* (London: Pinter, 1989), pp. 100–1.

3. Carla Kaplan, *The Erotics of Talk: Women's Writing and Feminist Paradigms* (New York: Oxford University Press, 1996), p. 13.

4. Susan Sniader Lanser, *Fictions of Authority: Women Writers and Narrative Voice* (Ithaca NY: Cornell University Press, 1992), p. 5.

5. Carson, p. 104.

6. William Linn, 'The Life and Works of the Hon. Emily Lawless, First Novelist of the Irish Literary Revival,' dissertation, New York University, 1971, p. 106.

7. Linn, p. 156.

8. Essex's real secretary on the Irish campaign was Sir Henry Wotton, who left no extensive record of the enterprise.

9. Robert Lacey, *Robert, Earl of Essex: An Elizabethan Icarus* (1971; London: Phoenix, 2001), pp. 223–4.

10. Review of *With Essex in Ireland*, by Emily Lawless, *Pall Mall Gazette*, 8 Jul. 1890, n. p. Clipping in Marsh's Library, Dublin. There is a similar comment in review of *With Essex in Ireland*, by Emily

Lawless, *Manchester Examiner*, 6 Jun. 1890, n. p. Clipping in the Lawless Papers, Marsh's Library, Dublin.

11. Edith Sichel, 'Emily Lawless', *Nineteenth Century and After*, vol. 76, 1914, p. 86; Daniel J. Murphy (ed.), *Lady Gregory's Journals, Volume Two, Books Thirty to Forty-Four, 21 February 1925–9 May 1932* (Gerrards Cross: Colin Smythe, 1987), pp. 153, 416.

12. Handwritten note in the copy of Emily Lawless, *With Essex in Ireland*, in Marsh's Library, Dublin.

13. Murphy (ed.), *Lady Gregory's Journals, Volume Two*, p. 416.

14. 'With Essex in Ireland', review of *With Essex in Ireland*, by Emily Lawless, *Boston Literary World*, Oct. 1890, n. p. Clipping in the Lawless Papers, Marsh's Library, Dublin. Similar praise of Lawless's recreation of Elizabethan style and thought appears in 'Recent Novels and Tales', review of *With Essex in Ireland*, by Emily Lawless, *The Times*, 21 Jul. 1890, n. p. Clipping in the Lawless Papers, Marsh's Library, Dublin; 'With Essex in Ireland', review of *With Essex in Ireland*, by Emily Lawless, *Spectator*, vol. 64, 1890, pp. 799–800.

15. Emily Lawless, *With Essex in Ireland* (1890; New York: Garland, 1979), p. viii. Subsequent references to this work will be given parenthetically in the text.

16. Emily Lawless, 'A Note on the Ethics of Literary Forgery', *Nineteenth Century*, vol. 41, 1897, pp. 84–5.

17. Lanser, p. 19.

18. 'Elizabethan Ireland', review of *With Essex in Ireland*,' by Emily Lawless, *Speaker*, 27 Sept. 1890, p. 359.

19. Review of *With Essex in Ireland*, by Emily Lawless, *Outlook*, 25 Oct. 1902, n. p. Clipping in the Lawless Papers, Marsh's Library, Dublin.

20. Lia Mills, 'Forging History: Emily Lawless's *With Essex in Ireland*', *Colby Quarterly*, vol. 36.2, 2000, pp. 137, 141.

21. Eve Patten, 'With Essex in India? Emily Lawless's Colonial Consciousness', *European Journal of English Studies*, vol. 3.3, 1999, p. 290.

22. Review of *With Essex in Ireland*, by Emily Lawless, *Saturday Review*, 4 Oct 1890, n.p. Clipping in the Lawless Papers, Marsh's Library, Dublin.

23. In her history of Ireland Lawless comments: 'There was but one method by which a success could be assured, and this was the

method which Mountjoy now pushed relentlessly, and from which Essex's more sensitively attuned nature evidently shrank. The enemies it was necessary to annihilate were not so much Tyrone's soldiers, as the poor, the feeble, the helpless, the old, the women, and the little children.' Emily Lawless, *Ireland: With Some Additions by Mrs. Arthur Bronson* (1887; London: Fisher Unwin, 1898), p. 213.

24. Ann Rosalind Jones and Peter Stallybrass, 'Dismantling Irena: The Sexualising of Ireland in Early Modern England', in Andrew Parker, Mary Russo, Doris Sommer and Patricia Yaeger (eds.), *Nationalisms and Sexualities* (New York: Routledge, 1992), p. 164.

25. Catherine Nash, 'Embodied Irishness: Gender, Sexuality and Irish Identities', in Brian Graham (ed.), *In Search of Ireland: A Cultural Geography* (1997; London: Routledge, 1998), p. 112.

26. Sue Best, 'Sexualizing Space', in Elizabeth Grosz and Elspeth Probyn (eds.), *Sexy Bodies: The Strange Carnalities of Feminism* (London: Routledge, 1995), p. 183.

27. Gillian Rose, *Feminism and Geography: The Limits of Geographical Knowledge* (Cambridge: Polity Press, 1993), p. 61. Essex and his followers were not the first invaders to experience the Irish landscape's active resistance. 'For the Anglo-Normans,' William J. Smyth writes, 'Ireland's complicated distribution of mountains, hills and boglands brought many enduring difficulties. The complicated border zone of interlaced woods, bogs and lakes that comprised the extensive drumlin and wet clay lands, running across the north midlands and south Ulster, formed one powerful barrier. The great midland bogs and woods also acted as refuges for resilient Gaelic Irish culture, for the Anglo-Normans did not like the wetlands, and neither did their horses.' William J. Smyth, 'A Plurality of Irelands: Regions, Societies and Mentalities', in Brian Graham (ed.), *In Search of Ireland: A Cultural Geography* (1997; London: Routledge, 1998), p. 26.

28. Lytton Strachey, *Elizabeth and Essex: A Tragic History* (London: Chatto & Windus, 1928), pp. 200–1.

29. Lawless, *Ireland*, p. 209.

30. Lawless, 'A Note on the Ethics of Literary Forgery', pp. 94–5.

31. Lawless's St Fechin is not the same as the St Fechin who was the abbot of Fobhar in Westmeath, died of the plague in 665 and was later canonised. His feast day is 20 January.

32. Emily Lawless, 'A Bardic Chronicle,' *Nineteenth Century*, vol. 30, 1891, p. 650. Subsequent references to this story are given parenthetically in the text.

33. See Seamus Deane, *Strange Country: Modernity and Nationhood in Irish Writing since 1790* (Oxford: Clarendon Press, 1997).

34. Emily Lawless, *Maelcho: A Sixteenth Century Narrative* (1894; London: Methuen, 1895), pp. 162–3. Subsequent references to this work are given parenthetically in the text.

35. Eileen Reilly sees Beara as an equivalent to Henry Rider Haggard's Ayesha, the protagonist of *She* (1887). Beara should then represent the dangerous power embodied in the colonial woman. She is certainly both powerful and terrifying, but she uses her power to protect Hugh from her even more terrifying father, Cormac Cas, not to control him or lure him away. Eileen Reilly, 'Rebel, Muse, and Spouse: The Female in '98 Fiction', *Éire-Ireland: A Journal of Irish Studies*, vol. 34.2, 1999, p. 138 n 7.

36. Pierre Bourdieu, *Distinction: A Social Critique of the Judgement of Taste*, trans. Richard Nice (1984; London: Routledge, 1994), p. 474.

37. Laurie Finke, *Feminist Theory, Women's Writing* (Ithaca: Cornell University Press, 1992), p. 8.

38. 'Maelcho: A Sixteenth Century Narrative', review of *Maelcho: A Sixteenth Century Narrative*, by Emily Lawless, *Athenæum*, vol. 104, 1894, p. 638.

39. Simon Schama, *Landscape and Memory* (1995; New York: Vintage, 1996), p. 6.

40. Frank Delaney, *The Celts* (London: Hodder & Stoughton, 1986), p. 92. In *Collins English Dictionary* (Glasgow: HarperCollins, 1991) the word 'druid' is said to derive from an Old Irish word meaning 'wizard', and *The Concise Oxford Dictionary* (Oxford: Oxford University Press, 1964) gives the original Old Irish meaning as 'magician'. Neither of these etymologies mention trees, but Delaney's explanation shows that there is at least a popular connection between druids and tree-lore.

41. Quoted in Críostóir Mag Fhearaigh and Tim Stampton, *Ogham: An Irish Alphabet* (1993; Indreabhán: Cló Iar-Chonnachta, 1997), n. p.

42. Daniel Corkery, *The Hidden Ireland* (1924; Dublin: Gill & Macmillan, n. d.), pp. 34–5.

43. Seán Ó Tuama and Thomas Kinsella, *An Duanaire 1600–1900: Poems of the Dispossessed* (1981; Portlaoise: Dolmen, 1994), p. 329.

44. Schama, p. 15.

45. *Ibid.*, p. 141.

46. Emily Lawless, *With the Wild Geese* (London: Isbister, 1902), pp. 35–7.

47. *Ibid.*, p. 36.

48. *Ibid.*, 36.

49. Emily Lawless, 'In the Kingdom of Kerry', *The Gentleman's Magazine*, vol. 28, 1882, p. 543.

50. Lawless, 'In the Kingdom of Kerry', p. 543.

51. *Ibid.*, pp. 543–4.

52. *Ibid.*, p. 543.

53. Linn, pp. 128–9.

54. Calendar of State Papers (Ireland) ccv, 113. Quoted in Lacey, p. 232.

55. Murphy (ed.), *Lady Gregory's Journals, Volume Two, Books Thirty to Forty-Four, 21 February 1925–9 May 1932* (Gerrards Cross: Colin Smythe, 1987), p. 423.

56. Emily Lawless, Letter to W. E. H. Lecky, n. d., Lecky correspondence, Trinity College Dublin, MS 1827–36/2482.

57. 'Maelcho: a Sixteenth Century Narrative', review of *Maelcho: A Sixteenth Century Narrative,* by Emily Lawless, *Athenæum,* vol. 104, 1894, p. 638.

58. 'Maelcho', review of *Maelcho: A Sixteenth Century Narrative,* by Emily Lawless, *The Times,* 30 Nov. 1894, 14.

59. 'Maelcho', review of *Maelcho: A Sixteenth Century Narrative,* by Emily Lawless, *Spectator,* vol. 73, 1894, p. 560.

60. Emily Lawless, Letter to W. E. Gladstone, 22 Oct. 1894, Gladstone Papers, British Library, MS 44519/149.

61. Emily Lawless, *A Colonel of the Empire: From the Private Papers of Mangan O'Driscoll, Late of the Imperial Service of Austria, and a Knight of the Military Order of Maria Theresa* (New York: Appleton, 1895), p. 21. Subsequent references to this work are given parenthetically in the text.

62. Valentine Browne Lawless, Baron Cloncurry, *Personal Recollections of the Life and Times, with Extracts from the Correspondence, of Valentine, Lord Cloncurry* (Dublin, 1849), pp. 18–21.

63. Sir Fenton John Aylmer, *The Aylmers of Ireland* (London: Mitchell Hughes and Clark, 1931), pp. 198–99.

64. Linn, p. 134.

65. Emily Lawless, Letter to W. E. H. Lecky, 5 Nov. 1895, Lecky correspondence, Trinity College Dublin, MS 1827–36/2477.

66. No title, *Irish Times*, 4 Nov. 1913, n. p. Clipping in the Lawless Papers, Marsh's Library, Dublin.

67. Emily Lawless, 'Collaboration – a Note', in Emily Lawless and Shan Bullock, *The Race of Castlebar: Being a Narrative Addressed by Mr. John Bunbury to His Brother Mr. Theodore Bunbury* (London: John Murray, 1913), n. p. The *Times Literary Supplement* review of the novel states that Lawless was responsible for the first nine and the last six chapters of the novel, but this does not correspond to the description given in the preface. 'The Author of "Hurrish"', review of *The Race of Castlebar*, by Emily Lawless and Shan Bullock, *Times Literary Supplement*, 1913, p. 589.

68. [Joseph Stock], *A Narrative of what Passed at Killala, in the County of Mayo, and the Parts Adjacent, during the French Invasion in the Summer of 1798. By an Eye-Witness* (Dublin: R. E. Mercier & John Jones, 1800).

69. 'Irish Literary Society', *Irish Book Lover*, vol. 7, 1916, p. 130.

70. Emily Lawless and Shan Bullock, *The Race of Castlebar: Being a Narrative Addressed by Mr. John Bunbury to His Brother Mr. Theodore Bunbury* (London: John Murray, 1913), pp. 48–56. Subsequent references to this work are given parenthetically in the text.

71. 'The Author of "Hurrish"', p. 589.

72. 'The Race of Castlebar', review of *The Race of Castlebar*, by Emily Lawless and Shan Bullock, *Bookman*, vol. 45, 1914, p. 283.

73. It should be noted that the whole O'Byrne episode amounts to very little in the end. Bunbury certainly manages to save the Colonel and get him out of the country, but this also means that his sister's family are still in possession of the castle and the title.

74. Emily Lawless, 'Irish Chronicles: Gerald the Great', *Nineteenth Century*, vol. 28, 1890, pp. 733–49.

75. Emily Lawless, 'Fragments of Irish Chronicles: Gerald the Great (Concluded)', *Nineteenth Century*, vol. 29, 1891, pp. 429–44.

76. Emily Lawless, 'How Art Kavanagh Fought Richard the King: A Fourteenth Century Chronicle', in Emily Lawless, *Traits and Confidences* (London: Methuen, 1897), pp. 243–72.

Notes to Chapter Six

1. Ernest Boyd, *Ireland's Literary Renaissance* (1916, rev. ed. 1922; Dublin: Allen Figgis, 1968), p. 374.

2. Lloyd R. Morris, *The Celtic Dawn: A Survey of the Renascence in Ireland, 1889–1916* (1917; New York: Cooper Square, 1970), p. 173.

3. Chanel [Arthur Clery], 'The Bread of Exile', review of *With the Wild Geese*, by Emily Lawless, *Leader*, 30 Aug. 1902, n. p. Clipping in the Lawless Papers, Marsh's Library, Dublin.

4. *Ibid.*, n. p.

5. *Ibid.*, n. p.

6. Review of *With the Wild Geese*, by Emily Lawless, *Bookman*, 22 May 1902, p. 70.

7. Horace Plunkett, Letter to Emily Lawless, 3 Oct. 1902, Lawless Papers, Marsh's Library, Dublin.

8. Daniel J. Murphy (ed.), *Lady Gregory's Journals, Volume Two, Books Thirty to Forty-Four, 21 February 1925–9 May 1932* (Gerrards Cross: Colin Smythe, 1987), p. 152.

9. Boyd, p. 207.

10. Murphy (ed.), *Lady Gregory's Journals, Volume Two*, p. 153.

11. Emily Lawless, *With the Wild Geese* (London: Isbister, 1902), n. p. Subsequent references to this work will be given parenthetically in the text.

12. Murphy (ed.), *Lady Gregory's Journals, Volume Two*, p. 152.

13. Gregory A. Schirmer, *Out of What Began: A History of Irish Poetry in English* (Ithaca: Cornell University Press, 1998), p. 202.

14. William Linn, 'The Life and Works of the Hon. Emily Lawless, First Novelist of the Irish Literary Revival,' dissertation, New York University, 1971, p. 204.

15. Review of *With the Wild Geese*, *Bookman*, 70.

16. Stopford Brooke, Preface, Emily Lawless, *With the Wild Geese* (London: Isbister, 1902), pp. viii–ix.

17. Mainchin Seoighe, 'Poems of the Wild Geese', *Limerick Leader*, 29 May 1999, online edition, http://www.limerick-leader.ie/issues/

19990529/seoighe.html, access date 8 Feb. 2005. See also Tim Pat Coogan, *The IRA* (1971; London: HarperCollins, 2000), p. 247.

18. Boyd, p. 207.

19. Rudyard Kipling's 'The Irish Guards' also deals with the Battle of Fontenoy, but the poem was published in 1918, and was obviously not known to Lawless.

20. Murphy (ed.), *Lady Gregory's Journals, Volume Two*, p. 418.

21. Emily Lawless, *Ireland: With Some Additions by Mrs. Arthur Bronson* (1887; London: Fisher Unwin, 1898), pp. 213–4.

22. See chapter 5. The forests were also cut down for timber, both by English and Irish landowners.

23. Chanel, n. p.

24. Linn, p. 206.

25. John Webster, *The White Devil*, ed. John Russell Brown (London: Methuen, 1960), p. 165.

26. John Russell Brown, editorial note to John Webster, *The White Devil*, V.iv.103–4, in John Russell Brown (ed.), John Webster, *The White Devil* (London: Methuen, 1960), p. 165.

27. Chanel, n. p.

28. The version of the poem included in the privately printed *Atlantic Rhythms and Rhymes* specifies the setting as Aranmore.

29. Chanel, n. p.

30. Horace Plunkett, Letter to Emily Lawless, 26 Jul. 1902, Lawless Papers, Marsh's Library, Dublin.

31. 'Miss Lawless's Poems', review of *With the Wild Geese*, by Emily Lawless, *Times Literary Supplement*, 1906, p. 417.

32. Mrs Humphry Ward, *A Writer's Recollections* (London: Collins, 1918), p. 263.

33. Hugh Alexander Law, *Anglo-Irish Literature* (Dublin: Talbot, 1926), pp. 289–90.

34. Liam Hourican, review of *The Poems of Emily Lawless*, ed. Padraic Fallon, *Dublin Magazine*, Summer 1965, p. 79.

35. Schirmer, p. 202.

36. Padraic Fallon, Introduction, *The Poems of Emily Lawless*, ed. Padraic Fallon (Dublin: Dolmen, 1965), p. 9.

37. Emily Lawless, *The Point of View: Some Talks and Disputations* (privately printed; London: Richard Clay & Sons, 1909), n. p.

Subsequent references to this work will be given parenthetically in the text.

38. Elizabeth Grubgeld, 'The Poems of Emily Lawless and the Life of the West', *Turn-of-the-Century Women*, vol. 3.2, 1986, p. 35.

39. Murphy (ed.), *Lady Gregory's Journals, Volume Two*, p. 152.

40. *Ibid.*

41. Emily Lawless, *A Garden Diary: September, 1899–September, 1900* (London: Methuen, 1901), pp. 197–8.

42. Edith Sichel, Preface, *The Inalienable Heritage and Other Poems*, by Emily Lawless (London: Privately printed, 1914), pp. vi–viii.

43. Hourican, p. 78.

44. 'The Last Poems of Emily Lawless', *Times Literary Supplement*, 25 Jun. 1914, p. 309.

45. Emily Lawless, *The Inalienable Heritage and Other Poems* (London: Privately printed, 1914), p. 25. Subsequent references to this work will be given parenthetically in the text.

46. Boyd, p. 208.

47. Emily Lawless, *Hurrish: A Study* (1886; Belfast: Appletree, 1992), p. 3.

Notes to Chapter Seven

1. Emily Lawless, *A Garden Diary: September, 1899–September, 1900* (London: Methuen, 1901), p. 195.

2. Simon Schama, *Landscape and Memory* (1995; New York: Vintage, 1996), p. 12.

Index